Electoral Politics in South Vietnam

Electoral Politics in South Vietnam

Edited by

John C. Donnell
Charles A. Joiner

Temple University

Lexington Books
D.C. Heath and Company
Lexington, Massachusetts
Toronto   London

Library of Congress Cataloging in Publication Data

Main entry under title.

Electoral Politics in South Vietnam.

"The essays in this book were initially presented December 10-11, 1971 to a conference of the Southeast Asia Development Advisory Group of the Asia Society in New York, and were later revised."
    1. Elections—Vietnam—Addresses, essays, lectures. I. Donnell, John C., 1919-   ed. II. Joiner, Charles Adrian, 1932-   ed.
JQ892.D65   324'.597   74-302
ISBN 0-669-91322-7

Published simultaneously in Canada.

Printed in the United States of America.

International Standard Book Number: 0-669-91322-7

Library of Congress Catalog Card Number: 74-302

Contents

1

Elections and Building Political Institutions in South Vietnam: An Assessment
Charles A. Joiner

For many years the government of the Republic of Vietnam (GVN) was losing the Indochina War, primarily because it was not building a viable political system. Ngo Dinh Diem's efforts, beginning in 1954-55, to construct national public service institutions and an apparatus for local administration had faltered significantly by 1959-60. When he fell in 1963, South Vietnam's political system had been reduced to a shell by the National Liberation Front (NLF) in much of the country outside urban areas. This institution destruction continued throughout most of the 1960s. By the criterion of viability of the GVN's political system, the NLF had nearly won the war by 1965. By its development of multiple hierarchies, including an extensive administrative system, the NLF appeared to have justified its claim to political legitimacy and to the Mandate of Heaven. As a vital revolutionary force it had undertaken complex programs in regions under its control, including establishing parties, youth groups, women's groups, farmers' associations, and a host of other structures that provided mass participation and linkage among diverse political echelons. To the extent that expanding structural differentiation and functional specificity in society, building political institutions and linkages among them, stimulating mass participation in political affairs, and augmenting the competency of political institutions to direct change are considered characteristics of "political development," the extensive political development in the NLF zones was undeniable.

Influx of massive American forces beginning in 1965 and the aftermath of the 1968 Tet offensive brought about a drastic change in the total configuration of political power. The end of 1971 found the NLF much weaker and increasingly "northernized" as it was more and more dominated by North Vietnamese regular military forces (PAVN), who assumed responsibilities carried out earlier by NLF military units. Further, the American presence was much less pervasive, and the GVN had become the administration for more of the nation than at any prior period. Undoubtedly, the last development was most important in terms by which the Indochina War was being fought.

Although not widely reported, South Vietnam had enjoyed a considerable amount of "political development" since 1967. The NLF suffered a decline in its competition for political legitimacy with both the GVN and with political forces assuming a posture of a "loyal opposition." New political institutions were established, including an entire national political system under the 1967 Constitution. A formal government with a national executive, assembly, and

1

judiciary had replaced rule by junta. Councils at provincial and village levels had been elected. Numerous local and national elections were held. Village chief positions became elective. Some decentralization through increased local-level financial, security, and general policy decision-making powers occurred. Political parties were somewhat strengthened and became more actively involved in electoral and legislative affairs. The military's paramount role in public administration lessened. Increased security was followed by a noticeable increase in actual governmental presence in most of the nation.

These characteristics of political development were dramatic, particularly to longtime observers of the Vietnamese political scene. Some saw it as implementation of a classic Western model of political development, although a long list of continuing deficiencies was evident. Implementation of the model was far from complete, a weakness certain statements in this book fail to stress. Among other deficiencies, the military continued as a dominant force of political and administrative affairs. The chief executive was authoritarian, refused to recognize the spirit of the constitutionally mandated separation of powers, seemed unqualified or unwilling to support political party development, and effectively rigged the 1971 presidential election to obtain an overwhelming vote of support in a single-candidate race. The National Assembly was still not a powerful force, and the judiciary remained impotent. Centralization continued in many public-policy areas. Village councils were not always selected in open elections but were often handpicked by the government. Elections for province chiefs had not replaced the appointment of military personnel to those highly important positions in the political system. Political parties were still greatly divided, and no one organization could claim national support. Corruption continued to be rampant, and economic and social problems were staggering. And progress noted by the authors in this work was much more evident in the far south, including the Mekong Delta, than in most of the rest of the nation.

No, the model was certainly still a quite distant ideal. Despite improved security, every aspect of political development remained contingent upon the nation's not being overrun by the PAVN and the NLF, as observers recognized. Still, changes had been so marked, signs of security so obvious (roads unsafe since World War II were safe to travel), progress in building village government so dramatic compared to anything seen in the past, that even disillusioned cynics began to acknowledge the growing political development.

The essays in this book were initially presented December 10-11, 1971 to a conference of the Southeast Asia Development Advisory Group of the Asia Society in New York and were later revised. The chapters by Ta Van Tai and Jerry M. Silverman and by John C. Donnell were written later to include pertinent political developments through most of 1973. When the conference was held, the significance of South Vietnam's electoral processes for the first time were being carefully analyzed. Judged by totally objective standards, elections for the Lower House and the Senate (in spite of the 1971 presidential election debacle) had displayed some growth of responsible and mature legal opposition. In particular the Buddhists (an historic opposition force) and the Progressive Nationalist Movement (a party often listed as progovernment but more accurately classified as an opposition group operating exclusively within the system) had made impressive electoral gains. Statements at the conference by leaders of those two groups, Senator Tran Quang Thuan of the Buddhists and Professor Nguyen Ngoc Huy, co-founder of the PNM, articulated programs as alternatives to government practices. Other statements, particularly by writers with broad American embassy and aid program experience in South Vietnam, such as Stephen B. Young and Theresa Tull, noted developments in electoral behavior and legislative and council activities which compare favorably with almost any underdeveloped nation's attempts to emulate the Western political development model. Even skepticism, voiced by Donald Kirk and Douglas Pike, about the applicability of the electoral process as a method for leadership selection within the Vietnamese culture was qualified by reference to instances where elections to a degree created a "new tradition."

One could simply dismiss the inherent optimism, individual and collective, of certain authors in this text. Their orientation was sympathetic to South Vietnamese, if not to the GVN. While they recognized the weak foundation for their optimism, they failed to spell out its total implications. This appears especially true of Pike and Young. Young witnessed actual change; he had seen broad structural adaptations and a revitalization of Vietnamese recognition of their own potential. Pike had studied the NLF more carefully than any other American. He understood the movement's evolution, traced its history step by step, and had his hand on the pulse of major changes in the NLF from its beginning. Still, despite the clarity of their perceptions, the orientation of their presentations lead the reader to overestimate the progress of South Vietnam's political development, to overestimate deterioration of the NLF movement, and to underestimate the extent to which the NLF continued to represent a legitimate alternative to many Vietnamese. Locally, political development was a thin veneer. Under appropriate circumstances, village government might potentially have been at a "takeoff" stage toward genuinely increasing political maturity. But stressful circumstances could easily result in a "throwback."

Primarily, local governments eulogized by most observers were subjected to two stress agents, the NLF and the GVN. The NLF could always muster resources adequate to destroy any given village government. The orientation of several essays implicitly underestimates this never ceasing threat. More significantly, the GVN continued its obstruction of localized political development. As both Huy and Thuan observe, national government representatives, especially military officers serving as province chiefs, were impediments to free elections, to building political party structures, and to effective local control. The GVN maintained policies depriving individuals of civil liberties in presumably "secure" regions. Province and district chiefs manipulated both village elections and council decisions. Military control of public administration precluded maturation of local administration. Government funds competed with the much more limited financial and personnel resources of political parties. The GVN and province chiefs rendered impotent the province councils, which legally should have become powerful links between local and national governments and should have strengthened local representative and decentralized government.

True, political development occurred despite tensions inflicted by the GVN and NLF. National legislative elections described by Tull and local council elections analyzed by Young were important. Political party growth, outlined by Young and Huy, was equally important. But the question remained whether electoral, legislative, and party institutions could survive pressures by the GVN executive and military and the PAVN-NLF. Of course, survival was not really the important question; for genuine political development these admittedly weak institutions would have to be strengthened, and the handicaps were enormous.

Nonetheless, elections had been more successful than was generally recognized, as shown by statistics on electoral behavior during 1966-71. Mass public participation through voting was meaningful and important to specific publics, certainly, as Young observes, in many villages and provincial council elections. Village government (and to a lesser extent provincial government) became more representative than it had been for a long time. Indeed, though historians differ greatly on the true position of village councils in Vietnam's evolution, this was the first time residents of most villages had opportunity to select local decision-makers by popular referendum rather than by co-optation determined by the "customaries" of individual villages. Provincial councils remained weak because province chiefs exercised basically unconstitutional powers. They provided, however, some representation in policy-formulation bodies for diverse interest groups (religious, ethnic, party) resident in each province. National Assembly elections also took on greater meaning as competition became more strenuous, membership became more consistent with national interest group percentages of the total population, and some Assembly members became more oriented to providing constituency services.

Each of these developments had a positive (though still limited) effect on the political system. Voter percentages, listed by Tull, show the trend toward greater public participation in various elections. As Huy's essay shows, certain major political parties became aware that electoral processes were providing greater potential for sharing power than previous political processes.

These recognized advances were offset to a great extent by several GVN actions. Despite the generally good record of Saigon's electoral administration apparatus, many elections were more or less fixed. Instances of blatant rigging by district and province chiefs of voting for village councils were not uncommon. Direct hindrances to opposition candidates and political parties by the GVN were well known. Bribery and sometimes overt but mostly covert threats against specific local electorates made many local elections a farce. Bloc voting by military units on leave upset local power balances.

All these deficiencies came to a head in 1971. Kirk's analysis of the 1971 presidential election is a penetrating review of events leading to Nguyen Van Thieu's one-man candidacy, but even if the race had been contested the result would have been a *fait accompli* before the voting began. Thieu had mustered the entire GVN apparat to insure he would not be embarrassed by a plebiscite. Ironically, he probably could have received a plurality in a relatively fair and open election, although a clear-cut majority in a three-or-more-candidate race was much less likely. He was not prepared, however, to risk an uncontrolled election as a method for ratifying his continued incumbency. Regardless of the the impact of prior elections, Thieu's actions seriously undermined the electoral process as an institution for leadership selection.

Tull's observation that the institution of elections gained strength by the victories of more oppositionists in the 1971 National Assembly elections is no doubt valid. Also, the thesis that Thieu gained temporarily in strength because he discredited both Vice-President Nguyen Cao Ky and the candidate of the militant Buddhists, General Duong Van Minh, is perhaps accurate, although, as Kirk observes, Thieu soon found his influence with both Catholic and military leaders lessened by his actions. Thieu outfoxed his opposition and displayed "ability" (the concept of *tai* discussed by Young) and shrewdness in manipulating events so that he could not possibly lose at the ballot box. Despite such "ability," he sacrificed involvement of the electorate in a procedure where they had competency to make a selection, genuine implementation of the spirit of the Constitution of the Second Republic, and the potential of added legitimacy to the political system.

All definitions of political development assume that it not only includes building political institutions but also involves creating in the minds of the citizens a greater legitimacy of the political system, its policies, and its leaders. The NLF was always aware of the importance of such legitimacy. From this perspective, the 1971 presidential election—not simply because it was a one-candidate race, but because its procedures were so contrived that only one candidate conceivably could have won—catalyzed the decline of the political system rather than its development. While not a fatal error, it weakened many gains made steadily from 1966 to 1971 in developing acceptance by politicians and citizens of elections as an integral aspect of political behavior.

Thieu also seriously undermined legislative and political party institutions during the 1971 elections. Huy's hope that a two- or three-candidate race might generate political party development was crushed by the one-candidate election. Instead of combining forces behind specific candidates, parties had no role in the presidential campaign. They were active in Lower House and Senate elections, and several made impressive showings. But these were not really national campaigns. Even in the at-large Senate election, parties depended mostly on regional strength. The parties were troubled by financial difficulties in costly campaigns, on occasion were restricted in their activities by district and province chiefs who supported their own candidates, and were plagued in some constituencies by election irregularities. Further, parties had no assurances of the loyalties of many candidates whom they supported.

This last problem was manifested in the National Assembly, where Thieu flattered, cajoled, and bribed even loyal opposition Assembly members to back government-sponsored legislation rather than party-supported programs. In addition, although the 1971 Lower House election proved even pro-Thieu incumbent members were likely to lose in re-election bids, this did not invariably indicate an electorate's demanding more responsible representation. There were examples of the GVN's opposing previously loyal representatives. Even the pro-Thieu bloc could not form a progovernment party under such circumstances. Many legislators voted against GVN proposals, and the National Assembly voted against Thieu programs on several occasions. Yet there were neither legislative bloc nor political party programs genuinely competing with executive-sponsored legislation.

As data provided by Tull indicate, the legislative system by 1971 was probably as representative of the population of South Vietnam as any previous national body. It was not a rubber stamp for the executive; militant Buddhist representatives like Senator Thuan would have never permitted this. The problem of the legislative system was that, while it could serve as a frequent administration critic, it was not permitted to exercise its constitutional function as a branch of government equal to, and independent of, the chief executive. While this is more usual than not in underdeveloped nations, a primary purpose of the electoral process was to build representative councils to make independent decisions concerning public policy issues.

To the extent the National Assembly could not and did not provide representative government, it lessened the meaning and utility of the entire electoral process. If the process is without significant meaning, prospects for future legislative and political party institutions remain bleak. Even if effective elections may not always be a prerequisite for political development, in their absence alternative institutions must be constructed.

The second set of pressures applied against electoral, party, and legislative institutions—those of the PAVN-NLF—naturally were more destructive than GVN executive and military leadership. There is an implicit assumption in some of the essays, and an explicit one in Pike's statement, that the NLF is no longer capable of challenging the political system effectively. These authors knew North Vietnam was fully capable of eliminating all or nearly all vestiges of GVN political development, but at a cost it might not be prepared to pay. Yet Young and Pike give evidence of how far local village council control had supplanted NLF de facto local government in most of the nation in 1971. While their evidence is based upon as valid data as were available, it was impossible to determine the extent to which NLF cadres were lying low and maintaining a clandestine but potentially effective infrastructure.

There is no way to know the true degree of NLF involvement in electoral processes. Pike's study assumes it was not great, and the NLF appeared ambivalent about its role. However, while weakened at the all-important village level, the NLF never lost its ability to harass voters, candidates, campaign workers, political party leaders and election officials. Nor did it lose its capability of threatening village councils and chiefs, provincial councils, and even members of the National Assembly. Guerrilla activities, including terrorism, shelling, and attacks on local facilities and communities, were always possible. In short, the NLF could always create tensions to disrupt GVN political system operations and actually destroy specific village governments.

The PAVN was a different equation, whose actions the authors naturally could not anticipate. Few analysts predicted that the PAVN would undertake an assault of the 1972 Easter offensive's magnitude, although a smaller offensive had been anticipated. That North Vietnam had the will, forces, and equipment for such an offensive was generally accepted. However, weighing alternative options available and the "objective conditions" Hanoi invariably considered prior to any major action (including the inevitable pullout of all American ground forces before the U.S. presidential election), PAVN's threat to political development did not appear imminent. In fact, by late 1971 most observers were speculating that warfare would center on guerrilla actions. This was particularly true for those who attached significance to North Vietnam's 1971 National Assembly elections, in which southerners were excluded for the first time, and to the combination of domestic emphasis upon industrialization and the apparent demotion of General Vo Nguyen Giap.

It will be a long time before the 1972 offensive's damage to different aspects of the GVN's political development in South Vietnam can be fully assessed. In many areas fruits of decentralization and increased elected village council control of local affairs described by Young were destroyed. Entire villages rebuilt after the 1968 Tet offensive were burned to the ground. Refugee and casualty figures swelled beyond those even of 1968. Local security either became precarious or ceased to exist in many areas. Although its role was secondary to that of the PAVN, the NLF did expand from regions of historic strength. While many regular GVN forces fought better than most commentators assumed they would, other units betrayed by their officers fled, abandoning village leaders and self-defense forces. All of Quang Tri Province fell. Still in many instances local defense forces fared extremely well, given the odds against them, albeit many fell back to find protection, leaving local populations to be influenced by PAVN and NLF proselytizers.

Whether performance of local units that held out against artillery and mortar fire and regular force attacks can be at all attributed to GVN political development between 1968 and 1972 is pure speculation. What is certain is that not even the most successful GVN or NLF local political bodies could provide competition for the mechanized horror of conventional warfare. They might withstand revolutionary warfare but never artillery and heavy tanks or well-armed regular forces if a shield of government forces was removed for tactical reasons. Elections, political parties, and legislatures notwithstanding, sheer firepower can eliminate almost overnight a decade of political development. Nonetheless, this did not signal the death knell for progress of political development in South Vietnam, as the last two chapters show.

Yet as a result of the Easter offensive and of Saigon's political as well as military reaction, many parties were weakened locally. Reappearance or re-emergence of NLF cadres in many locales automatically insured this decline whether or not occupying forces were PAVN elements. Also, Thieu's temporary alterations in the status of village and hamlet leaders, shifting power from elected to appointed officials, eliminated a local power base useful to various political parties in future electoral processes and upset many gains Young describes in his essay on local development. The Democracy party pushed by Thieu beginning in 1972 might have been an alternative step toward political development, substituting for local vestiges of other parties, but this was an artificial instrument, as the last two chapters indicate. As the papers by Silverman and Tai and by Donnell note, its vast enrollments were largely the products of overt and covert coercion, rather than of carefully formulated organization.

This was the political situation following the 1973 cease-fire, but it was not distinctly different from 1963 when Diem fell, or even 1954—or, for that matter, 1945-46. The Communist party itself, by whatever name, was representative of a minority. Resistance to foreign "imperialism" was always nearly universal, but this was the whole point in both Indochina wars. The Hoa Hao, the Cao Dai, the VNQDD, the Dai Viet—to name but a few obvious examples— all wanted an independent state. However, they were unprepared to work together and share power to achieve it.

A feeble GVN attempt in February 1973 to inaugurate a People's Front to Safeguard Peace and to Realize the People's Right to Self-Determination representing nationalist interests showed the continued plight of the Vietnamese party system. The participants probably represented, nominally at least, a majority of the electorate. But all were cautious, and many factions of their groups were absent. Even Senator Tran Quang Thuan, whose views are presented in the Appendix and who attended, did not represent the total "militant" Buddhist interest.

Indeed, Senator Thuan is representative of much of nationalist politics. He is vigorous, thoroughly grounded in the intricacies of Vietnamese history, economics, and political processes. He holds Vietnam's first doctorate in anthropology, and was a leader of the Young Buddhist Association imprisoned during the last day of Diem's regime, an activist involved in all antigovernment Buddhist demonstrations during the 1963-65 ministerial musical chairs era, a minister of social welfare, an army officer who refused to participate in military life while his movement was protesting government actions, a member of the Constitutional Assembly, and chairman of the Senate Foreign Affairs Committee. He has been a longtime Buddhist lay leader and a leading organizer of his movement's attempt to become a truly mass-based national force. Nonetheless, at the People's Front gatherings he represented only one of numerous factions of the Buddhist movement.

As one means to alleviate this fractionation of the political process, Huy, a leader with as much interest in his party's obtaining government positions as any other political personality, suggests political development defined as structure building: party building, legislative strengthening, provincial and other council growth in responsibility, electoral mechanisms providing avenues and legitimacy for claimants to political power at all levels, and building of executive and judicial institutions according to a separation of powers scheme already formalized in the Constitution. The failures of political development mean such structure building simply has not occurred. Allan Goodman's disappointment in the National Assembly's failure to become a viable, independent structure, spelled out in the Appendix, is but one piece of evidence of such failure. Structures have developed through considerable expenditure of energy by many political parties and political personalities. Each structure has been undermined—by the GVN, by the NLF, and by centrifugal pressures exerted by numerous nationalist interest groups.

As a consequence, the post 1967-68 attempts at political development appear at best an empty shell. From a wider perspective this evaluation is less than accurate. The irony, the tragedy has not simply been failure; this was anticipated, especially under wartime conditions. The real tragedy is that a considerable amount of political development transpired, at least in terms of building political institutions. Although those political institutions were unable to direct major changes systematically in economic and social institutions, they did provide a degree of public access to government. North Vietnamese 130 mm artillery and GVN authoritarian reaction to the 1972 Easter offensive plus continued emphasis upon military leadership crushed many advances. Devastating as they were, these factors were secondary to the refusal of forces in South Vietnam's complex pluralistic political milieu to agree to any order requiring minimal cooperation with other elements. Even granted that Thieu could have amassed a sizable minority in 1971 to assure his re-election, the legal opposition was too divided to offer effective competition.

This is the tragedy. If South Vietnam obediently had followed forecasts of many political analysts, there would have been no political development. A simple dictatorship would have spelled out rules, and it would have failed completely to generate popular or interest group support against the NLF. The scenario was not played in this neat fashion. After 1967, interest groups, political parties, local councils, and the National Assembly did succeed in building improved organization structures. Significant numbers of people were enmeshed in the legal political process.

During late 1972 and early 1973, structures built with such meticulous care showed signs of crumbling. They did not, however, disintegrate—surely a sign of change not believed possible before the mid-1960s. When the cease-fire was promulgated in 1973, the degree of development attained, much more than Thieu's control of the GVN itself, represented what true potential there was for competing politically with the NLF. The depth of this potential was very much open to question. Opposition parties certainly had neither organization nor cohesiveness to outdistance Thieu. Factions of the Hoa Hao, Cao Dai, Buddhists, Catholics, Dai Viet, VNQDD, et al. might defeat the NLF in specific locales without devising unified organization structure. Yet this had little meaning on even a regional, let alone national, basis.

As for the NLF, the simple fact is that its true strength as a political force at the time of the 1973 cease-fire will never be known. Its armed forces were more active in Binh Dinh Province, the Mekong Delta, and in selected other areas than evidence available to Pike indicated. Yet he unquestionably is accurate in noting that much terrain occupied by PAVN forces could not be counted on by the NLF for electoral support in anything approaching open elections— not, at least, unless elections were delayed long enough for application of the NLF's traditionally effective political organization techniques. Indeed, much of that terrain had been abandoned by a significant percentage of its population. Pike also assumed no national-level agreement was possible. At one level of analysis this assessment appears inaccurate, because those who initialed the Paris accords considered them applicable to all of South Vietnam. From a different perspective Pike's pessimism may still prove warranted. Certainly the NLF disagreed with Thieu's position that future elections should include a nationwide presidential election, which he felt confident he could win.

In any formula for future elections the NLF will fare better in specific constituencies rather than in races involving a single nationwide constituency. The formula suggested in the Appendix by Ithiel de Sola Pool of a parliamentary system could serve as a better guarantee of NLF representation in national decision making and in probable holding of ministerial portfolios. It also could permit representation of various nationalist opposition parties, including "neutralist" and non-neutralist parties alike. However, a parliamentary system would also run the risks mentioned by Huy.

It is impossible to predict whether either the GVN or the NLF would permit others to challenge them even locally for any period of time. In the unlikely event that a multiparty or even a three-party system emerges, as Huy envisages, and competes freely in an era of relative peace, vestiges of political development already begun could conceivably bear significant fruit for both nationalist parties and the NLF. And if there is a viable southern political system, it is even conceivable a peaceful northern-southern *rapprochement* on a confederation basis might occur in time.

Naturally this is unlikely. Hanoi, Saigon, the NLF, and the varied nationalist groups, all are more likely to pursue their own perceived interests so as to undermine changes for political development they do not completely control. Recognizing this, however, it would be a mistake to underestimate the ability of the southern Vietnamese, including both communist and non-communist nationalists, to struggle again one more time to build and rebuild what they have lost. The non-communist political system remains fragile; "political development" remains more promise than reality; the perennial centrifugal interests continue unabated; and foreign allies can no longer be depended upon.

However, attempts at political development will continue, perhaps under two separate Vietnams or under some form of unification of North and South Vietnam. Political forces in Vietnam will never relinquish ambitions to protect their groups and build a nation governed by a viable political system. The Mandate of Heaven may never be bestowed upon a single group in Vietnam during the twentieth century, but, as Young eloquently observes, the constant search for the mandate will continue. Perhaps this search and its attendant political processes will provide a much better and more appropriate Vietnamese model for political development than that offered in any Western textbook.

2

The Mandate and Politics in Vietnam
Stephen B. Young

This will be an initial attempt to provide a crude outline of the major contours on Vietnamese political culture. In full knowledge that I am setting off into deep water without a sure rudder, I nonetheless hope this attempt to bring related disciplines of historical analysis and social anthropology to bear on Vietnamese politics will be useful. My basic method, over which I have only an amateur's command, is to imitate Ruth Benedict's approach to the Japanese in her *Chrysanthemum and the Sword*. (And I must also apologize to my Vietnamese colleagues for a clumsy and imperfect effort to explain their politics.)

The central concept that runs through Vietnamese life is the ultimate power of heaven and its mandate over human affairs. Heaven, or the cosmos, or destiny assigns all of us our particular fate and sets up basic laws of social and natural relationships. Careful statistical analysis would be required to show just how many Vietnamese still believe in this heaven; let it suffice that such a root concept is held by all Buddhists, Ancestor-worshipers, Cao Daists, Hoa Hao, and other traditional believers. And there are good grounds to argue that this traditional concept has not been rejected by those who received extensive Western education or follow the Western ideologies of Catholicism and communism.

The Mandate of Heaven is called *mang troi*; basic social change, or revolution, is *cach mang*—a different mandate. Thus, Marxist revolutionary social theory can be expressed and accepted in very traditional terms. When heaven's mandate incorporates earth, there is peace, *hoa binh*, but this concept does not mean simply lack of war: social relations are harmonious, families happy, sons filial, and people prosperous. Thus, in a period of mandate-loss every Vietnamese desires peace. The problem lies in who has the mandate or who should have it. Conflict will not end and harmony reign through more compromise of rivals. There must be clear political predominance for one who, in addition, must be accepted as chosen of heaven. Struggle and conflict in Vietnamese history are long-term propositions and the norm in politics. A mandate and peace do not easily arrive.

The issue of war or peace is a fundamental question of which mighty force will prevail. And prevail it must. As long as there is only compromise between powers, heaven has not yet made its will clear and there must be more struggle. Either there is a mandate with order and peace, or there is not and all is in flux and persisting uncertainty. Without the mandate, things are at sixes and sevens; there are no standards of behavior, no guides as to whom to follow; all is chaos

13

and disorder; war and corruption blight mankind. The only security lies in the quality of one's self-defense. With a mandate, however, crops are lush, the people happy, craftsmen diligent, husbands faithful and fathers just, wives virtuous and children filial, the state upright and beneficent. And the mandate comes to earth through an individual. Some national leader must receive heaven's favor and establish just rule to bring heaven and earth into harmony. It should come as no surprise that most Vietnamese discussions of politics revolve around leadership: *who* is fit to be leader; why so-and-so is not worthy; if only Ngo Dinh Diem or Lyndon Johnson or Nguyen Van Thieu would do right, then all would be well.

Mention of the mandate usually evokes thoughts of Confucian formalism, with mandarins, annual rites on the alter of heaven and earth, and an uncomfortable sense of a dusty past now swept away by the fires of revolution, Western rationality, and modernity. Few Vietnamese are Confucian in the fashion of their great-grandfathers, just as the formal Confucian bureaucracy with the court and nine ranks of mandarins has passed away. But if we throw out the book when the cover falls off, we miss the profound, living reality of a vibrant folk culture and world view engraved in varying degrees within each Vietnamese. This culture provided common maxims and a social outlook and context within which the formal Confucian system could flourish. Now, though the emperor no longer makes offerings and the court exists only in tombs and memories of Hue, heaven still controls; fate is constant, and spirits of ancestors and magic beings still survive. Stars continue to influence our births. We are still under the thumb of the ultimate unknowable. In this overarching world we must find keys to the thought and behavior of Vietnamese.

The two most readily available and instructive guides are the *Book of Songs* in the Confucian classics and the *Romance of the Three Kingdoms. The Book of Songs* contains odes probably written between 1000 and 600 *B.C.,* long before Confucious, and provides much raw material from which he fashioned his theory of state and society. Lao Tzu took the same body of material and fashioned a different theory. The *Songs* show us the soul of a people before it became rationalized. They tell of good kings and bad, soldiers weary of endless wars in foreign lands, wives longing for distant husbands, lovers pining for illicit loves, ministers complaining of kings who ignore good advice, ministers moaning over loss of the mandate. The frame of the Vietnamese world view is there: the way of heaven, the people, leaders, right and wrong. History tells us the Viets were a distinct people with a sophisticated bronze culture in South China when these odes were composed. They are mentioned in early Chinese histories and they probably were in contact with the Chinese in Shang and Chou times. I would even infer a common East Asian culture in those times, one in which Viets and early Chinese shared such basic concepts as ancestor worship, spirits, and an overlord in heaven.

We may never know exactly which parts of contemporary culture are exclusively Vietnamese in origin. Yet the Vietnamese sense of unique ethnic identity and tradition is so strong they would have been unable to accept Chinese high culture if there had not been a compatible, pre-existing folk culture. Indeed, full Confucian practice flourished in Vietnam only by the fifteenth-century Le dynasty. The culture revealed in the *Songs* allows us to understand more clearly the basic themes underlying the formal intellectual accomplishments of China and Vietnam. In a sacrificial ode to the memory of a great Shang dynasty king, we find a stanza with a curiously modern ring:

> "When Heaven's high glance this lower world surveys,
> Attention to the people first it pays.
> Aware of this, our king impartial was,
> Nor punished so as justice to o'rpass.
> 'gainst idleness he took precaution sure,
> So o'er the states his rule did firm endure,
> And all his life he made his happiness secure.
>   (Arthur Legge Trans.)

The *Romance of the Three Kingdoms* tells of the House of Han around A.D. 200, as emperors took counsel from women and used eunuchs to rule. Greedy soldiers grabbed power, famine fell across the land, and each man lived by might and cleverness in a dog-eat-dog world of warlords and rebellions. The novel shows how those fit for heaven's favor rise and those incapable, unjust or unlucky fall by the way (usually decapitated by rivals). And yet turns of fate are such and the Han so ill-favored that an able and true man, a scion of the imperial house, cannot reunite the empire. Even with great virtue he cannot overcome the ultimate disposer, fate. Thus, the novel poses the basic moral dilemma of Sino-Vietnamese culture: What is the point of being good if fate determines our reward? Even today these stories are given in the *hat boi*, a form of opera, in annual ceremonies at the village shrine. The minister of state for culture in 1970, Mai Tho Truyen, struggled to preserve this art form to remind people of the ethics of their race. Contemporary pop-opera, *cai luong*, has attracted the best talent and plays to full houses. When *cai luong* is shown on Saigon TV every Friday, the power drain brings down the voltage throughout the city. These new stories take old issues and plots and combine them with sex, romance, and magic or add a modern setting. As a result there isn't a Vietnamese who can't name characters in the *Romance* or describe an incident or quote an aphorism. Contemporary political and military tactics are also discussed by Vietnamese with reference to the *Romance*.

In this novel and in the *Songs* we see basic individual drives operating within the Vietnamese world view. Guides to behavior (what is good and what is bad) are there for all to follow in ordering their own lives. The *Romance* also lets us predict actions of figures in today's world, for the novel's characters are not so

much individuals as character-types. We see what kinds of men form solid relationships and which are not to be trusted, the roles of fate, heaven, the good
leader, the evil man, or the well-intentioned but incompetent statesman. Just
how relevant these traditional patterns are in the modern world is possibly the
most thorny question facing most Vietnamese as they stand in tradition and
look over to the ethic of progress founded on Western rational faith in man's
control of his destiny. Vietnamese wonder if what is theirs must give way to
the alien style and drive. But Western modernity has been modified in Japan
to leave room for much of the traditional. Studies in different cultures also
attest to the power of older patterns to survive, especially where tied to fundamental religious beliefs about the purpose of man. This hold of tradition is
bound to be strong on politics, where conflicts of purpose are resolved involving
morals as well as narrower questions of interest. A people's politics are shaped
by their notions of good, and their social structures bear the impress of their
general perceptions and beliefs. Thus, since the mandate concept is part of
nearly every Vietnamese's understanding of how the universe works, it will
continue to exercise pervasive influence and to modify his adaptations of
of Western institutional forms.

The key to any mandate in the *Songs* and the *Romance*, as well as everywhere in Vietnam (once we look for it), is the individual. Only the right kind
of person can inherit a mandate, someone always respected and trusted as a
source of social harmony. It does not stretch reality too much to say that
Vietnamese society functions well only when individuals appear who meet
the rigorous standards of right conduct. Otherwise, affairs remain in a state
of tension—between brothers, within families, in a group or association, in a
ministry, or in the nation. The traditional ethic has prescribed loyalties
between father and son, husband and wife, brother and brother, etc., but
under observation these appear to be only very formal, external standards.
They do not insure smooth and satisfactory emotional relations. Children
will perform rites for ancestors and use respectful language towards parents,
but at the same time nourish deep disgust for the entire family or feel that
their father is an old fool and tyrant. But these formalities have penetrated
deeply the personality structure, so the conflict of form with feeling generates
both a heavy burden of guilt and simultaneous resentment of guilt. In fact,
not a few families break under the resulting tension, a frequent subject of
novels and plays. Superficially, Vietnamese culture provides for order and
regularity, and it often seems very regular to the stranger. But the inner emotional reality of the person and the family is constant stress, tension, and conflict. A family, for example, is only happy if the father is a "good" man and
his wife has sufficient character to recognize her obligations to a "good" man.

So the important questions a Vietnamese asks about anyone is: What kind
of a person is he? How does he conduct himself? How did he act in the past?
Anecdotes and gossip necessarily play a profound role here. They are more

than interesting; they reflect and determine how people treat each other. And in Vietnamese politics, where the game is for the mandate, a man's personal life is more critical. We generally tend only to ask about a man's position, where he stands on issues or whether his interest is similar to ours. In Vietnam one assumes that if the man himself is right, his policies will be right and his self-interest will correspond with the general good. But there is a paradox in Vietnamese political culture: right actions may not lead to wordly success, and worldly success may fall to those considered "bad." If fate predetermines everything, then even our ability to be "good" is fixed. Life is a puppet theater. This is one pole in Vietnamese thought and underlies the abdication of responsibility often seen in the South. At the other extreme is the belief that humans have power to shape their behavior and subsequently their fate. Other Vietnamese believe their fate has been predetermined but that their good deeds will improve the lot of their children and grandchildren. At the pole of belief that behavior can release one from the dead weight of the past is Buddhism and its emphasis on self-control. The more complex middle position, including Confucian and Taoist ideas (Taoist thought easily sliding into Buddhist belief), holds that fate is nothing more than the sum of cosmic, terrestrial, and human energy, each manipulable to some degree. While the larger outlines of one's life are determined by celestial and terrestrial energy, there is a separate level of human energy more under our control which can affect the pattern of our days. The three levels of energy are generated by the unknowable cosmos, the ultimate unity, and consist of flows of yin and yang. The difference between Confucian and Taoist traditions is that the first controls human energy through observance of formal ritual relationships and the second demands actual physical control of energy within one's body. In Confucianism there is a tendency to believe the man who ignores social proprieties does so by choice and so can correct his ways. The *Songs* tell of ministers lamenting that if only the king would see the "right" and abandon his concubines and revels, the state would become healthy again. Even here there is acknowledgment that human energy alone is too insignificant to deflect terrestrial and celestial forces, especially when they act in combination.

Inner workings of these latter forces are known by men to some degree. Heavenly forces of the cosmos or earth can be studied to predict and interpret events. Americans have recently developed a fascination for the I-Ching with its sixty-four basic combinations of yin and yang. This book was written to give political guidance to princes of ancient China, but it is only one way of ascertaining fate. The first discipline remains astrology. The thrust of celestial forces at the precise moment of one's birth defines possibilities for one's life. A successful imperial ruling house with a firm mandate might pass to an emperor born under the wrong stars. The mandate would then begin to crumble. We know Vietnamese frequently consult astrologers over each major event in their lives: funerals, betrothals, weddings, business deals, and family problems. The

1970 Cambodian operation was postponed a day because General Do Cao Tri's astrologer had advised him against fighting on that day. And General Tri is said to have died because he disobeyed the astrologer's warning to remain indoors for three days. Returning to the field on the third day, he was killed in a helicopter crash. A province chief I worked with would begin to build outposts only on auspicious days. Astrologers make a living interpreting the combination of the five elemental forces (fire, water, earth, gold and wood) dominant at the hour, month, and year of their client's birth. The cycle of these five forces differs for the hours, months, and years, so working out the dominant combination for a given individual is very complicated.

There is a second science, geomancy, which interprets the flow of yin and yang within the earth to determine the shape of terrestrial forces. These forces modify and supplement celestial ones. They act through the location of the graves of one's paternal male forebears, the place of one's birth, and the siting of one's house. An ambitious man often moves his father's grave to a more auspicious location. Changing the site of a great-grandfather's grave brought greater longevity to a family whose members for several generations had died short of the age of fifty. Every man considers a proper grave site for himself to be advantageous for his offspring. Having one's body left on the battlefield has terrible consequences for one's children and grandchildren. Thieu's father and grandfather are buried under the lee of a dragon rock in an auspicious village, and it is therefore regarded as no accident that Thieu has risen to high power. He has done better than his brothers, possibly because his stars are more favorable than theirs. Many still believe one reason for the Nguyen dynasty's decline was Emperor Tu Duc's refusal to consult a geomancer on location of his tomb. He chose a spot with pond and trees, favored during his life for picnics and contemplation, but all wrong for a grave, as it did not focus earthly energy on the tomb itself but let it all run off.

A favorable location of birth may balance the ill fortune of having one's ancestors buried in inauspicious places. Thieu is said by intimates to believe in his right to rule partly because he was born in a village capable of producing a national leader. He has ordered the village council not to sell any land to Chinese for fear they will set graves there and obtain advantages for their race. But unfortunately for Thieu, energy flows in the region surrounding his village in Ninh Thuan Province do not generate great potential and limit the effect of energy within the village. The mountains run close and parallel to the sea, so energy runs north and south along the coast and does not concentrate around the village, though whatever energy passes through the village is trapped and held.

In Vietnam, the great reservoir of energy lies in the Mekong Delta, the flat plains through which run the nine mouths of the Mekong River. The Mekong is called the Nine Dragon River because flowing water is a major carrier of terrestrial energy, and an energy flow is a "dragon." One of the first Vietnamese settlements in the Delta was Vinh Long, meaning "Eternal Dragon." The province's location was considered the most auspicious in the central Delta. It is the origin of Vice-President Tran Van Huong and many leaders of the southern branch of the Dai Viet nationalist party. Vinh Long sits between two main branches of the Mekong. Since energy flows from high to low and the Mekong rises in the highest mountains in the world, the Himalayas, a vast flow of energy cascades down its course to finally come to rest in the Delta. (It is not believed to flow out to sea.) This lower Delta energy concentration explains why Vietnamese were able to move from the Delta and conquer Cambodia, why Gia Long could come from the Delta with a few followers and a weak claim to the throne and yet establish a new mandate and unite the nation. At present, many Vietnamese nationalists believe this southern energy will prevent Hanoi from taking over the south. There is also good reason to expect that the man who will bring a new mandate and make peace will come from the Delta.

The geomancy of one's house is also important for success, because if the lay of the land lets energy flow away, one's achievement potential is reduced. For this reason people consult geomancers when they build, buy, or rent a house. An example of the ill effects of mislocation is Saigon. It lies on the wrong side of the Saigon River to collect the amount of energy needed to power a national government. If it lay on the other side of the river, it would have the Saigon River on its right and the Dong Nai River to its left. In this way energy would flow on both right and left to meet where the rivers join. Yin flowing on the left and yang flowing on the right would meet, and opposite energies would spin in circles within the ambit of the two rivers to provide a great well of energy for citizens of the city. Now the yin energy in the Saigon River flows out to sea. No energy is brought in on the right, leaving a constant drain of power away from the city. This explains the consistent weakness of the government based in Saigon. For all their technical skills, the French, who built the city, were ignorant of this Achilles Heel. They also built what is now the Presidential Palace and made a similar mistake: The palace grounds are higher in front, so energy runs alongside the palace following the slope of the land, again draining the palace of strength and power. This presents a very real problem for Thieu, who is badly advised on geomancy and has been more concerned with the popular notion that there is a physical dragon in the earth under the palace, cathedral, and other buildings in the area. To hold down this dragon's tail and bring stability to the central government, Thieu had a new statue built on Chien Si Circle. The director of city planning told me Thieu insisted on a heavy statue and water, to keep the tail weighted down and cool. However, the geomancer I consult told me it was a waste of effort and that Thieu's real problem was the palace.

The third element whereby cosmic forces determine fate is *tuong*, or features of one's face. As we read palms, so do Vietnamese read the face, only more intently. I cannot stress enough how important this face reading is for interpersonal relations. People judge you from your face even before you speak a word, for it tells what kind of person you are and how they should treat you. Ambassador Ellsworth Bunker had a fine *tuong*, but Ambassador Henry Cabot Lodge was not similarly blessed. President Richard Nixon's *tuong* shows that he will be successful in foreign policy and military combat. A young Vietnamese friend, a second lieutenant, has such a *tuong* of leadership he has commanding influence over full colonels. People can spot honesty, friendship, hypocrisy, greed, and other traits in one's face. They look to the thickness and curve of the eyebrows, shape of the ears, height and width of the nose, thickness and curve of lips, shape of eyes, slant of forehead, etc. For example, a high forehead shows the intelligence required in a leader (Chairman Mao). Thieu is favored with a forehead curved like a calf's liver. Unfortunately, other aspects of his face betray selfishness and opportunism. General Duong Van "Big" Minh has the *tuong* of a nice, honest, dedicated man, but one without decisiveness or ability. Marshal Nguyen Cao Ky's *tuong* is of a man of violence and momentary passions. His teacher advised him to grow the mustache and wear high-collared suits to give an air of dignity and purpose, but few were fooled by such superficial changes. One leader of an effective modern political movement in South Vietnam told me that the great weakness of the nationalists was the lack of anyone with a *tuong* of mandate-bearing proportions. Until heaven sees fit to send forth a man born under the right stars, with impressive *tuong* and presumably from the Delta, then the South can only muddle through. And so the stars, flows of yin and yang in the earth, and shapes of faces combine their cosmic influences over men's destinies.

These energies known to man but not controlled by him can still be modified by the third level of basic energy, the human level between earth and heaven. The Confucian approach to this level of energy is to regulate social and political relations through a worldly moral code to maximize the human energy potential in the scheme of fate. Taoist teaching emphasizes solitude and self-discipline of the individual to master elemental forces open to our control. A man who lives by Confucian tenets shows his devotion to heaven by so doing. At least he will improve the fates of his descendants and may even be rewarded with personal good fortune. The five virtues in the Confucian code are: *nhan*, humaneness; *nghia*, righteousness; *le*, correctness of social intercourse; *tri*, intelligence; and *tin*, faithfulness or fidelity. These virtues evoke a paragon; he who lives up to them in all circumstances is indeed a man of special quality. He will always take the correct path in a conflict of loyalties; his intelligence will give him the upper hand in the world's practical affairs; he will never break his word and will know when not to give it; he will never lose his temper or wrong an innocent; he will deeply respect his parents, remain faithful to his wife, and upright before his children. With such an exacting model before them, it is no wonder Vietnamese have difficulty finding leaders under whom they feel comfortable.

The individual who lives up to this standard stands apart from his friends and associates, and they assume he has been selected for a higher destiny. Such a man possesses *dao duc*, the way of virtue, or simply has *duc,* virtue. He must (1) be concerned for the welfare of all and never intentionally bring another to avoidable harm, (2) know to whom and for what his life must be dedicated, (3) be neither subservient nor condescending, (4) correctly analyze and predict events, and (5) never give cause for mistrust. Achievement of all this is the ultimate, but usually one finds men who realize one or two elements of virtue only. But they merit the accolade of *duc* nonetheless. Some combination of *nghia, le,* and *tin* is considered the threshold. And it is my impression most Vietnamese feel *duc* can be attained by mere application of will.

Possession of *duc* in this ordinary sense is still insufficient for political leadership. The man of virtue may mean well and be very just, but if he can neither influence events or men, he is of no political consequence. His worldly insignificance is prima-facie evidence that no strong combination of cosmic forces supports him. He is not *hop thoi,* or right for the times. To lead, a man must above all else be significant, be able to make a difference. Thus, he must have ability, *tai,* as well as virtue, *duc.* With both he can bring currents of heaven and earth into phase. His mastery of affairs of men must be guided by correct moral purpose, otherwise people will not flock to him, and he must not rule through naked force or manipulation of interests and passions. Once a mandate holds firm sway over earth, heavenly forces see to it that men of right and ability emerge to help in government. But when an unfit ruler comes to power, the mandate is threatened. His more prudent officials desert, then the people fall away, and finally the regime collapses. When the mandate is lost and not yet restored, men of virtue know heaven will not supplement their own meager efforts with higher energies to bring order to the land, so they retire to seek solace in books.

Men possessing only ability, unencumbered by moral scruples, lunge for mastery and struggle for spoils of power only to confirm loss of the mandate by conflict and fratricide. Men of virtue take comfort in the wisdom of their decision to withdraw from public life, and government sinks further into venality. Diem's fall presents a classic case of mandate loss. The regime strayed from the correct path, then good men left the government, the people turned uncooperative, and finally all collapsed. The will of heaven became obscure and up swirled duststorms of chaos. Only the most greedy and selfish went to any lengths to maintain power. Men of thought and concern refused to participate because the government was unworthy. Third-stringers took over the team against professional communist opposition. The Vietnamese, a nation of permanent political bookmakers, shifted the odds even more against the government and remained apathetic. The Buddhists' struggle against Diem, General Nguyen Khanh, and Ky represented a national demand for leaders of *duc,* who could end the declining spiral of government power. The Buddhists did not seek power for themselves, because they lacked the necessary *tai*, or ability, but they sought to build a political force to pressure the government into cleansing itself in the eyes of heaven. With good leaders the people would see that the government deserved to rule. Consequently, the masses would come forward to help, thus confirming the mandate. Even NLF followers would see the new mandate arising and desert to join heaven's cause. This scenario is still the core to oppositionist thought in Vietnam and was the rationale for General "Big" Minh's 1971 presidential campaign. There is an implicit belief among all Vietnamese that the good leader will resolve all problems.

In the 1971 presidential election, the initial candidates were Thieu, credited with *tai* for the successes in the pacification program, "Big" Minh, a man of *duc* but not much ability, and Ky, who lacked both *tai* and *duc*. The differences between Thieu and Minh supporters centered on whether a man of *tai* or of *duc* was more important for the country. Before Minh withdrew, I sensed that the Thieu people were having the better of the contest. The presumption seemed to be that the man with *tai* was more right for the times than the man of mere virtue. Increased rural security and prosperity testified that Thieu was at least competent, and it was considered easier for the man of ability to acquire *duc* than for the man of virtue to become able.

In calculus of leadership, the twin variables of *tai* and *duc* join in the concept of *uy tin,* a three-factor equation of ability to bring about one's intent, moral purpose, and an aura of magical prowess. The true mandate-maker has more than a combination of *tai* and *duc*. He must have a touch of the supernatural: propitious face, stars, and birthplace. He must fuse in himself moral conduct and practical achievement and link these human energies to higher cosmic ones. A man of *uy tin* is the cultural ideal of Vietnam, the sought-after Galahad, a paladin of the people. Only he can bring earth under the beneficence of heaven, as if he were the spout of a funnel opening up to the heavens to pull all blessings down on the earth below. People will come from far and wide to follow his banner. They will sacrifice themselves for him, and he will never want for material comfort as people supply his needs in recognition of his special calling. But his way is precarious, for the slightest blemish or fault flaws the aura of greatness. A series of military setbacks, a political program that fails, or selfish indulgence with women, money, or possessions will trigger doubts about the firmness of his *uy tin.* He must always try to balance the power of *uy* with the moral purpose of *tin* so that he always does what he promises and his promises are morally correct. He is rated on degree of accomplishment and on morality of purpose. Actions alone maintain *uy tin,* which is why Vietnamese warn newly arrived Americans never to judge a man by his words, but always wait to observe his acts. Words alone do not give stature; it must be won and constantly defended. Anyone can tell what are the right things to do, but only a few can do them.

Mistakes are long remembered. More political alliances have aborted or foundered in Vietnam because of some past error, inconsequential to American observers, on the part of one principal. We look at the error as a lapse or more probably as irrelevant, given the pressing need for political unity among Vietnamese. But to Vietnamese the wrong goes to the core of the man and disqualifies him completely. If political union is achieved, it will be burdened with deep mistrust, suspicion, and a reluctance by all parties to rely on any other. It is theoretically possible to atone for mistakes, but this rarely happens. The communists directed much of their village-level appeal against local notables and elders. In general, this has been successful in limiting formal authority held by village elders. However, the particular fate of individual notables and their families has depended more on their individual *uy tin* than class status. *Uy tin* is distinct from class and has an independent life. Wealth and class prerogatives may help gain *uy tin,* but they do not guarantee it. Many local notables were deferred to by the Viet Minh or Viet Cong because of their individual *uy tin* among villagers. In general, those who were rich notables or prominent officials in the 1940s and 1950s became so through cooperation with the French. But benefiting from a foreign power destroys one's *uy tin,* so this structure of formal village authority crumbled easily before the communists, and no one cared to defend it. By emphasizing the national cause and the Mandate of Uncle Ho, the communists recognized the primary motive forces were individualistic and not class.

It is important to note that *uy tin* is an egalitarian notion. Everyone, regardless of class, can obtain society's recognition to the extent that he lives up to the demands of his milieu. An effective farmer, artisan, father, or businessman will gain some degree of *uy tin* in his field. Still it seems in village society, while many can achieve *duc,* the status of *uy tin* is held by the well-to-do who have economic, social, and political resources with which to accomplish things.

In time of stress like the present, *uy tin* falls on those who can cope with the situation, regardless of their class or origin. Thus, from low beginnings arose founders of the Han and Ming dynasties in China. In Vietnam, Tran Hung Dao, Le Loi, and Nguyen Hue came from unprepossessing backgrounds and yet saved the nation. These three are the great national heroes (not the least because they each defeated the Chinese). Tran Hung Dao, having defeated the enemy, retired and returned full power to his emperor. Le Loi established a new dynasty to the acclaim of all and reformed the state. Nguyen Hue is a slightly lesser light, for, though he swept up the people, eliminated corrupt government, and defeated the Chinese, he became selfish and made himself emperor when there was a rightful ruler on the throne. Thus, his *uy tin* is reduced by his imperfect *duc.*

Since *uy tin* works for the humble as well as the mighty, everyone can judge who is qualified to be leader. Farmers as well as mandarins can discuss fitness of the emperor to reign. Politics does not consist of an esoteric body of fact and special considerations known only to urban savants, but is the property of all. Villagers may comment extensively on national affairs, in sharp contrast with

Thai political culture, for example. Every individual has a very real stake in the mandate, for when his society obtains a mandate, he like all others prospers. Whether or not the emperor was fit to rule was always an issue of profound importance for the common man. For rural folk, harvests depended on the emperor's ability to keep heaven and earth in celestial harmony. When harvests failed, floods ravished the land, or wars broke out, everyone looked to the ruler for a remedy, if not for the cause. When the conclusion spread that the ruler had brought about the distress or was powerless to end it, local leaders would spring up proclaiming their *uy tin* and their intent to bring a new mandate to the land. Depending on their character and reputation, men would flock to their standard. Examples are the Tay Son, the Hoa Hao, the Cao Dai, and the VNQDD of 1927-30. In China there were the Taipings, the White Lotus rebellions, and even founders of several dynasties in this pattern of messianic mandate building.

Today there are men of *uy tin,* though government and army leaders have no such pretensions. The charisma of Ho Chi Minh revolved around his *uy tin,* but the great respect he attracted from most Vietnamese did not pass to his party upon his death, for his unique, individual fate could not be transferred. Possibly the most noted man of *uy tin* on the non-communist side is Lieutenant General Ngo Quang Truong, First Military Region Commander, who during North Vietnam's 1972 offensive turned the rout from Quang Tri into an agressive holding and defense within one week. When rioting soldiers heard he had been given command, they went back to their units and order was restored to Hue. That was *uy tin* in action. Lieutenant General Nguyen Chanh Thi is another leader of *uy tin,* as are Colonels Duong Hieu Nghia and Le Van Than. For a while, Thich Tri Quang had much *uy tin,* but people came to feel he was too political, which conflicted with his spiritual calling. Further, he had failed in the 1966 struggle movement. Prime Minister Tran Thien Khiem's considerable *uy tin* was sullied by the corruption of his close relatives. Thieu lost considerable *uy tin* when the 1971 election turned into a fiasco.

It is significant, Vietnamese would say, that the palace clique around Thieu contains no one of *uy tin*. With four or five exceptions, no senior Vietnamese general has *uy tin.* Worst are the few generals who provided Thieu with his support of last resort: Dang Van Quang, Ngo Dzu, Hoang Xuan Lam, Nguyen Van Toan, Nguyen Van Minh, and the late Do Cao Tri. Their *uy tin* quotients tend towards minus infinity. They know very well who has *uy tin* and usually prevent such men from gaining power. It is no wonder ARVN morale is low. Personal histories of these powerful generals have involved the piling of intrigue upon intrigue in quest for personal aggrandizement and riches under the aegis of foreigners. Their skills are not those of the leader but of the flunky who knows how to manipulate in troubled times. These men joined with the French at the beginning of their struggle to reimpose colonialism on Vietnam. They did not even make a pretense of joining the Viet Minh and then leaving after its takeover by the communists. They rose always at the expense of their own people, violating both *nghia* (righteousness) and *nhan* (humaneness). They thus lost any pretense to *uy tin*. Their primary interest has been to cut themselves into monopolies over legal and illegal profit-making operations. They preserve themselves through payoffs to superiors and obsequious subservience to senior American officials who direct the financing of the war and the economy. Two of the only generals respected by their troops were removed from tactical command under overt American pressure, and the careers of Dang Van Quang, Ngo Dzu, and Nguyen Van Minh have been advanced at critical points by favorable American recommendations. One well-respected, ranking American civilian official came repeatedly to the defense of a Vietnamese general held in contempt by his compatriots and accused of heroin smuggling. While these men may have some military competence, their political liabilities are immense. It is not selfishness alone which brings these generals into disrepute, so much as service for the foreigner and success built on the blood of their countrymen.

For the Vietnamese, concern for national loyalty is not just a normal adjunct of citizenship but a basic demand of Sino-Vietnamese culture. The man of *nghia* and of *le* (propriety) knows he owes his existence to his ancestors, first to the ancestor of the Vietnamese race and then to all male descendants between that personage and himself. He owes his own identity to his racial heritage, personified in his mother and father and acknowledged at every Tet. He is obligated to pass on to his progeny what he has received from his forebears.

Vietnamese must be loyal to their heritage and the Chinese to theirs, so the two nations can war against each other though both hold to an ethic that forbids the killing of men. Loyalty to one's own is higher value, so war against an intruder is just. Both parties recognize the other's right to struggle, with the outcome determined by heaven. That the Chinese always lose is seen by Vietnamese as confirmation of their own special destiny. A similar obligation of gratitude exists for one's emperor, because his family has defended and advanced the people. He therefore must be defended against rebels and usurpers, unless their claim of a new mandate appears sound. The great moral issue for the protagonists of the *Romance of the Three Kingdoms* is whether the Han dynasty has so lost its mandate that obligations of loyalty to its current emperor are forfeit.

The kind of nationalism that derives from allegiance to the roots of one's culture is more akin to a sense of peoplehood or ethnic solidarity than the nationalism defined by Western political science. Nationalism is not a modern development in Vietnam, for the Vietnamese have had a strong sense of their own identity and a fierce loyalty to their ethnic group since they entered recorded history in South China thousands of years ago. Of all tribes in South China, only the Vietnamese retained (after Chinese domination) their own identity as an independent people directly under heaven. The others became Cantonese or other groups of present-day southern Chinese. Having moved to the Red River Delta, the Vietnamese continued to nourish this sense of

separateness under a thousand years of Chinese administration. Nationalism
long preceded the French and was used, not fomented, by the Viet Minh. It
is woven throughout the primary culture of the country. The key concept
here is *dan toc,* people, race. The men of great *uy tin* are also known as *anh
hung dan toc,* heroes of the people. Dedication to the ethnic group is manda-
tory for one who aspires to *uy tin.*

Because this nationalism grows from primary obligations placed on individuals by culture and reinforced by family patterns, it is strongest in areas of
tradition: in the villages, among the sects, in families where some ancestor
did high service for the land. Struggles for national survival stimulated great
political forces both for the Viet Minh and the NLF across rural Vietnam.
The local governments established by Ho in 1945 did legitimately replace old
village councils, because they were to lead towards a new mandate for the race
with freedom from foreign domination. The populous zones of pervasive Viet
Minh or NLF influence, such as Quang Ngai and Kien Hoa, had long histories
of resistance to the French owing to intense loyalty to the throne prior to
communist initiatives. The communists grafted themselves onto a hardy root.
They used tradition against itself.

The Catholics have always been a core of resistance to the communists,
but not out of nationalism. They too used the national banner to advance
sectarian interests but were less successful than the communists, since their
power was a direct function of French rule. Most Vietnamese still harbor deep
suspicions that Catholic Vietnamese have alienated themselves from the thrust
of Vietnamese destiny. Many Catholics cannot avoid a sharp twinge of con-
science that they have betrayed their own. Since that religion led to French
colonization, Catholics have much to overcome before they acquire sufficient
uy tin to rule. To keep themselves within the greater Vietnamese family,
Catholics rationalize that they must remain filial to a decision taken by their
forebears or that Catholicism is also a way of morality (*dao duc*) under heaven
and so not incompatible with other aspects of heaven's heritage. But major
change is taking place in relationships between Catholics and non-Catholics
owing to Vatican II and the Council of Asian Bishops. The Church has now
given a clear command for Catholic accommodation to local customs and
national traditions. The leader of this movement within South Vietnam is a
nephew of Ngo Dinh Diem, Bishop Ngo Dinh Thuan. And Thieu, a Catholic,
pays public homage to tradition with joss sticks and bows to national heroes
on very un-Christian altars.

But primordial national loyalty has influenced recent Vietnamese history
more than estrangement of the Catholics. This was the case in the emasculation
of the nationalist parties when they were forced to choose between the communists and the French in 1946. From then until 1954 they were trapped
between two alien foreign ideologies: colonialism and Marxist-Leninist class
warfare. With communists in command of the overt nationalist leaders, and

foreigners leading so-called "nationalist" forces on the other side, there seemed no way to fulfill their obligations as Vietnamese men. The trauma of that experience was deep, for it looked as if history had acquiesced in dissolution of their heritage no matter what happened. Where was their special destiny? The ego and self-confidence of each individual depended on approval of those ancestral generations personalized in his superego. The nationalists only had three choices, none satisfactory: they could join the communists to fight the French; join the French to defeat the communists and then oust the foreigners; or simply do nothing and await events.

Cooperation with the French was the most corrosive of one's ego and reputation. Few pursued that course with any vigor. Alliance with the communists was morally preferable but suicidal for those who remained nationalists first and communists second. The third position of *attentisme* was buttressed by reasoning that heaven had ushered in a period of such chaos that the nation had no choice but to pass through a terrible trial before a new mandate would emerge. And nationalists had seen what happened to their great leaders—Huynh Phu So of the Hoa Hao, Truong Tu Anh of the Dai Viets, even Nguyen Binh of the Viet Minh—all killed by communists acting alone or in combination with the French. They saw the communists rise to power with assistance of the foreign enemy and on the corpses of Vietnamese patriots, and yet they could do nothing. An entire generation of nationalist leadership was crippled by a sense of profound impotence and irrelevance. They had no *uy tin*. Yet the power of Vietnamese nationalism is such that the active non-communist wing of the movement, though bereft of capable leaders and led by colonial, dictatorial, or corrupt regimes and without hope for success, still thrives as a social force and refuses to acknowledge the communists as legitimate holders of the mandate. There is a deep faith that heaven is on the side of the non-communists and that in the long run they will win.

This potent sense of Vietnamese peoplehood is not based exclusively on obligations of Confucian formalism. Vietnamese hold a strong mystical presumption of being a chosen people. In their origin myth a water element, the dragon, united with a spirit from the sky and the mountains to bring forth their race. Thus, a completed circle of yin and yang strengthens the spirit of the people, providing an unusual concentration of cosmic energy. And the geomancy of the nation puts the Vietnamese under special protection of the dragon. They are a dragon people near water at the mouths of great rivers. They also live in the South, the quarter always faced by the emperor in Peking. Dragon ancestry gives them masculine, martial tendencies, while the earth and sky spirit gives them warm, feminine traits and high energy and intelligence. Even many Vietnamese who do not accept such myths believe that they are a special people. No matter how long they live abroad or how well they speak French, they retain a powerful sense of identity as Vietnamese. Like all Vietnamese, they refer to their nation as *dat nuoc*, earth and water, not as *quoc*, the Chinese loanword for "state." There is a clear parallel to the Japanese origin myth and the powerful sense of ethnic pride and tradition; this has not gone unnoticed by the Vietnamese, particularly the Dai Viets and Cao Dai, who actively sought Japanese support against the French. Vietnamese nationalists also compare themselves to the sea between great empires. They also frequently cite Israeli strategy, defense, and kibbutzim as solutions for their war.

This mystic feeling for peoplehood, an identity nurtured in each Vietnamese child from birth, is not only a powerful political force; it must be obeyed by those who seek *uy tin*. Correct behavior and ability in a man working for the wrong cause will win him no loyalty. But when the elements of *uy tin* (including nationalism) are present, then the man generates *chinh nghia,* the principle of righteousness. Every political figure of any standing must have a *chinh nghia* as proof of his *uy tin*. Usually such a cause becomes a complex, abstract philosophy to explain all earthly events and show by its comprehensiveness a mastery of heaven above and earth below, Eastern truth and Western thought. Politics must link the individual with the ultimate; it cannot be propelled by a mere social force, as some demand. The communists have dialectical materialism; the Catholics have Christ and the Bible; the Cao Dai sect has mediums in constant touch with the Cao Dai, the "Great on High"; the Dai Viets have social darwinism, Diem had personalism. Even Colonel Nguyen Be, former director of the Vung Tau training center, had his philosophy to explain everything: "Victory through Love and Sincerity." All these theories and personal world views tend to make political confrontation harshly antagonistic, contributing to fragmentation. Disagreements between politicians are not merely matters of interest, solvable by compromise. Each difference, no matter how small, is an aspect of a larger fundamental premise of one party's *chinh nghia*. Since the cause cannot be compromised, the issue in dispute cannot be compromised either. If the Communists accept a solution short of their stated aims, they must lose the mantle of historical inevitability and righteousness. "Face" is not just a matter of personal pique; it is fundamental to one's power.

Finally, it is perhaps an anomaly that premises of *uy tin* are followed even when there is no mandate and no compulsion to support or follow any existing system of order. Of course, people feel that loss of mandate is only one aspect of the general theory of truth that always obtains. But it is well to remember that politics is shaped by other forces than correct behavior. The pressures of selfish advantage, class interest, bonds of kinship or friendship actively concert to divert one from the correct path. Most succumb to the pressure at one time or another. No one can escape conflict between what is right and what one would like, but compromise here is more damaging to one's political stature than in America. One's *uy tin* is measured by what resolution of the conflict is chosen. In times of mandate loss when there are weaker pressures pushing for good behavior, selfish choices become more common as everyone seeks his own advantage waiting for the brighter dawn. Everyone remembers *uy tin* but is constrained from working for general good out of fear of being taken advantage of.

Using this tentative and limited approach to Vietnamese political culture, it would be possible to analyze elements of national tradition manifest in different political groups and the *uy tin* of individual politicians. Whether or not elections can be incorporated into the Vietnamese political scheme is an open question, and there are signs of strain in their adoption, which is none the happier for having been forced by American pressure. On balance, though, elections can mesh with tradition and even allow for tradition to modernize into a more rational, functionally specific and objective, and less emotional system. And when all the elections from hamlet to president are considered, a good case can be made that Vietnamese electoral democracy is off to a better start than in most modernizing countries.

There are three reasons why the mechanism of elections is most compatible with the basic political culture: first, elections select leaders on qualifications as individuals; second, there is a likeness between the will of the people expressed through elections and the will of heaven as conceived in tradition; and third, elections simplify political calculations. Elections integrate societies through good offices of individuals who as candidates seek to maintain a coalition of voters. It is a *man* who runs for office, though in stable, complex industrial societies the candidate runs as representative of a group and voters chose between aggregations of social and economic power with competing interests. Parties emerge, not as inevitable camp followers of elections, but as vehicles fashioned by unique social, economic, political, and cultural forces in each polity. Since Vietnamese society already hangs together around worthy individuals, elections are appropriate means to select leaders because they emphasize the individual's qualification against other individuals. Elections can easily become a forum for comparing different bearers of *uy tin*.

Consider, for example, the method and results of leadership selection in non-communist Vietnam from 1946 until 1967. Leaders, such as Bao Dai, Diem, and Khanh had to be acceptable to a small, special interest minority— first the French, then conservative wealthy and Catholic elements, and then the generals. That political system was *not* designed to bring out the kind of men most acceptable to Vietnamese, and consequently it was unsuccessful. Further, it could not remove men from office once they compromised their *uy tin*, as in the case of Diem. Vietnamese need a procedure not only to get right people into power, but more importantly to remove them quickly and legitimately when their time has passed. The reason Vietnamese are so sensitive to the issue of genuinely free election is that an effort to thwart the natural tendency of an election by rigging it prevents the man qualified by heaven and recognized by the people from coming to the fore. By denying free expression of the will of heaven, an administration acknowledges its lack of mandate and subjects the state to mandate loss under fraudulently elected leaders.

Second, there is an old saying: "*Y dan la y troi*"—the people embody the mind of heaven. This notion appears throughout the *Songs* and is found in the passage quoted above. Nothing so perfectly brings the mind of heaven into our lives as following the wishes of the common people. And in theory no political mechanism does this better over time than elections. In the past, confirmation of a mandate came with rural prosperity; if famine, flood, or drought plagued the land, the king had no reliable mandate and rebellion was expected. Before the advent of elections, a society could only look to external signs of military victory, success of specific policies, and general prosperity to make up its mind over the ruler's legitimacy. There was no device to transfer legitimacy automatically without decline, struggle, and renewal. Now elections can maintain traditional values and leave the ultimate decision with the people, but at the same time provide routinized political change. If elections are free, the people will express preferences and the men so selected must by necessity be in harmony with those desires and by inference must also be blessed of heaven.

Elections are a modern technique to accomplish traditional goals. Thus, when Diem stage-managed his elections to achieve an 89 percent majority and prove he had a mandate, he misunderstood the role of elections vis-à-vis the mandate. If they only confirm a power arrangement made by men, they say nothing about the higher harmony of that arrangement with heaven. An election may in fact confer legitimacy upon a man already in power. It is no coincidence that Diem began to lose *uy tin* after the uncontested election to the National Assembly in 1959 and a simultaneous decline in the price of rice. Both events cast doubt on his fitness to hold a mandate. When he reneged on promises made to defuse the coup of 1960, Diem again cast doubt on his possession of *duc*. When self-immolations by monks showed how out of line heaven and earth were, Diem was deserted by all.

Third, elections are compatible with Vietnamese political culture, for they simplify political life. Previously, assessments of politics and resulting decisions had to be made on the basis of gossip about personal behavior, inside stories of the latest intrigues, and imprecise calculations of who had what kind of influence. Good judgments were hard to make in such confusion, and there were many differing versions of how things *really* stood. Actors and onlookers were caught in a ceaseless undulation where friendships, understandings, and alliances were always subject to change with the latest rumor or development. There were no fixed points of reference. Calculations had to start with power at the top and trace it down. The system was Saigon biased. Since the advent of elections, however, and particularly local ones, there is a clear guide as to just who represents what political strength, who is gaining power or losing it, and who has *uy tin*—all of this confirmed by the imprimatur of heaven acting through voters. Now one must look to the local areas to make political assessments. Saigon alone provides increasingly fewer answers. Whoever controls a bloc of voters in Long An or Binh Dinh, for example, is now critical for operational politics as never before. He forms one of many fixed points which can be woven into a field view of what is happening. This changing scene, while still complex and far from stable, is less ephemeral than previous ones and produces a greater sense of some order in political life.

For example, the role of the Revolutionary Dai Viets is no longer a function of the claims Ha Thuc Ky has on Thieu, but of how well the party did in elections. Recently they have been doing badly, for An Quang-supported candidates won in the RDV's central Vietnam stronghold. The party's inability to rig the 1971 Lower House elections in Hue brought them into a furious struggle with the province chief, who had An Quang support. The Hoa Hao and Cao Dai have gained steadily in influence as they have developed the technique of bullet voting for their single slate to triumph among the inevitable plethora of candidates who split all other votes. Yet unionist Tran Quoc Buu is finding it difficult to translate his labor advantages into votes. His candidates usually win only where they are supported by the local administration.

The political standing of these individuals and groups is taking on more and more the coloring of hard realities (which can be relied upon for political calculations) and less of salon conjecture. Vietnamese political cognoscenti are rapidly becoming analysts of voting behavior, candidate appeal, and bloc combinations. This new certainty about politics means that the man who wins an election, or better yet several, commands some position in making alliances, for he offers proven respect and willingness of others to deal with him. His *uy tin* is established, for he trades in hard political currency. In the 1970 Senate elections and the 1971 House election, a detailed *quid pro quo* was established between An Quang and the Progressive Nationalist Movement, an unusual event in older days. An Quang would concentrate on Binh Dinh to the north and throw second-choice votes to the PNM, which would reciprocate in Military Regions III and IV. While alliances featuring compromise are made more feasible, it is not clear they have become more probable, because cultural factors of *chinh nghia* and fragility of *uy tin* still have a fragmenting impulse. At least now there are countervailing pressures for accommodation.

In assessing the fit between electoral democracy and traditional political culture in Vietnam, points of friction between the two are equally impressive. There are three obvious ones, and more may be lurking under the surface. First, running for election calls for a lot of talk and making many promises. Even in Vietnam, an important dimension of any campaign is showing how you will do more for people than the many other candidates. (There were eighty-seven candidates for one Saigon seat in the Lower House.) Many of those elected find themselves trapped by grandiose promises and are unable to perform. If they get their just desserts they will be defeated the next time around and subsequently harbor some resentment at the system—particularly if they are defeated

by someone who makes even more outlandish promises than they did. Elections
up to now have been remarkable for the high turnover rate of officeholders,
though generally this has brought forth better quality men. Not many incumbents run for re-election, and of those who do, few are selected again. But more
important than candidate frustration is popular frustration arising from elected
officials' inability to meet expectations generated by a campaign. Given the
importance of standing by your word in Vietnam, a system unable to produce
expected results presents a constant invitation for a colonel's coup by dedicated,
relatively honest, and dynamic officers frantic to do away with petty politicians
and get things done for the people. The political culture would reward with
high *uy tin* men like this who proved effective on behalf of the public weal even
if they weren't elected. Elections must produce hard results to become accepted
as the acknowledged instrument of heaven's will.

Second, an electoral system over time tends to foster alliances between
small, well-organized minorities trading blocs of votes and guaranteeing each
some measure of power. As long as vast numbers of candidates enter the lists
and parcel up the prize of votes, it is practically impossible to displace incumbent representatives of small disciplined groups. The tendency in Vietnam has
been for groups to fly apart, but now there are new incentives for groups to
aggregate voting power and avoid internal splits. And usually control of only
15 percent of the vote is sufficient for victory in local elections. If organized
groups are able to dominate elections blatantly, they will add a seeming stability
to the political process but at a cost of frustrating the popular wish to have the
most qualified individual win. Legitimacy is not won by government by granting
an opportunity to make a choice among a limited number of candidates but
rather by assuring that men are selected through open contests in which *only*
individual qualifications are relevant. In America if one group consistently wins
elections, the system as a whole is still responsive, while in Vietnam this would
probably be seen as evidence of something wrong. Social forces should only
dominate after winning heaven's approval. The group's candidate will only
threaten the structure if he is incompetent and owes his election to status within
a group that gives him blind loyalty. The other 80 percent of the electorate may
not feel that his election is just.

A third, less important conflict between electoral behavior and tradition is
the constraint on compromise owing to emphasis on rigid consistency of position. To avoid losing *uy tin*, a politician must not be seen as a selfish oppor-
tunist, only as a man of long-standing principle. If he becomes too identified
with a particular position, it is very difficult for him to change his stance without serious loss of prestige, thus obstructing alliance and the passage of legislation.

Moving to a more abstract level of Western analysis, several electoral developments seem auspicious for the future. One major weakness of the non-communists has been lack of an acceptable *chinh nghia* (righteous cause) after the

Viet Minh usurped the banner of national self-determination. Diem's cause of personalism was a studied attempt to take advantage of respect for the leader and the individualism inherent in Vietnamese culture, but it was too ersatz and unsupported by outward signs of cosmic approval. The 1967 Constitution, with its dedication to electoral democracy, provides a more valid political cause. In contrast with communist totalitarian rule on behalf of the once-dispossessed, the Constitution offers a system where many flexible aspects of traditional culture can play a role. It incorporates many essential elements of past political life, with which Vietnamese feel comfortable, into a system that offers a more organized, rational approach to social problems and national development along with a measure of greater social justice. Around this cause most non-communist Vietnamese can rally. The Constitution can subsume most of present *chinh nghia's*. The constitutional cause also offers a most respectable reply to the communists: If they renounce force and compete with others according to the rules, they can be included under the constitutional umbrella through amendment of a few clauses, such as the one outlawing communism and pro-communist neutralism. Note however that in so doing the communists would have to relinquish claim to an exclusive *chinh nghia.*

Second, the entire electoral structure brings out many individuals at different levels with a claim to *uy tin* and legitimate authority. No longer does the entire political structure hang on the quality of the few men at the top. There is now a middle and a bottom around which people can cling. Already this expanded structure is providing Vietnam with extra stability without the need of repression.

My assumption is that first concerns of most citizens lie in local politics. If their needs can only be met through action at the national level then the system is top-heavy and unstable. Substantial local power is essential for political health. However, owing to the mandate theory, Vietnamese politics has hung the legitimacy of local government on the legitimacy of the one man at the top. Local government depended on perfection at the national level. When the leader fell the entire system collapsed. Now, with local elections, local power rests on local legitimacy. For example, politicians' involvement in the 1971 Lower House election defused the intensity of their concern with the Presidential election crisis. What formerly would have paralyzed political circles passed without undue fuss. The administration continued to function smoothly, the army fought on, the politicians were wrapped up in local politics, and the people looked on. And the electoral selection of many good men for the Lower House, particularly in Saigon, added prestige to the constitutional structure to counterbalance the presidential non-election's negative impact. Lack of one man at the top whose *uy tin* is accepted by all no longer cripples the polity but only slows it down.

Third, the process of elections should enhance both stability and the articulation of popular concerns by encouraging constituency ties and formation of more clearly defined constituency groupings. Politicians who maintain good standing with their districts and produce reasonable results can expect re-election. I have already seen Vietnamese politicians on the hustings, not kissing babies, but attending weddings, funerals, and communal hall ceremonies. In seeking out voters, or more accurately those with *uy tin* in a community who influence voters, politicians participate in a dialogue with the people. At the very least, this process allows citizens to get a crack at the power structure by venting their dissatisfactions. A greater popular sense of participation and interest in the system's workings should follow. Acceptance, even on that level, adds stability to the whole. One can talk of an emerging political community.

Simultaneously, with strengthening of interest articulation, the electoral process rewards groups controlling a sizable share of the vote. This adds stability to the internal cohesion of these semipolitical organizations and facilitates deals between them. Deals are the first steps towards more lasting combinations. Through elections groups can bring power to bear on local issues and pull individuals from social roles into politics, insuring an interface between polity and society. In short, pressures generated by elections encourage groups and individuals to take actions that lead to contact, communication, and cooperation. The system develops more give and take, becomes less brittle.

Fourth, development of interconnected levels of elected representatives at village, province, and in the Lower House provides a vertical channel to move issues up until they hit a power point where action can be taken. Now there are political pressures on bureaucrats to perform, if only to avoid having their *uy tin* publicly disparaged. Administrators at each level must also now consider the elected representative's chance of obtaining a favorable hearing at a higher level. As a result of these prods on the administration, effectiveness and responsiveness of government should improve. Responsive government has a better chance of resolving particular problems and gaining the kind of over-all mastery of problems associated with winning a mandate. Government that works and demonstrates substantive changes in the life of the people is given a strong presumption of possessing a mandate. Again, consequences of a proper system of elections should go far towards giving Vietnamese politics a novel stability and order, happily devoid of the familiar choke-hold of the wrong few at the top. It is highly probable that legitimate desires will continue to be frustrated in varying degrees, but the important point is that there is now sufficient pressure to move the system where before no pressure has ever existed.

Here, however, as with everything else in Vietnam, it is treading too close to folly to offer firm conclusions. It is, after all, possible heaven has given the democratic trend in Vietnam only a few years' warranty.

3 Broadening the Base: South Vietnamese Elections, 1967-71
Theresa A. Tull

From 1967 to 1971 the average Vietnamese had opportunity to vote in nine elections. He chose officials to run his hamlet and to govern his country. He voted for his hamlet chief, his village council, his provincial or municipal council, twice selected an entire Lower House of the National Assembly, elected an initial sixty-man Senate for the National Assembly and initiated the triennial replacement of one-half of that body, and twice voted for a president and vice-president.

What has this almost bewildering series of elections meant to Vietnam? Although political development has been an uneven process, the present political situation is a marked improvement over the difficult years between the overthrow of Ngo Dinh Diem on November 1, 1963, and the series of elections held under the 1967 Constitution has contributed to the improved situation. Although each election was unique, with its own character and impact, some broad, tentative conclusions can be drawn concerning the over-all process:

1. *Legitimacy.* The elections have lent legitimacy to the Republic of Vietnam's top leaders. As a consequence of the September 1967 presidential election, Nguyen Van Thieu and Nguyen Cao Ky were elevated from positions of "first among equals" in the ruling military group to the status of constitutionally elected president and vice-president. Presidential legitimacy has been weakened to some extent, however, as a result of the uncontested presidential election in 1971.

2. *Stability.* Political stability enjoyed by the Republic of Vietnam since initiation of the Second Republic is attributable to many factors: military acquiescence in the Thieu presidency, Thieu's consolidation of control over the government's administrative structure, improved security, and a general disinclination to revert to the instability and uncertainty of the immediate post-Diem period. The elections, however, also contributed to political stability by providing a constructive channel for opposition activity, a mechanism for orderly change, and opportunities for upward political mobility. The politically active can progress from local to province to national-level office. The 1970 decision of the An Quang Buddhists to participate in the Senate election, and subsequently the 1971 Lower House election, was a positive contribution to political stability.

3. *Broader Participation in Decision Making.* The popularly elected National Assembly and provincial, municipal, and village councils have

broadened popular participation in decision making. The National Assembly has defended fiercely its interpretation of its constitutional prerogatives, if not always successfully, and is a force to be reckoned with in governing the country. The national government increased the authority of provincial, municipal, and village councils, broadening their role in government.

4. *Accountability.* Elected officials have been held accountable by voters for their actions. Many incumbents were unseated in the June 1970 provincial and municipal council elections. In August 1971 only 41 of the 119 incumbent deputies who sought re-election were returned to the Lower House.

5. *Increased Political Party Activity.* By providing a purpose for such activity, the series of elections held since 1967 have stimulated nationalist political party activity. Parties have done well in local elections or in the constituency-based Lower House election. The failure of political parties to make an appreciable impact in elections in which the entire nation is the constituency (presidential, senatorial) may provide an added stimulus for coalescence among the myriad diversified parties and factions competing on the political scene.

On the other hand, elections have not yet given the Vietnamese people:

1. *Civilian Government.* Although the top levels of the Vietnamese government are ostensibly civilianized, it cannot be said the government has become a civilian government. The military hierarchy seems to eschew politics, apparently content to leave the task of government in the hands of individuals publicly identified as responsible for that task, but it remains a potent force for conservatism, stability, and vigorous pursuit of the war. Thieu has gradually assumed a civilian political image, but he is still a general. His would-be 1971 opponents for the presidency, Duong Van Minh and Ky, are generals. The prime minister, also a potential aspirant to the presidency, is a general. Key government programs—pacification, defense, interior—are run by generals; province chiefs are military officers. The electoral process has introduced significant civilian elements into the governing process, but has not yet returned the reins of government to civilian hands.

2. *Unity.* The impetus provided by frequent elections has not been sufficient to overcome South Vietnam's principal shortcoming, a lack of national unity. Elections have not forced coalescence of Vietnam's multiple political parties into a few meaningful progovernment and opposition groupings. This failure was particularly apparent in connection with the contested 1971 presidential election. Vietnam continues in its debilitating diversity, faction-plagued, its politicians paying generous lip service to the necessity of national unity, but most remaining unwilling to submerge personal identities or organizations in a larger grouping to achieve that unity.

In spite of these shortcomings, however, it can be argued that the Vietnamese body politic is healthier even after the 1971 presidential election than it was in 1967, because of the series of elections since the adoption of the Constitution. A close examination of these elections supports this conclusion.

Presidential Elections, 1967-71

The Republic of Vietnam's Constitution, promulgated April 1, 1967, calls for the election of a president and vice-president every four years. Accordingly, on September 3, 1967, Vietnamese voters went to the polls. They were also asked to elect a sixty-man upper house of the National Assembly.

The 1967 elections have been examined extensively, and there is little to add to that examination, but one feature of the 1967 presidential election had considerable bearing on the evolution of the 1971 presidential contest. In 1967, the military slate of General Nguyen Van Thieu and Air Vice-Marshal Nguyen Cao Ky, then chief of state and prime minister, respectively, was opposed by ten civilian slates of candidates and was elected with only 34.8 percent of the total votes cast. The 1967 candidates, in order of finish, are shown in table 3-1.

Table 3-1
1967 Presidential Returns
(As released by the Provisional National Assembly, Sept. 5, 1967)

Slate	Votes	Percent of Vote
Nguyen Van Thieu Nguyen Cao Ky	1,649,561	34.8
Truong Dinh Dzu Tran Van Chieu	817,120	17.2
Phan Khac Suu Phan Quang Dan	513,374	10.8
Tran Van Huong Mai Tho Truyen	474,100	10.0
Ha Thuc Ky Nguyen Van Dinh	349,473	7.3
Nguyen Dinh Quat Tran Cuu Chan	291,718	6.2
Nguyen Hoa Hiep Nguyen The Truyen	160,790	3.5
Vu Hong Khanh Duong Trung Dong	149,276	3.2
Hoang Co Binh Lieu Quang Khinh	131,071	2.9
Pham Huy Co Ly Quoc Sinh	106,317	2.2
Tran Van Ly Huynh Cong Duong	92,604	1.9

Of the 5,853,251 registered voters, 4,868,266, or 83 percent of those registered, actually voted. The Suu-Dan slate won in Danang, Hue, and Thua Thien, thanks to Buddhist support. Tran Van Huong, twice mayor of Saigon, won in the capital city. The Dzu-Chieu "peace" ticket took Quang Ngai, Binh Duong, Hau Nghia, Tay Ninh, and Kien Phong. The Thieu-Ky slate won all other electoral jurisdictions, running particularly well in the Delta and in the Central Highlands.

The plethora of candidates and the resultant "minority" victory was not forgotten by the successful candidate, to whom the opposition applied the label of "minority president." As the 1971 presidential election approached, Thieu was determined to avoid a repetition of his minority victory. His determination to win a clear-cut majority of total votes cast led him and his supporters to an excess of zeal and to miscalculation of his 1971 opponents, which backfired into the embarrassment of a totally uncontested election.

Evolution of the 1971 Uncontested Election

Reflecting President Thieu's conviction that a president could govern more effectively if elected by a majority of the people, the election law passed by the National Assembly to govern the conduct of the October 3, 1971, presidential election stipulated that all candidates must obtain endorsements of either 40 National Assembly members or 100 provincial and/or municipal councillors. Proponents of this controversial provision contended it was designed to discourage nonserious candidates lacking proven popular support. Opponents of the endorsement provision argued it was a device to exclude opposition candidates to the benefit of the incumbent president. They alleged that the provision, which had been removed by the Senate (Upper House), was reinstated by the Lower House in response to bribes and executive branch intimidation. They also contended the provision was unconstitutional. The Supreme Court, nonetheless, in response to a formal challenge, upheld the provision's constitutionality.

Thieu's principal presumed opponent, retired General Duong Van Minh, had no difficulty obtaining necessary endorsements. He collected signatures from 44 National Assembly members. Vice-President Ky, however, who as a result of a rumored arrangement with Minh had concentrated his efforts on councillors, encountered difficulty. The vice-president claimed province chiefs were obstructing his efforts to establish his candidacy and alleged that councillors has been intimidated into endorsing Thieu. (The president and his running mate, Tran Van Huong, collected 452 of a possible 552 councillor endorsements, together with 104 National Assembly signatures.)

Ky still filed his candidacy, presenting 61 properly certified councillor endorsements and an additional 41 uncertified endorsements from councillors who initially endorsed Thieu but wished to switch their endorsements to the vice-president. The Office of the Supreme Court, a special three-member body which accepted the Thieu and Minh candidacies, provisionally declined to accept the Ky candidacy because he had not submitted the required 100 certified endorsements. The Court observed that the vice-president could appeal this preliminary ruling. Ky declined to appeal the Court ruling. He denied the authority of the Office of the Supreme Court to provisionally exclude his candidacy and contended it was up to the entire Supreme Court to resolve the issue.

On August 20, General Minh withdrew his candidacy. Minh said he had concluded the election would not be fairly conducted. He alleged that the central government had issued detailed instructions to province chiefs calling for improper intervention by them and other government officials on behalf of the incumbent president. Although the Supreme Court, meeting as a whole, ruled August 21 that the Ky candidacy was valid, Ky refused to be a candidate, alleging the election would not be fairly conducted. He demanded his name be removed from the candidates' list, and the Court ultimately acceded to his request. Thieu was left the sole candidate, to run unopposed.

Thieu would not be dissuaded from continuing with the election as scheduled. He told the Vietnamese people he would consider the election as a referendum, and if the results demonstrated the people were dissatisfied with his leadership, he would resign. He subsequently explained all invalidated ballots would be counted as votes of "no confidence." (A ballot is invalidated by being torn or marked, or if an empty envelope is cast.) Thieu said he would not remain in office if he received less than 50 percent of the total votes cast. He flatly rejected Ky's suggestion that they both resign to permit the Senate chairman to organize a new election (as permitted under one interpretation of Article 56 of the Constitution).

Politically outmaneuvered by his opponents, Thieu declined to accede to their demands for a new election, but decided instead to risk the embarrassment of running uncontested rather than chance the possibility of prolonged instability or the weakening of his own position as a consequence of a delayed election.

The opposition, spearheaded by Ky, was unable to organize an effective election boycott. A major element in their failure was the moderate approach adopted by the An Quang Buddhist organization. Its leaders called upon the faithful to "deny" the results of the election but did not actively oppose it or attempt to prevent it by joining in street demonstrations. An intensive get-out-the-vote campaign was undertaken by government administrative personnel, and on October 3 the people went to the polls steadily and in large numbers. When the votes were counted, Thieu could claim to have received his mandate, since 5,971,114 voters, or approximately 83 percent of the total registered voters, had cast valid, or pro-Thieu-Huong, votes. Table 3-2 compares the 1971 returns with the 1967 Thieu-Ky totals.

Table 3-2
Presidential Election

Voter Turnout	1971	1967
Total registered voters	7,192,660	5,853,251
Actual voters	6,327,631	4,868,266
Percentage	87.9	83

Votes Cast	1971	1967
Valid Votes (i.e., pro-Nguyen Van Thieu-Tran Van Huong)	5,971,114	1,649,561[a]
Percentage of total votes cast	94.3	34.8
Invalid Votes (i.e., anti-Nguyen Van Thieu-Tran Van Huong)	356,517	
Percentage of total	5.7	
Valid votes as percentage of total number of registered voters	83	

Breakdown of 1971 Vote by Military Regions and Major Cities

	Total Votes Cast	Turnout Percent- Age	Total Valid Votes	Percentage Valid Votes
Nationwide:	6,327,637	87.9	5,971,114	94.3
Military Region I	972,079	85.9	886,585	91.2
Military Region II	1,165,094	90.1	1,123,823	96.5
Military Region III	1,847,820	82.1	1,672,173	90.4
Military Region IV	2,337,558	92.3	2,283,691	97.6
Saigon	516,312	76.5	432,099	83.6
Hue	42,045	67.2	27,059	64.3
Danang	122,081	76.0	90,829	74.4
Qui Nhon	59,017	87.1	58,395	98.0
Nha Trang	66,213	83.3	53,841	81.3

[a]Refers to total number of votes received by Nguyen Van Thieu-Nguyen Cao Ky slate in 1967 presidential election against ten competing slates.

The high voter turnout figures and high percentage of valid votes cast have been criticized as excessive. Doubtless in some localities some returns were inflated; how much will never be known. Allowing for some inflation, however, the returns were not surprising, and there is some correlation with known Thieu strong and weak spots. Voter turnout and percentage of valid votes cast were highest in Military Region IV, which includes the populous Delta, where Thieu ran well in 1967. The high rural turnout can be attributed to the efficiency of local officials and greater receptivity of the rural voter to official suggestion that he vote, but the efforts Thieu made between 1967 and 1971 to win rural support, including his land-to-the-tiller program, should not be overlooked in assessing rural turnout. In the cities, particularly Saigon and Hue, where Thieu's support has traditionally been weakest, voter turnout was lowest and percentage of invalid votes was highest.

Because Thieu ran without an opponent, the October 3 election was not a conclusive test of popular support for his government. Nonetheless, the election results can be examined in terms of other criteria.

First, the returns, even though possibly inflated, indicated a considerable administrative capability on the part of the central government. Second, the returns were a convincing measure of the improved security situation between 1967 and 1971, since during that time an additional 1,300,000 people were placed on voter rolls. Third, it can be argued that the high turnout and low percentage of invalid votes cast indicated lack of an organized opposition capable of seriously challenging the present occupant of Independence Palace. The prompt return of political calm following the election supports this contention.

The First Senate Election

The initial sixty-man Upper House of the National Assembly was elected on September 3, 1967, concurrently with the president and vice-president, in a unique electoral process. The Constitution specifies that the Senate is to be elected at large, using a system of list voting, with winners determined by plurality. The electoral law required candidates to group themselves into lists of ten members; the six highest-ranking lists were elected in their entirety. Voters were allowed to cast ballots for as many as six lists. There was no provision for a runoff or for any sort of pre-election nominating process. As a result, forty-eight lists, or 480 candidates, were certified to run. (Sixteen lists were disqualified for having "incomplete dossiers" or, in a very few cases, for alleged pro-communist connections.)

The Senate election process placed a premium on voter discipline. Should many voters select ballots in fairly random fashion from among the forty-eight ballots presented to them at the polls, slates that could garner a solid bloc vote were at an advantage. The most likely recipients of this sort of disciplined support were thought to be those slates identified with Catholics, Hoa Hao, or Cao Dai religious organizations, or with nationalist political parties, particularly the VNQDD (Vietnam Quoc Dan Dang) and Dai Viet, or a combination of these groups.

Only the Catholics were sufficiently disciplined to take full advantage of this unusual voting process. Catholic voters, following the lead of parish priests, knew which of the forty-eight slates to back and voted accordingly. Four of the six winning slates were favored by Catholics. The biggest vote-getter, however, the Worker-Farmer-Soldier slate of retired General Tran Van Don, was not Catholic and apparently drew a heavy Buddhist vote, particularly in Military Region I. The Don slate received support from a wide spectrum of the Vietnamese population, owing to the popularity of its leading members (Don, Ton That Dinh, Tran Dien, who was to lose his life during the 1968 Tet offensive, and Dang Van Sung) and to a well-organized campaign. Don's slate won with almost one million votes, far more than his closest runner-up, the slate of respected southern Catholic Nguyen Van Huyen. The slate that finished sixth was also non-Catholic and had a decidedly Revolutionary Dai Viet cast.

The lineup of the first Senate included approximately thirty Catholics, nineteen Buddhists, four Cao Dai, two Hoa Hao, three Confucianists, one animist, and one of unknown religious affiliation. There were twenty-three northern-born senators, sixteen central Vietnamese, and twenty-one southerners. Two senators were Montagnards. The upper house included eleven former members of the Constituent Assembly, a civilian directorate member, four retired generals, six attorneys and judges, six professors, a former chairman of Diem's National Assembly, and several former cabinet ministers of either Diem or post-Diem vintage.

Table 3-3
Official Senate Results, 1967

(Announced by Central Election Council September 18, 1967, and subsequently validated by the upper house itself)

List 13	headed by Tran Van Don	980,474
List 40	headed by Nguyen Van Huyen	631,616
List 8	headed by Nguyen Gia Hien	600,720
List 31	headed by Huynh Van Cao	569,975
List 3	headed by Tran Van Lam	553,720
List 21	headed by Nguyen Ngoc Ky	553,632

1970 Senate Election

The Constitution specifies that senators will be elected for six years, with one-half of the upper house elected every three years. In December 1969 the Senators elected in 1967 drew lots to determine who would serve six-year initial terms and who would have to seek re-election or bow out. Twenty-nine senators drew three-year terms, it having been agreed the term of assassinated Senator Tran Dien would be regarded as of three-years' duration. The election was scheduled for August 30, 1970. An interesting race developed, stimulated by the fact that leaders of the first four winning 1967 slates drew three-year terms and had to gain re-election or leave the Senate. After much speculation and negotiation, a total of eighteen slates of ten candidates each (plus alternates) filed to run for the upper house. Only three slates, or thirty senators, were to be elected. Of these 180 candidates, the Central Election Council disallowed a total of six. Four were disqualified, in accordance with the election law, for having directly or indirectly worked for communism or pro-communist neutralism. One candidate was disallowed because of a criminal conviction. In all but one case the lists affected by these disqualifications had named alternates who were then moved into the vacated positions on these slates. One slate, headed by a relative unknown, had a member disallowed and failed to nominate an alternate, so the entire slate was disqualified for insufficiency of membership. One other slate subsequently withdrew of its own volition, so that sixteen slates—160 candidates—finally made the race, for a candidate-to-position ratio of 5.33:1.

Adding spice to the contest was the appearance of a list headed by Ngo Dinh Diem's onetime foreign minister, Vu Van Mau, an active An Quang Buddhist layman. Abandoning its anti-election stance, An Quang actively supported the Mau list, which included several prominent An Quang laymen.

The participation of the Mau list probably accounted for the absence of a prominent senator from the contest: Tran Van Don, whose list came in first in 1967, did not seek re-election. Don had assumed leadership of the opposition in the first upper house. With two very strong Catholic lists in the race (Huynh Van Cao, who was believed to be Thieu's preference, and the Senate chairman, Nguyen Van Huyen), it did not seem likely, if Catholic voting discipline held, that more than one opposition list could be successful. Saigon rumor suggested Don had been offered a place, but not the leadership position, on the An Quang-backed list. Not heading a list, in view of his 1967 performance, would have been a step backward for Don, and heading a losing slate was unthinkable. For reasons known best to him, he decided not to participate. Don did return to the political arena in 1971, when he was elected to the Lower House from Quang Nam with An Quang support.

The campaign period was quiet, brief, and generally issueless. Most campaigning was done by means of television, radio, and distribution of posters and leaflets. Quiet visits to opinion leaders throughout the country were the rule instead of appearances by candidates before large groups.

When the polls closed August 30, a total of 4,301,139 voters (approximately 65.4 percent of the 6,578,082 registered voters) had cast ballots. Although each could have voted for as many as three slates of ten candidates each, in practice each voter cast an average of 2.28 ballots, indicating that some groups made an effort to discipline followers and to discourage random voting.

When the returns were announced by the Central Election Council, chaired by the chief justice of the Supreme Court, the opposition slate of Vu Van Mau was in first place, followed by the progovernment list of Huynh Van Cao. In third place was the independent list of Nguyen Van Huyen, upper house chairman. Of the twenty-two incumbents who sought re-election, eleven were successful.

It can be argued that the determining factor in the success of these three slates was religion. The Mau list received ardent backing from the An Quang Buddhists and ran particularly well in the areas of greatest An Quang strength: Military Region I, the coastal portions of Military Region II, and Saigon.

The Cao and Huyen lists had strong Catholic identification. However, even though two of the three winning lists were headed by Catholics, the upper house election revealed a slackening in Catholic political discipline. With the prospect of only three winning lists, Catholics fielded five slates of candidates. The hierarchy reportedly let it be known the Cao and Huyen slates were to be supported by the faithful, but permitted "local option" for the third selection.

The lack of political parties with national strength was again demonstrated in the upper house election. Religion and personal prestige were the factors that carried most weight with Vietnamese voters. Yet the election provided an excellent opportunity for the regionally based political parties to test their national strength. Several parties participated, and some did relatively well. The fourth-, fifth-, and sixth-place finishers out of the sixteen-slate field all represented political parties. The fourth-place finisher, headed by southern Catholic Truong Vinh Le, included elements of one faction of the Nhan Xa party, a Catholic party formed in 1968, and VNQDD personality Pham Thai. In fifth place was the Progressive Nationalist Movement's slate, headed by the party secretary-general, Nguyen Ngoc Huy. (The PNM, a party with a moderate opposition stance and organized in 1968, included elements of the Tan Dai Viet party and numbered many National Institute of Administration graduates among its members.) The Revolutionary Dai Viet offering, headed by Nguyen Van Canh, came in sixth, probably aided by the presence of an RDV member in the cabinet. (Had the Dai Viets and the Nhan Xa not been split into competing factions, either of them might have been victorious.)

None of the winning slates, it should be noted, relied exclusively on the appeal of its predominant religious affiliation for votes. The Mau and Cao lists offered the voter a cross-section of the population. Since victory required national support, each of these lists presented a coalition of individuals representing various religious, regional, and ethnic elements. Although heavily An Quang oriented, the Mau list included oppositionist Senator Ton That Dinh, Montagnard Senator Ksor Rot, a Hoa Hao figure, and a Cham. Senator Cao's list re-elected four other incumbent Catholic senators, but also included prominent Cao Dai and Hoa Hao figures, a Montagnard, and an ethnic Cambodian.

Senator Huyen did not go the "coalition" slate route, but relied heavily on regional loyalties to reinforce the religious coloration of his slate. Eight of the ten candidates on his slate were southern; seven of the ten were Catholic. Adding particular southern flavor to his list and moderating its top-heavy Catholicism

was his trump card: Tran Van Huong, twice prime minister, twice mayor of
Saigon, longtime friend of Huyen. Huong's presence may well have provided the
additional support required to bring Huyen's slate home ahead of the govern-
ment-supported, also Catholic, fourth-place Le slate.

The election did not drastically change the composition of the upper house.
It became somewhat more southern and slightly less Catholic than the body
elected in 1967. With the presence of An Quang laymen, the Senate came
closer to reflecting the Vietnamese body politic.

Table 3-4
Comparison of Composition of 1967-70 and 1970-73 Senates

By region of birth:	1967-70	1970-73
(including ethnic-minority members)		
Northern	23	20
Central (both sides of 17th parallel)	16	11
Southern	21	29
Total:	60	60
Ethnic-minority members:		
Montagnard	1	2
Chinese[a]	1	1
Nung	1	–
Cambodian	–	1
Cham	–	1

[a]In addition to one full-blooded Chinese, Lam Van Hiep, alias Lam Hap (1967–70
and 1970–76), there are others with some Chinese blood, e.g., Tran The Minh
(1967–73) and La Thanh Nghe (1970–76).

By religion:		
Catholic	30	25
Buddhist (Vietnamese Mahayana)	19	18
Cao Dai	4	5
Hoa Hao	2	3
Confucianist	3	3
Animist	1	2
Moslem	–	1
Theravada Buddhist (Cambodian)	–	1
Unknown	1	2
Total:	60	60
By age (as of date of election):		
70 and above	1	2
65-69	3	3
60-64	2	5
55-59	6	10
50-54	14	10
45-49	7	9
40-44	11	15
35-39	10	5
30-34 (30 is minimum age)	6	1
Total:	60	60

Table 3-5
Official Senate Election Results, 1970

(Announced by the Central Election Council September 14, 1970, and subsequently validated by the upper house itself)

Winners	No. of Votes
List 11 headed by Vu Van Mau	1,149,597
List 1 headed by Huynh Van Cao	1,106,288
List 3 headed by Nguyen Van Huyen	882,274
Unsuccessful Slates	
List 6 headed by Truong Vinh Le	800,453
List 4 headed by Nguyen Ngoc Huy	654,833
List 9 headed by Nguyen Van Canh	628,992
List 14 headed by Nguyen Dai Bang	611,351
List 7 headed by Truong Cong Cuu	591,258
List 15 headed by Mrs. Nguyen Phuoc Dai	533,692
List 13 headed by Nguyen Van Lai	492,131
List 10 headed by Phan Ba Cam	453,168
List 8 headed by Nguyen Gia Hien	430,465
List 16 headed by Nguyen Tien Hy	420,688
List 12 headed by Nguyen Huu To	399,767
List 2 headed by Nguyen Anh Tuan	342,416
List 5 headed by Nguyen Cao Hach	320,365

Lower House Elections: 1967-71

The Constitution specifies that the Lower House will contain from 100 to 200 deputies, elected as individuals from separate constituencies no larger than provinces. The deputy's term of office is four years, and the entire body is elected at the same time.

The 1967 Contest

The first Lower House under the Constitution of the Second Republic was elected October 22, 1967. Seats were apportioned among constituencies on the basis of one for every 50,000 voters. Voters in a given constituency could cast as many votes as there were seats allotted to the constituency. Sixteen seats were reserved for representatives of minority groups in constituencies where they were most numerous. Under this provision, seats were set aside for six southern Montagnards, two northern Montagnards, two Chams, and six Cambodians. In these constituencies, voters of all ethnic backgrounds voted both for Vietnamese and for minority representatives.

With 137 seats at stake, 1172 candidates competed, a candidate-to-seat ratio of 8.6:1. Of the 5,853,251 registered voters, 4,270,794, or 72.9 percent cast ballots. The decrease in voter turnout percentage from the September election figures may have reflected a feeling that the Lower House election was somewhat anticlimactic after September's presidential and upper house elections.

The successful candidates were a diverse grouping, with every color of the legal political spectrum represented. Approximately thirty-five deputies were Catholic, sixty-five Buddhist, thirteen Hoa Hao, four Cao Dai, two Protestant, and one Moslem. Of the thirty-five Catholics, approximately ten were affiliated with the Northern-led Greater Solidarity Force. Approximately twelve to fifteen deputies had some association with "political Buddhism." Twenty-one deputies were associated with General Tran Van Don's Worker-Farmer-Soldier group. The Revolutionary Dai Viet party elected ten to twelve members or sympathizers, the various factions of the VNQDD (Vietnam Quoc Dan Dang) approximately ten, the Movement for the Renaissance of the South approximately twelve. Four deputies were backed by the Vietnamese Confederation of Labor (CVT). A majority of the successful candidates proved to be generally progovernment.

By regional and ethnic origin, the 1967 Lower House was broken down as follows: northerners, twenty-seven; central Vietnamese, forty-one; southerners, forty-eight; Chinese, five; southern Montagnards, six; northern Montagnards, two; Chams, two; and Cambodians, six. The average age of the deputies was thirty-nine.

1971 Lower House Election

The election to replace the Lower House elected in 1967 was conducted in the highly charged political atmosphere surrounding the uncontested presidential election. The election was held August 29, one week following Duong Van Minh's withdrawal and Nguyen Cao Ky's decision not to participate in the presidential election on the stated grounds that the election would not be fairly conducted. The atmosphere was rife with allegations of government pressures against opposition Lower House candidates and of government intervention on behalf of favorites, and candidate threats to withdraw from the race.

Despite dissatisfaction with the presidential election situation, the threatened mass withdrawals did not materialize. Some 1404 candidates initially filed for the 159 seats at stake, but 118 were disqualified by local election councils, including three incumbent deputies. Appeals to the Central Election Council, chaired by the chief justice of the Supreme Court, succeeded in reinstating sixty-five candidacies, including two of the initially disqualified Lower House deputies, southern Catholic oppositionist Deputy Ngo Cong Duc from Vinh Binh Province, and Deputy Nguyen Van Dau from My Tho. Ninety candidates voluntarily withdrew following the second posting of candidates, leaving 1242 people in the race on August 29, a candidate-to-seat ratio of 7.8:1. The very high number of candidates unfortunately insured that very few deputies would be elected by a clear majority. In some multicandidate races, winners garnered less than 15 percent of the vote cast. Increases in population under government control accounted for the increase in Lower House seats, which continued to be allotted at the ratio of 1 seat per 50,000 population. Sixteen seats were again reserved for ethnic minorities.

Predicted voter apathy, expected by some to be generated by the uncontested presidential election, did not materialize. Of the 7,085,943 registered voters, 5,567,446 people, or approximately 78.5 percent, cast ballots. The election proceeded smoothly; Viet Cong-North Vietnamese forces made some effort to disturb the balloting but succeeded in closing only a few polling places.

The election results gave the progovernment forces a clear majority in the Lower House and at the same time introduced a more homogeneous, potentially better organized opposition than the outgoing body had provided. While estimates of the political tendencies in the new House must be regarded as tentative, preliminary assessments suggest that approximately 53 percent of the newly elected deputies might be considered progovernment, 37 percent oppositionist, and 10 percent independent.

Progovernment forces did best in the countryside, particularly in Military Regions III and IV. Opposition candidates were strong in Saigon and Central Vietnam, taking seven of the eleven Saigon seats, and at least eighteen of the twenty-four seats in central Vietnam. The An Quang Buddhists took the election seriously, attempting to build on their 1970 Senate election success. The effort paid off. An Quang adherents, particularly strong in central Vietnam, swept all seats in some constituencies (Danang and Thua Thien) and elected approximately twenty-five adherents or sympathizers nationwide. Catholic political groupings, more plagued with factionalism and less disciplined than in 1967, had little success. The northern Catholic-based Greater Solidarity Force leader Nguyen Gia Hien, defeated in a 1970 bid for re-election to the Senate, failed in an attempt to enter the Lower House. The Greater Solidarity Force only elected two members nationwide. Four members of the predominantly Nhan Xa party won seats. Approximately twelve Hoa Hao were elected.

Incumbent deputies seeking re-election fared poorly. Only 41 of the 119 incumbents running were re-elected; opposition deputies did much better on a proportional basis than progovernment figures.

Political parties participated actively in the campaigning, and some made gains. The Progressive Nationalist Movement elected approximately nineteen members, the Worker-Farmer party approximately fourteen. The old-line parties, including various factions of the VNQDD, and the Revolutionary Dai Viet party did less well but elected a few members each. In Military Region I, the VNQDD and the RDV came off second best to the An Quang candidates.

The elections were net gain for political parties as a whole, providing organizational and proselytizing opportunities denied them in the presidential election.

Campaign Issues

No single national issue emerged through the election campaign to focus voter attention on one theme or particular group of candidates. Given the multiplicity of Vietnamese political groups and the lack of clearly differentiated platforms among competing groups, this is not surprising.

Instead, issues varied from one constituency to another and tended to be oriented to personalities and the locality. Was the candidate of good reputation? What had the incumbent seeking re-election done for his province in concrete terms: road improvements, marketplaces? What would the candidate do for his constituency if elected? Allegations of poor performance of incumbents, government corruption, and government attempts to rig elections were popular campaign themes in many provinces. In general, candidates sought support on the basis of personality or identification with a particular group, party, religion, or with respected local leaders rather than on the basis of their stance on a particular issue.

The universal desire for peace was articulated to some extent by candidates across the range of the political spectrum. The question of how to achieve peace, however, did not emerge as a major national issue. Although the subject's sensitivity doubtless imposed some constraints, other factors also account for the fact that the Lower House election cannot be regarded as a referendum on the Government of Vietnam's handling of the peace issue. As already suggested, no one person or group had a monopoly on the desire for peace. Certainly no politician would gain election by calling simplistically for a continuation of the war! Moreover, there is no clearly defined difference between the peace position of the government of Vietnam, personified by President Thieu, and his opposition. Accepting Duong Van Minh as de facto spokesman for that unorganized opposition, and comparing his peace position with that of Thieu's, no major difference is detectable. Minh has publicly rejected a coalition government with the Communists as a solution to the war. His peace position is largely based on personality. In Minh's view, he is better equipped personally than Thieu to lead Vietnam towards peace. There is, therefore, little of substance to debate at the local level concerning the pursuit of peace.

It might also be noted that Lower House deputies are not regarded as having much influence on negotiating a peace, nor is this viewed by their constituents as a major part of their duties. The achievement of peace is generally believed to be in the hands of higher authority, at the presidential level. A candidate would be more likely to win votes by speaking to his would-be constituency of bread-and-butter issues than by concentrating on the universally desired but elusive abstraction of peace.

The election results in some constituencies were quickly challenged in the courts as provided for in the election law. The final judicial arbiter of these cases, the Supreme Court, ultimately heard appeals involving twenty persons (polling officials as well as some deputies) and affecting nine provinces. The most significant Supreme Court action was confirmation of a lower court's annulment of the election of Vu Van Quy in Phuoc Tuy. But the election law gives the Lower House final responsibility for validating the elections, and on November 12 the House voted to seat all of the apparent winners, rejecting the Supreme Court attitude concerning Quy, and in effect whitewashing the entire process.

Reported heavy-handed tactics by some government officials on behalf of favored candidates aroused resentment. On September 23 the Senate, lending credence to some of these allegations, passed a resolution stating that Lower House elections in Bac Lieu, Vinh Binh, Phuoc Long, Binh Long, Gia Dinh (constituency thirty-two), Binh Thuan, Phu Bon, An Giang, Chuong Thien, Tay Ninh, Kien Phuong, and Bien Hoa "were not held in a free and democratic spirit." The resolution recommended that the executive dismiss "and apply legal sanctions against the province chiefs who have blatantly violated the 1971 Lower House election law, especially in Bac Lieu, Vinh Binh, Phuoc Long, Phu Bon, and Binh Thuan." On September 30 the Supreme Court issued a rare communiqué, which stated that the province chiefs of Binh Thuan, Vinh Binh, and Bac Lieu had "engaged in actions disdainful of the courts and contemptous of national law" in connection with the Lower House election. The Court called on Thieu to dismiss the Binh Thuan province chief and to transfer the province chiefs of Bac Lieu and Vinh Binh.

It is difficult to evaluate the validity of charges of irregularities and the extent to which irregularities affected election results. It is widely accepted that at least two outspoken Thieu critics, incumbent deputies Ngo Cong Duc (Vinh Binh) and Duong Van Ba (Bac Lieu), were defeated as a consequence of blatant government determination to unseat them. Neither incumbent had an organized following; both provinces are in the less politicized Delta. The well-organized opposition grouping of the An Quang Buddhists, however, operating in the highly politicized center and major cities of Vietnam, elected its candidates in elections that prompted very few allegations of fraud.

No sweeping generalization regarding the honesty of the elections, positive or negative, can be supported. The elections were neither universally honest nor hopelessly rigged. The upper house resolution, the broadest credible denunciation that surfaced, suggested elections in approximately one-fourth of the electoral constituencies were tainted to some degree by irregularities. The bulk of the constituencies cited by the upper house are in the southern region of the country, not the most politically sophisticated region.

Official favoritism, it might be noted, did not guarantee election. A comparison of pre-election reports of province chief pressure on behalf of preferred individuals with actual election results reveals that in some cases reported favorites were elected (Gia Dinh, Bien Hoa, Vinh Binh, Bac Lieu), but in other provinces (particularly in Military Region I and the coastal area of Military Region II), the province chief's supposed selections lost. Nor did relatives in high places automatically assure election. In two instances, both in the Delta, brothers of the local province chief ran for the Lower House. In An Xuyen, the brother was elected easily without major controversy. In Kien Phong, opposition reaction against the brother's candidacy persuaded him to withdraw from the race.

On the whole, the election results appear to reflect fairly accurately what is known of the political attitudes of the country's various areas, urban and rural, southern and central.

Table 3-6
Composition of the 1971 Lower House

Political Affiliation
Political parties and groups represented in the Lower House elected in 1971 (all numbers are estimates):

Unified Buddhist Association (An Quang)	25
Progressive Nationalist Movement	19
Worker-Farmer Party	14
Hoa Hao (Tuong Faction)	9
Hoa Hao (Minh Faction)	3
Revolutionary Dai Viet Party	5
Nhan Xa Party	4
Movement for the Renaissance of the South	4
Greater Solidarity Force	2
VNQDD (Vietnam Nationalist Party)	
Unified faction	3
Southern faction	1
Khanh faction	1
National Salvation Front	1

Religious Affiliation (where known; approx.)
Buddhists	49
Catholics	21
Hoa Hao	12
Cao Dai	3

Regional Origin (where known)
Northern Vietnamese	36
Central Vietnamese	51
Southern Vietnamese	64

Ethnic Origin (where known)
Vietnamese	143
Southern Montagnard	6
Northern Montagnard	2
Chams	2
Cambodian	6

Table 3-6 (Continued)

Age	
25-29	16
30-34	34
35-39	33
40-44	32
45-49	27
50-54	10
55-59	4
60-69	3
Occupation	
Military personnel	43
Incumbent deputy[a]	41
Civil Servant	15
Councilman (provincial or municipal)	13
Teacher	13
Pharmacist	7
Farmer	7
Medical doctor	6
Businessman	5
Lawyer	4
Employee	2
Judge	1
Religious	1
Journalist	1

[a]119 incumbents sought re-election

Sex	
Male	154
Female	5

Table 3-7
Official Results, Lower House Election, August 29, 1971 and
Comparison with 1967 Results

	1971	1967
Voter Turnout		
Total registered voters	7,085,943	5,853,251
Actual voters	5,567,446	4,270,794
Percentage	78.5	72.9
Candidates		
Seats at stake	159	137
Number of candidates		
First posting July 8	1,404	1,650
Second posting August 9	1,332	1,240
On ballots August 29	1,242	1,172
Candidate-to-seat ratio on election day	7.8:1	8.6:1

4

Presidential Campaign Politics: The Uncontested 1971 Election
Donald Kirk

The 1971 presidential campaign in South Vietnam appears, over the perspective of a year characterized by military lull and then intense fighting, to have had a curiously ambivalent effect. First, the nature of the campaign and election vastly solidified the personal power of President Nguyen Van Thieu and his entourage, at least in the short run. Despite outraged cries of "farce" and "fraud" by opposition politicians and foreign observers, Thieu does not appear, from the short-range vantage, to have bungled or seriously erred in manipulating the campaign so that his two most serious opponents finally felt compelled to withdraw from the race. In fact, by running alone, supported by a military establishment of over a million men, Thieu capitalized on an unparalleled opportunity to impress the electorate with his regime's strength. It seemed symbolic of his growing power, if not his real popularity, that he could now claim 94.3 percent of the votes cast as opposed to a mere 34.8 percent in his first presidential election victory in 1967.

In contrast to his show of strength, however, Thieu's 1971 "victory" may have had quite another effect in the long run. Thus, even though he seemed to have decimated, silenced, and humiliated an entire spectrum of opponents during the campaign, the ultimate tendency of the "single-candidacy phenomenon" may have been to weaken the political system Thieu's government was pledged to defend. There was little possibility, for instance, that Thieu's serious opponents, ranging from radicalized students and war veterans to leftist Buddhist monks to conservative generals eager for the Saigon regime to adopt a more aggressive military and political attitude, would rally around the government in the periods of crisis that lay ahead. Indicative of the underlying lack of unity, much less loyalty, was the opposition's response after the North Vietnamese launched a massive military offensive on April 1, 1972. After the offensive's initial shock had worn off, Thieu's opponents decided to contest his request for approval by both houses of the National Assembly of a bill giving him sweeping "emergency" powers. The Senate on June 2 rejected, by a vote of 27 to 21, a version already endorsed by the Lower House of the Assembly. The Senate would probably have rejected a second, somewhat softened version of the bill but for a comic-opera maneuver in which Thieu's allies, meeting after the 10:00 P.M. curfew, declared a quorum and finally passed the bill, 26 to nothing.

Widespread sentiment against Thieu was apparent from the range of senators opposed to the bill. Predictably, the Senate's leading Buddhist member,

Vu Van Mau, became a focal point of opposition, but so also was the Senate speaker, Nguyen Van Huyen, politically viewed as an "independent." Senator Huyen, apprised that pro-Thieu senators had met in secret after he had adjourned the session of the sixty-member body, declared the vote on the bill "illegal and valueless." In fact, said Huyen, the action constituted a "usurpation of power" and was a "sad event for the nation." Despite such denunciations by Huyen, Mau, and other senators, the Thieu regime had merely demonstrated again that it still wielded final power in regions of South Vietnam not occupied, overrun, or heavily influenced by the National Liberation Front or the North Vietnamese. The outcry among senators, many of them not normally identified with opposition groupings, closely resembled that of political opponents incensed by the machinations of the Thieu government in the 1971 presidential campaign. The ease with which Thieu seized upon the North Vietnamese offensive as a device for further extending his own personal writ was in part a consequence of solidification of his power during the 1971 campaign. The voting in the National Assembly may not itself have been particularly significant, since Thieu had already declared a state of national emergency immediately after the North Vietnamese opened their offensive, but it did indeed symbolize his fundamental approach toward constitutional democracy.

Omnipotent though Thieu might still have appeared after the maneuvering by the Senate minority, his over-all policy ran the risk of foundering entirely as the United States continued to withdraw troops from the country and even considered the possibility of drastically reducing arms and airpower, both vital to the Saigon government's survival. Then, as Thieu's government weakened militarily, Thieu's opponents, some of them allied with the NLF, could seize the political initiative and attempt to force his resignation. The NLF and North Vietnam doubtless hoped the spring 1972 offensive would accomplish this aim, but American arms and airpower were finally enough to blunt the thrust after North Vietnamese troops occupied the entire northernmost province of Quang Tri and portions of several other provinces as well. Still, many of Thieu's opponents in Saigon and other major centers questioned how much longer he could count on overwhelming American support and openly predicted that the North Vietnamese would mount another major offensive in a year or two if negotiations in Paris or elsewhere failed to produce some form of compromise settlement. The nature of this compromise, before or after another offensive, would determine the leadership in Saigon—and, in all probability, reveal the precariousness of Thieu's position. Military factors aside, the long-range impact of the 1971 single candidacy was to weaken the political system in general in terms of recruiting leaders, encouraging credibility among the populace, or developing any semblance of a favorable "consensus" on its efficacy, responsiveness, and capacity for open political processes.

One obvious sign of the sense of insecurity beneath the veneer of strength was the decision by Thieu and his advisers to investigate and arrest student agitators and to confiscate, if not entirely ban, antigovernment newspapers. In the winter of 1972, while Thieu was warning of the imminence of a North Vietnamese offensive, his aides initiated the most far-reaching roundup of minor political opponents in four years. The series of arrests, many if not most of them never officially disclosed or explained, appeared in large measure to have been a direct result of the 1971 election campaign. Ten students went on trial before a military court in late March on charges of "sabotaging national security" by removing large poster photographs of Thieu during the campaign. Those actually tried represented only a small portion of the total number arrested. One reason for the government's failure to try most of them was that the students could easily turn such occasions into opportunities for gaining international publicity and sympathy. On the trial's first day in late March one student drew blood from his arm and scrawled slogans in blood on the courtroom walls.[1]

Government fears vis-à-vis all serious opposition increased markedly during the period of the North Vietnamese offensive. For the first month or six weeks of the fighting, major organized opposition against the regime appeared to have ended in what American diplomatic and intelligence sources viewed as "patriotism" and "nationalism" among anti-communist Vietnamese. The government, through the official Vietnam press agency and on national radio and television, publicized statements by political organizations rallying for victory. In a joint communiqué issued April 16, for instance, the Vietnamese Peasants and Workers party, the Revolutionary Dai Viet party, and the Progessive Nationalist Movement not only declared their determination to aid the government but handed a check for 300,000 piastres (approximately $750) to the director of the Political Warfare Agency, for medical aid for sick and wounded soldiers and dependents of war victims. On May 11, ten days after the fall of Quang Tri, Thieu wrote a letter to the leaders of the newly organized Nationwide Anti-Communist Invaders' Front praising them for their efforts and declaring "Now, more than ever before, the unity of mind and heart of the whole people and armed forces is a decisive factor to save the country from danger."[2]

The fighting at first aroused general concern among urban Vietnamese of all political persuasions that it might actually engulf them, as during the 1968 Tet offensive. After the fall of Quang Tri, the road south from Hue was clogged with vehicles as Vietnamese stampeded toward Danang and Saigon in an effort to escape what they imagined would be a holocaust similar to that which had befallen Hue in February of 1968. In the general rush to abandon Hue, twenty miles south of Quang Tri on Route One, differences between political factions seemed to have evaporated. Anti-communist military officers and leftist intellectuals, members of the faculty of the University of Hue, were united in their private concerns with their families and possessions. The flight from Hue, the former imperial capital and still an important cultural and commercial center with a population of approximately 300,000 seemed to this witness to epitomize the primal human concern with individual survival. It also dramatized the absence of a real sense of nationalism, beyond lofty statements, among urban cultivated Vietnamese—the very ones on whom Thieu and his government relied for survival.

Acceleration of the campaign of arrests, while it may have provided short-term security for members of the government, was not likely to promote a spirit of genuine nationalism among non-communist Vietnamese. Even before the fall of Quang Tri, the president had launched a special program, originally drafted in the aftermath of the 1968 Tet offensive, for rounding up saboteurs and opponents throughout the country. Prime Minister Tran Thien Khiem, in his other capacity as minister of interior, and Lieutenant General Cao Hao Hon, secretary-general of the pacification program, were responsible for the new plan, which was far more extensive than the wave of arrests immediately preceding the offensive. It was an irony of the entire campaign that Vietnamese officials often relied upon techniques introduced to them by the Phung Huang, or Phoenix program, an intelligence-coordinating system inaugurated with American aid and advice after the Tet offensive. In the first weeks following the fall of Quang Tri, Vietnamese national policemen arrested 1300 persons in Hue along on suspicion of collusion and complicity with the enemy. Hundreds were also picked up in Danang, while a thousand more were arrested in Saigon and 4000 in the Delta. Some were released after questioning; many more were held in "preventive detention."

The campaign not only reduced the Thieu regime's popular credibility but also alienated young Vietnamese, on whom the government eventually would have to depend. The victims, for the most part, were not established, known politicians, whose arrest or mistreatment might arouse adverse publicity and a strong antigovernment reaction in the midst of the offensive, but obscure figures who had worked quietly for Thieu's major opponents, Many of them, particularly those in large cities, were seized in systematic house-to-house searches and charged as draft dodgers or deserters. Hundreds, if not thousands, of those arrested were never officially reported under "preventive detention" or even "investigation." They simply disappeared with no mention and little notice beyond their own family and circle of friends. For this reason, details of the campaign, probably the most severe since Diem, were often unknown and elusive. Yet the over-all pattern, including figures cited above for the numbers arrested, was corroborated by political sources, South Vietnamese journalists, and even government officials and American advisers.

The government crackdown, in a real if not precisely definable sense, was necessitated by the lack of confidence engendered by the 1971 election. "If we have a fair election, that means the democratic regime in the South is a real democratic regime," said Ly Quy Chung, a deputy in the Lower House of the National Assembly, publisher of two newspapers often identified with the An Quang pagoda, headquarters of the Buddhist antigovernment faction, and author of numerous critical articles and commentaries. "Then the National Liberation

Front cannot say the regime does not represent the people of the South," said Chung, interviewed by the writer in June 1972 in the back room of a restaurant run by his wife beside an American billet and post exchange. "If the president were elected by the people, we would have more support from the people," Chung went on. "If we had had a fair election in 1971, we would not have had the communist offensive beginning in April." Chung reasoned that North Vietnam would have refrained from attacking because the people of the South would have fought "with all their strength" for a government they had voted into office in a freely contested election. "But in this case the North Vietnamese knew the government of the South was not elected by the people," said Chung, talking above the strains of a popular American song broadcast over the Armed Forces Radio Network, operated by the U.S. Military Assistance Command. "They knew the government in the South has not the people's support."

Chung argued, however, that the North Vietnamese and the National Liberation Front could not win militarily, because "the South does not support the communists either." The net result, he said, was an impasse in which neither the communists nor the Saigon regime could win the war politically, because both lacked popular support. "We need a new government or Thieu will lose on every front—peace, war, economically, socially, politically." For the moment, said Chung, Thieu could defeat his non-communist opposition only by arrests and de facto press censorship. As an example of censorship, he pointed out that government police had seized fifty-one issues of one of his papers in two months. "We can sell just a few papers in Saigon and then the police pick them up," said Chung. "It is impossible to send any to the provinces, because police control is very hard." At the same time, he explained, the government dared not close the papers entirely because a press law finally passed in 1969 forebade any outright restrictions. (The government, in August 1972, devised another method for eliminating opposition papers: a presidential decree on August 5 requiring each of the capital's forty-odd papers to place a deposit of 20 million piastres, approximately $50,000 in the national treasury as "security" against possible fines levied under the press code or libel claims by individuals. Two papers, including one owned by Ly Quy Chung, promptly ceased publication.)

Chung's viewpoint, representative of much of the thinking of antigovernment but non-communist political figures in Saigon, may have been vastly oversimplified. First, it is not entirely certain Thieu would have lost, as many of his opponents seemed to assume, if he had had to run against two well-known, popular contenders in a genuinely free and open election. Second, if a contender more amenable than Thieu to reconciliation with the enemy had won, it is even less likely North Vietnam would have abandoned its master plan for an offensive. Indeed, if a leader interested in compromise had been running the government in Saigon, the North Vietnamese and NLF strategists might have decided a military offensive was all that was needed to persuade him to agree to some form of leftist coalition. Such counterarguments to Chung's thesis, however, do not contradict the general impression that Thieu was perhaps more distasteful to his political opponents as a result of the 1971 election than he had been before the campaigning—and manipulating—had begun. The 1972 offensive, while it frightened urban Vietnamese of all political persuasions, failed to unite government and antigovernment factions in real common cause against the enemy.

It could not be denied, though, that Thieu succeeded temporarily, as a direct result of the election, in strengthening and unifying a government apparatus once noted for unpredictable disunity and political weakness. Thus, despite initial losses suffered in the 1972 offensive, despite simmering political opposition in urban centers, Thieu still had enough control over civil and military branches of his administration not only to keep his armed forces basically intact but actually to launch a counteroffensive. The first substantive sign of Thieu's strength—founded, to be sure, on American arms and airpower—was his decision, on May 3, to relieve two commanders primarily responsible for loss of Quang Tri. One, Lieutenant General Hoang Xuan Lam, had been commander of Military Region I covering South Vietnam's five northernmost provinces, since the bloody Buddhist uprising in Hue and Danang in 1966. Regarded as a vacillating, politically oriented administrator, Lam was replaced by Lieutenant General Ngo Quang Truong, commander of Military Region IV, including the Mekong River Delta. Truong, who had served during the 1968 Tet offensive as commander of the first division in Military Region I was much admired by Vietnamese and American officials alike for military experience and aggressiveness.

That Thieu could relieve powerful generals without risking his position clearly testified to his own relative power and security against the most severe communist threat in four years. In the same month Thieu also relieved the commander of Military Region II, covering the Central Highlands and coast, and shifted important airborne, ranger, and marine units from one trouble spot to another. Military observers, including American advisers, often criticized the performance of individual commanders and units, but certainly Thieu demonstrated more resolution under pressure than his enemies, political as well as military, had really expected. At the same time, political considerations still influenced military appointments in many cases. "All four of the top commanders in the strategically critical Military Region III, surrounding Saigon, are regarded as Thieu men," observed an American correspondent in early June. "And three of the four are best remembered for former political posts rather than for military performance in the field."[3] Perhaps the best known of the three was Lieutenant General Nguyen Van Minh, whose lack of military aggressiveness and know-how was widely regarded by American advisers as responsible for the failure of three divisions of South Vietnamese troops to reopen the road to the besieged provincial capital of An Loc, sixty miles north of Saigon, for more than three months.

It was partly by playing politicians against each other, by favoring those whom he could trust politically, that Thieu was able to build and maintain his power through periods of severe stress. A lucid summary of the basic conflict confronting Thieu in the 1971 election was provided by the politically independent *Tieng Vang* (*Echo*) in an editorial published on September 6 of that year. That was eight days after the elections for the 159-member Lower House, in which Thieu retained a majority of political allies despite sizable gains by politicians sponsored by the An Quang pagoda.

> In the current political crisis in Saigon, there are two contradictory opinions or observations. On this side, one observes that a one-slate election is "unpleasant to the eyes" but agrees that under present conditions, there is no other way for President Thieu . . . a decision to resign or to postpone the election will prove the failure of his present policy, will jeopardize his prestige and will open the road for numerous concessions to the opposition faction.
>
> On the other side, one notes that the administration has achieved success in the Lower House election and President Thieu has decided to organize a one-slate election in defiance of all protests.[4]

Such action, said the newspaper, "has obviously driven the opposition faction into a corner and constitutes a challenge to this faction." Thieu himself, *Tieng Vang* explained, might "be driven into an isolated position" if he resorted "to violence to suppress his opponents," particularly if the opposition were united "in creating a movement to oppose the election under various forms."[5]

As *Tieng Vang's* analysis indicated, the 1971 single-candidate election's main significance was not the voting but the interplay between Thieu and his opponents, both before and afterward. If the Saigon government had had to confront the threat of military defeat and economic disaster, the "opposition" cited by *Tieng Vang* might have been far more successful than it was in mustering popular support. As it happened, Thieu's political ability, dramatized by the election campaign, may have momentarily enhanced his image as a relatively stable, if not appealing, political leader.

Even in the minds of some opponents, Thieu appeared, after the election, as perhaps the best of any available alternative. "No one likes Thieu," said Senator Tran Quang Thuan of the Lotus, or An Quang, slate, whose ten candidates ranked first nationally in the senatorial election in August 1970, "but we are afraid we will only help the National Liberation Front by inciting violence against him." Besides, said Senator Thuan, "we do not have the strength to oppose him. Right now, he has all the power."

The remainder of this paper, then, will analyze the single-candidate election in terms of not only Thieu's power but also its impact on long-range acceptance and growth of representative institutions and competitive elections generally.

As part of this discussion, we shall recount recent South Vietnamese political history and Thieu's own experience in his first full term under the 1967 Constitution, as they directly affected the 1971 campaign. Then we will examine effects of Thieu's political success on his allies and opponents, assess prospects for continued opposition to him, and offer some evaluation of Thieu's political strength in a period of declining American aid.

Background of the Second Presidential Campaign

First, it should be recalled that in 1967, Thieu, with the aid, collusion, and tacit support of American authorities, prevented his two or three leading opponents at the time from running against him. The case of Thieu's rivalry with Premier Nguyen Cao Ky was perhaps most significant. "General Ky and myself are not going to fight each other," said Thieu, who held the largely honorific position of chief of state. "General Ky's candidacy is a good thing. Nothing will happen between us, and everybody will witness that."[6] On June 30, however, Thieu and Ky, pressured personally by Ambassador Ellsworth Bunker as well as senior commanders of the Vietnamese Joint General Staff, agreed to run together with Thieu heading the ticket. Although Ky had served as premier for approximately two years, Bunker was convinced Thieu would provide the kind of mature, responsible leadership Vietnam needed. And besides, the bland, greying Thieu, then forty-four, appeared far more palatable politically than did Ky. At thirty-seven, the dashing premier still wore his air force pilot's uniform and often uttered statements that embarrassed the Americans, such as his oft-quoted remark in praise of Adolf Hitler's qualities as leader of Nazi Germany.

Once Ky had been eliminated from the candidacy for president, Thieu faced only one, or at most two, other serious opponents. The first was General Duong Van "Big" Minh, leader of the 1963 coup against Diem. Minh served as chief of state for approximately three months and then was overthrown by another general, Nguyen Khanh, and forced into exile as "ambassador-at-large" in Thailand. The Constituent Assembly accepted Minh's petition, filed on June 30 by his wife in Saigon, to run for president, but the Assembly on July 19 rejected his candidacy, ostensibly because his vice-presidential running mate, leftist attorney Tran Ngoc Lieng, was still a French citizen. Thieu and Ky had both publicly stated they did not think Minh should return to Vietnam, and the nation's highest-ranking generals personally protested to the Assembly against his candidacy. Nearly four years after the coup against Diem, "Big" Minh was still too much of a threat for the ruling generals to tolerate.

The other serious contender in 1967 was, in effect, more dangerous as a symbol, an intellectual provocateur, than as a competitor for power. He was Au Truong Thanh, a former minister of economics under Ky, whose campaign label was a bomb covered by an X. Thanh urged a cease-fire and peace negotiations as soon as possible, a stand perhaps even more repugnant to Vietnam leaders in 1967 than in 1971, since American warplanes were still bombing North Vietnam, and negotiations seemed only a distant prospect. The Assembly, under military pressure, rejected Thanh's candidacy the day before it eliminated Minh from the ballot. Thanh, who lacked influence and power beyond a small circle in Saigon, left Vietnam for the United States in mid-1968 after having served six weeks in prison without any charge against him. "I am for peace," he told the writer on August 26, 1967, a week before the presidential election. "There is nothing I can do here. If I stay, I will be in danger." Thanh now lives in self-imposed exile in France.

The government's rejection of serious opposition in 1967 provided ample insight into Thieu's view of the Western ideal of "open elections." Like the late President Diem, Thieu wanted to preserve certain democratic forms, but, also like Diem, he was anxious to secure and insure his own position. The only real issue in 1967, as in 1971, was the government's attitude toward negotiations and concessions to the NLF and the North Vietnamese. Since Thieu—and Ky at that time—viewed any gesture toward more than token concessions as contrary to basic national interests, they felt entirely justified in opposing the candidacy of anyone showing signs of advocating compromise with the enemy. Allied with Ky, Thieu knew he could easily defeat any or all other candidates as long as none tried to rally votes on a "peace" platform. The government might have kept Truong Dinh Dzu, a Saigon attorney hitherto known largely for his financial manipulations, from running had Thieu suspected the use to which Dzu would put this issue. As it was, Dzu amassed 17.2 percent of the vote, second only to 34.8 percent for Thieu, by calling for cessation of the bombing of North Vietnam and a peace conference.

If Dzu's success as a "peace" candidate offered some clue to the electorate's mood, the government's hostility toward him in the following months provided convincing evidence of Thieu's unyielding position. "I still believe we must enter into negotiations with the National Liberation Front," said Dzu, interviewed at his home on April 20, 1968, more than two months after the Tet offensive. One week later, Dzu was arrested, tried by a military court on charges of undermining "national morale" by calling for peace talks, and sentenced to five years in prison. The government's harsh action against this otherwise secondary politician, who decorated his home with pennants of American Rotary Clubs and was noted for exorbitant fees he charged American clients in petty legal matters, turned him into an international *cause célèbre*. For Thieu, it was far preferable to remove a political irritant with a popularly appealing viewpoint than to heed outraged cries of Western liberals, particularly since the American Embassy in Saigon completely supported his regime.

Although the Saigon government soon was compelled to enter negotiations, the main political issues and rivalries never changed. Indeed, events of 1967 formed the framework within which those of 1971 may be understood, if not exactly justified. President Johnson, bowing to domestic pressures, ordered a halt to bombing of all North Vietnam shortly before the American presidential election of November 1968, but Thieu refused initially to support this gesture or to acquiesce to proposals for negotiations including separate delegations from North Vietnam and the NLF. It was only after Bunker explained that Washington could not tolerate any other diplomatic position that Thieu agreed finally to send a delegation to "expanded" peace talks in Paris at the beginning of 1969. At the same time Thieu began to define his totally nonconciliatory policy of "four no's": "no" coalition with the enemy, "no" territorial concessions, "no" neutral foreign policy, and "no" communist political activities in South Vietnam.

Thieu was equally concerned with tightening his grip over the government while undercutting the power of Vice-President Ky, whom he had placed on the ticket merely to help guarantee victory. Thieu seemed to have buttressed Ky's waning prestige by asking him to lead the South Vietnam delegation to the peace talks in 1968, but this gesture was just that, a gesture. More significant than Ky's temporary assignment to Paris was Thieu's decision, in May of 1968, to dismiss Prime Minister Nguyen Van Loc, a Saigon attorney identified with Ky. Thieu replaced him with one of the unsuccessful presidential candidates, Tran Van Huong, who had picked up 10 percent of the votes in the field of ten slates. A favorite of the American embassy, Huong, at sixty-seven, exuded the impression of an honest, if noncontroversial and malleable, southern Buddhist whose presence might counterbalance the influence of the generals, many of them from central or northern Vietnam. In mid-1969, however, Thieu gently eased Huong out of office to make way for his powerful interior minister, General Tran Thien Khiem. An experienced if ruthless administrator, Khiem proved far more successful than Huong in coordinating the government, manipulating military commanders, discouraging dissent—and greatly decreasing possibility of effective opposition in 1971.

Bored with the peace talks and cut out of the decision-making process in Saigon, Ky sulked in his office in the palace or else went skin diving and water skiing near his coastal villa at Nha Trang. At the urging of American diplomats, however, Thieu adopted a totally different strategy vis-à-vis General Minh. Apparently in hopes of winning over Minh and his political allies, Thieu invited him to return from exile at approximately the same time he was removing Loc as prime minister. In an interview in October 1968, shortly after his return, Minh hinted at both the strategy and the policy he would follow in 1971. No, he said, he would not serve as an "adviser" or minister on Thieu's cabinet, as widely rumored. He had already conferred with Thieu and foresaw no further discussions. Yes, he had also met with some monks from the An Quang pagoda and, what's more, might see them again.

More significant was Minh's view on war and peace. "So many Vietnamese from all sides have died," he said. "Is the bombing necessary?" Although not quite ready to call openly for compromise, he hoped fervently both sides might meet, discuss differences, and reach some kind of "understanding." A year later, after conferring secretly with political and religious figures opposed to Thieu, Minh began to show his hand. On November 1, 1969, the sixth anniversary of Diem's fall, he and Senator Tran Van Don, one of the generals with whom he had joined in the coup, appeared together at a reception, where they exchanged pleasantries amid renewed expressions of interest in "national reconciliation." Minh and Don, who had formed his own National Salvation Front, seemed for the moment to have molded a viable alliance.

The relationship between Minh, Don, and the monks at the An Quang pagoda appeared even stronger at the same time the following year. On October 30, 1970, General Minh, speaking at a reception proferred by Don, called for a government composed of "genuine representatives" of the people. "Everyone wants peace and a cease-fire," he told the enthusiastic gathering, "but a cease-fire can only be made operable by a government that the people trust." Then, two days later, on the seventh anniversary of the fall of Diem, Minh showed up at another reception, this one at the An Quang pagoda, where he strongly indicated his desire to run for president. Although he said he was not yet a candidate, he remarked that he and his allies were ready to challenge the government if the election were held as provided by the Constitution. Earlier in the day, at a reception at his home for some of the generals with whom he had participated in the coup against Diem, he reiterated his desire for peace and "national reconciliation." "Big" Minh by this time posed perhaps the strongest threat Thieu had confronted since he settled the 1967 election by running with Ky while keeping Minh in exile in Bangkok.

Underscoring the popularity of candidates allied with the An Quang pagoda was the election on August 30, 1970, for half the seats in the sixty-man Senate, in which sixteen ten-man slates competed nationally. The leader in the election was the Lotus slate, led by Vu Van Mau, a Saigon attorney and professor who had resigned as Diem's foreign minister in protest against Diem's repressive policies toward the Buddhists. Professor Mau, supported by the An Quang pagoda, won 1,149,597 votes as opposed to 1,106,288 votes for the progovernment Sun slate led by Senator Huynh Van Cao, a former army major general. Third was the White Lily slate, which won 882,274 votes, far ahead of the fourth-ranking slate, dominated by Diem supporters, which received 800,453 votes.

Confronted by this kind of challenge, Thieu struck back in two ways. First he emphasized more strongly than before his continued opposition to compromise. Eschewing conciliation, he declared in a National Day address on November 1 that his government would "never enter into a coalition with the Communists" and attacked those advocating this solution as "cowards and defeatists." Then foreshadowing his manipulation of the next election by legislation, his government submitted a bill requiring that each candidate for president or

vice-president be supported by forty members of both houses of the National
Assembly or by one hundred municipal or provincial councillors. The measure,
approved by the Lower House on December 23, 1970, by a vote of 72 to 24,
was clearly part of an effort to keep most of his potential opponents from
challenging him before the campaigning had ever begun. "Thieu doesn't want
the kind of mad scramble we had in 1967 with ten candidates running against
each other," was the facile explanation to visiting correspondents proferred by
an American diplomat. "We still hope for a genuine test of public opinion."

Thieu had in mind a somewhat different kind of contest. After the Senate,
in February 1971, rejected the election law, the government rounded up the
fresh majority of House votes required by the Constitution to override the will
of the Senate. The search for votes assumed a certain urgency in the minds
of government officials as it became increasingly clear Thieu and Ky would not
run together on the same slate. Ky himself at first seemed to waver, possibly
to test Thieu's reaction, but palace sources indicated in February and March of
1971 there really was no chance of reuniting them. Ky began looking for support among antigovernment Buddhists, whom he had suppressed with military
force in the 1966 uprisings in Hue and Danang while he was premier. Finally,
on June 3, amid outraged charges of bribery, Thieu's allies rammed the electoral bill through the Lower House by a vote of 101 to 21.

Not even an American diplomat, at this stage, would have argued that Thieu
was not deliberately attempting to ruin his opposition, which posited its strategy
on the hope Minh would pick up An Quang and independent votes while Ky cut
into progovernment forces. Thieu would probably have preferred to keep one
candidate in the race, but he plainly regarded the prospect of two formidable
opponents as intolerable. Minh had no difficulty finding enough assembly
deputies to support his candidacy; Ky had to obtain the signatures of forty
provincial and municipal councillors already committed to Thieu. A number
of them claimed their signatures had been forged by Thieu-appointed province
chiefs, but the Supreme Court ruled in early August that Ky could not run on
the basis of a petition including names of councillors who had already endorsed
Thieu on another petition.

This pivotal decision, as it turned out, eliminated any prospect of a serious
test of the voters' confidence and turned the campaign into what Thieu seemed
to have wanted all along: a chance to spread his own influence and power without seriously risking his job. After the Supreme Court disqualified Ky, the
question was not so much whether Thieu would win as whether his inevitable
victory would be so tainted, so blemished by adverse reaction, both internal and
foreign, as to negate its value as a symbol of his strength. The monks at the An
Quang, highly skilled at judging public response and political nuance, decided
after Ky's disqualification that the best strategy, the easiest way to embarrass
both Thieu and the American Embassy, would be to persuade Minh to withdraw
voluntarily. The result, they hoped, would be the single cadidacy American

officials feared might jeopardize the entire program of American aid, assistance, and aerial combat support after withdrawal of American combat troops. Minh himself, according to Vietnamese and Western sources interviewed by the writer, was still not averse to remaining in the campaign. Running alone against Thieu, he might have obtained 45 percent of the votes, enough perhaps for him to bargain for a position of some stature in Thieu's administration.

The Americans, the An Quang, and Thieu all knew such a campaign would immensely enhance Thieu's power—and at the same time sharply decrease the political influence of An Quang. Hence the An Quang monks advised Minh he could no longer expect support if he did not withdraw. Minh, who had announced his candidacy at a reception at his villa on July 25, officially reversed himself on August 20 in a prepared statement in which he declared he could not "lend a hand to a dirty farce which would only make the people more desperate and disillusioned with the democratic system."

Ambassador Bunker, returning from ten days of talks with officials in Washington, met Minh for an hour and a half on August 19 to try to convince him to stay in the campaign. Bunker was widely believed to have offended Minh during the session, but reports to this effect were probably exaggerated by Minh's aides, anxious to improve ties with An Quang.

The Campaign and the Consequences

Minh's withdrawal from the campaign appears to have come as a genuine surprise to Thieu, for though he did not wish to run against both Minh and Ky, he had hoped to compete with one legitimate, major opponent. Since he would almost certainly obtain a comfortable majority in the voting, he could overcome the 1967 election stigma of having won on the basis of only a third of the votes. It was partly to establish the key campaign issue on which to trounce Minh that Thieu had been castigating "neutralists" in speech after speech and declaring he would never agree to coalition. While Thieu had easily outmaneuvered Ky by keeping him out of the campaign, he thought he could dispose of Minh as a political threat by the opposite strategy of challenging him to run. If Thieu had hoped all along that Minh would withdraw, he could have set up a "straw man" candidate by turning over 100 of his 452 provincial councillor endorsements to some relatively harmless politician. Thieu permitted the filing deadline to pass, however, in anticipation of fighting—and thoroughly defeating—the lone rival who seemed to epitomize the most dangerous political forces around him.[7]

Despite his disappointment, Thieu might have been content at this stage with running by himself were it not for pressure applied by the American Embassy somehow to open up the campaign. The embassy, responding to urgent pleas and queries from the White House and the State Department,

informed Thieu of possible consequences of a one-man election on American
public opinion, on Congress, and, finally, on continued American aid and support. The result was that members of Thieu's palace staff, probably acting on
his instructions, secretly asked the Supreme Court to reverse its earlier decision
ruling Ky off the ballot. The Court, although theoretically independent from
the executive branch, complied exactly two days after Minh's withdrawal. The
basis for the new decision was invalidation by the court of endorsements
for Thieu's candidacy by provincial and municipal councillors. The court ruled
as valid those pro-Ky endorsements it had earlier invalidated on grounds the
names had already appeared on Thieu's application. The new ruling did not
affect Thieu's candidacy, since he had obtained the required number of signatures from members of the National Assembly, but it meant Ky had enough
names to go on the ballot.

It was largely, then, as a concession to the United States that Thieu and the
nine-member Court connived to allow Ky to run after Minh had dropped out
of the campaign. Thieu was even more certain of defeating Ky than he was of
beating Minh—and viewed the prospect of competing with his vice-president
as one way of appeasing anxious American officials. It is not certain, of course,
that Thieu expected Ky to reenter the campaign, but at least he, Thieu, could
argue he had given his long-time rival a fighting chance.

Although Ky had some support among students, veterans, and military
officers, he was basically isolated and weak—and he attempted to compensate
by angry attacks on Thieu. In so doing, Ky not only destroyed whatever
immediate chance he may have had of wresting power from the president but
also may have eliminated himself permanently as a major figure in Saigon
politics. First Ky, like Minh, decided, after consultation with advisers, to
reject the pleas of Ambassador Bunker and refuse to participate in a two-man
campaign he knew he would lose. Unlike Minh, however, Ky made the grave
mistake, at a crowded press conference in the government guest house, of confronting Thieu with a direct challenge. He demanded Thieu postpone the
election and organize a new campaign in which all candidates could participate
without interference by the electoral law or the courts.

"The nation is now in a crisis that can bring about great peril unless it
is resolved," said Ky, implying but not stating directly he might attempt to
rally support for a coup d'etat if Thieu did not yield. By committing himself
openly to Thieu's political destruction, Ky merely gave the president a chance
to defy him—and thus to humiliate him. The remainder of Ky's vendetta
against Thieu illustrated Ky's own desperation rather than the weakness of
the Thieu regime, which was determined not only to counter but to exploit
Ky's threat. An integral factor in Ky's defeat was the reluctance of either the
An Quang pagoda or the American embassy to support him.

The An Quang monks, to whom Ky had appealed for months by calling
for negotiations rather than continued war, wanted Ky to run in order to divert

votes from Thieu—and thus enable Minh to win the election. But with Minh out of the contest, the pagoda had no use for a man whose anti-Buddhist role in the 1966 riots was still a fresh memory. "Ky has met with some of us but not with our leaders," an An Quang spokesman informed me. "He knows he cannot see them personally in view of the events of five years ago." Just as Ky failed to win any semblance of An Quang support, so was he totally unsuccessful in persuading the American Embassy and the government in Washington to apply pressure for postponement of the election. One of Ky's top advisers, Dang Duc Khoi, son-in-law of Thieu's foreign minister, Tran Van Lam, flew to Washington in early September to discuss this possibility. The State Department and White House rebuffed his inquiries, explaining the election was a "Vietnamese affair" in which the United States could not participate.

It was against the backdrop of these rebuffs—none publicized by the American press in its voluminous reporting on the campaign—that Ky on September 3 attempted to convey the impression he personally would lead the revolt against Thieu. The vehicle by which Ky signaled this notion was a two-hour "background" conversation with correspondents at his home at Tan Son Nhut airbase. He evidently believed the correspondents would attribute the threat to "informed sources" or "sources close to the vice-president," but major newspapers and news agencies, much to his embarrassment, identified him personally as the source. After some hesitation Ky conceded he had been quoted accurately but claimed, in a statement released through his press office, that he was merely engaged in an "informal talk." Ky's effort at intimidation, far from influencing American or South Vietnamese positions, appeared as a rash remark that had backfired.

The single candidacy also weakened Minh and the An Quang Buddhists—but only for the short run. The central difference between the An Quang and the vice-president was that the former realized they had no immediate chance of forcing Thieu to yield. An Quang leaders also sensed that Minh, despite his reputation and popularity, probably lacked the personal strength and intellect to upset Thieu's plans in the few short weeks remaining before the election. "We admire General Minh for his role in the overthrow of Diem," said the Venerable Huyen Quang, secretary-general of the United Buddhist Church, in an interview with the writer at the pagoda six weeks after the election. "You are correct," the monk added, when asked if An Quang leaders had decided Minh no longer seemed to suit their purposes. Huyen Quang did not specify what Minh had done to arouse the An Quang's displeasure, but political and diplomatic sources intimated that he had perhaps been too willing to compromise, and then had not been tough enough in his protests.

Just as Minh appeared to have lost sympathy of some monks, the An Quang entered another period of relative political quiescence. An Quang candidates won more than twenty seats in the National Assembly elections on August 29, but one of the strongest antigovernment deputies, Ngo Cong

Duc, a Catholic from the Delta province of Vinh Binh, was defeated amid charges of "fraud." (Not long after the election, Duc fled Vietnam, reportedly via Cambodia, and eventually emerged among the Vietnamese emigré community in Paris.) Although An Quang held twice as many seats as in the previous Lower House, pro-Thieu politicians still commanded a majority among the 159 members. Some of An Quang's more outspoken voices evidently preferred to await another opportunity in the indefinite future rather than risk the embarrassment of a futile challenge against the government. Deputy Chung, a victorious candidate from Saigon, pleaded for a boycott of the presidential election and organized antigovernment demonstrations but readily conceded Thieu held the real power. "Thieu is strong enough because he has the army," said Chung, in December 1971. "He can stay in office even though the majority of people do not like him."

Another factor overlooked in foreign reporting was the success of candidates representing the Progressive National Movement led by Professor Nguyen Van Bong, rector of the National Institute of Administration. Although Professor Bong, not himself a candidate, opposed some of Thieu's policies, he supported Thieu's stand against coalition or compromise. "Thieu may not be ideal," Bong remarked in May, five months before the election, "but he is the only man who can really keep the government together." Bong's movement, an outgrowth of the old Tan or New Dai Viet, seemed to epitomize the kind of "loyal opposition" American diplomats yearned to see in Vietnam. Members of the Progressive National Movement won twenty-one seats in the August 29 elections, only four fewer than the number claimed by An Quang.

The real influence of the Progressive National Movement, as might have been expected of an organization motivated by intellectual, almost libertarian ideals, was not entirely clear. Since it was "loyal" to the government against the enemy, its leaders did not seem at all disposed to unite with much more extreme antigovernment intellectuals sympathetic with Minh or the An Quang. Yet as the government adopted an increasingly repressive attitude toward all forms of criticism, particularly during the 1972 offensive, the strong possibility emerged that some members of the Progressive National Movement might veer to the left in defense of their ideals. The question of the ultimate direction of the movement lay close to the heart of the debate over who was responsible for assassinating Professor Bong by tossing a firebomb into his car on November 10, 1971. Some of Bong's relatives and political allies charged he was marked for death by pro-Thieu officials angered and intimidated by his hard line against corruption. The national police, however, reported having cracked a "cell" of communist saboteurs, one of whom eventually "confessed" to having participated in the assassination.

"I was only the agent for the execution," said Vu Quang Hung, aged twenty-seven, at a crowded press conference arranged by national police officials in Saigon on June 28, 1972. Hung, arrested a month before the press conference, said he drove the motorbike from which his accomplice, Le Van Chau, threw the firebomb. "I had no other choice" but to confess, said Hung, after others had implicated him in the plot. "I only know a limited number of communist cadre," he added. "Each one has his own duty. The motive or purpose I don't know." On the basis of these remarks, observers found it difficult to discern whether Hung's confession was reliable.

As the 1971 election approached, Thieu seemed increasingly confident of his own political prowess and security. At a dinner with foreign correspondents at Independence Palace on September 15, he could even afford to engage in political witticisms at the expense of some of his critics. Regarding Senator George McGovern, who had left Saigon the same day after a brief and controversial visit, Thieu remarked, "I watched him on the seven o'clock TV news. He was much more impressive at his press conference than he was when he saw me." Of Ky, he said, "If a vice-president can't help the president, he should not disturb him." On politicians, he went on, "I think I'm more a general than a politician. Politicians have a bad reputation in Vietnam." But he was altogether serious when asked to reiterate his views on negotiations. "As I have said, everything is negotiable. Everything except my four no's. One, coalition government. Not negotiable. Two, territorial integrity. Not negotiable. Three, the communist party in the republic [of South Vietnam]. Not negotiable. Four, neutralism. Not negotiable.[8]

The mood of the president, in short, was relaxed but firm. One reason for this attitude, aside, perhaps, from elimination of his two major contenders, may have been that many of his severest opponents, the political and religious figures surrounding the An Quang pagoda, were somewhat divided among themselves. The pagoda on September 15, the day Thieu chose to chat with correspondents at the palace, issued a formal statement urging a boycott of the election. Political sources soon revealed that actually the monks were in sharp disagreement on whether or not to involve themselves openly in the campaign. The most militant Buddhist voice was that of the Venerable Tri Quang, who had led the 1966 revolt and then, plagued by chronic asthma and constant fear of arrest, had retreated to the role of behind-the-scenes political strategist. Tri Quang, from central Vietnam, was responsible for organizing Buddhist support in the cities of Hue and Danang, from which most of the An Quang deputies were elected in the 1971 Lower House contests. The chairman of the pagoda, the Venerable Thien Hoa, from the Mekong River Delta region, was believed to favor a somewhat softer, quieter approach, although he too entirely opposed the single-candidate election and espoused reconciliation with the Front.

The disciples of Tri Quang finally decided to publicize their cause by limiting themselves to spirited but largely nonviolent protests. Their purpose clearly was to embarrass Thieu, internationally as well as nationally, without provoking reprisals that might endanger the viability and legitimacy of their movement while Thieu was still in power. One of the leftist politicians, Tran

Ngoc Lieng, whom Minh had chosen as his vice-presidential candidate in 1967, engineered a series of demonstrations in the final two weeks before the election. As chairman of a radical group known as the National Progressive Force, Lieng strengthened ties between the An Quang and antigovernment students' and veterans' organizations. On October 1, two days before the election, national police broke up a gathering of three hundred persons inside the pagoda. One of the monks managed to read a statement renewing the plea to boycott the voting, but militant politicians were unable to hold a news conference they had scheduled for the occasion. The international publicity accorded the raid more than compensated for this omission.

Although Thieu's repressive tactics did not enhance his international image, he did appear, in the fall of 1971, to have temporarily stifled serious opposition. "We are doing nothing now," Lieng conceded in an interview with the writer several weeks after the election. "We have many difficulties in broadening our group. Police are watching us all the time." Among other examples of the use of force by the government were arrests of most leaders of the National Students' Union, harassment of critical newspapers, and interrogation of members of veterans' organizations. A prominent radical intellectual, Madame Ngo Ba Thanh, allied with Lieng, was jailed without charges on September 26, a week before the balloting.

Although he was anxious to suppress real opposition, Thieu knew he ran the risk of inspiring popular animosity and official disfavor in Washington, both of which could ultimately upset his regime. Thus, he attempted to soften the harsh tone of his policies by a series of statements aimed at appeasing domestic as well as foreign critics without offering substantive concessions. In this spirit Thieu tried to give an impression of "choice" in the election by stating, in his initial campaign speech broadcast on September 11, that he would not serve as president if more than half the voters signified their opposition by tearing up their ballots or casting blank ballots. Another sign of Thieu's desire to appear as something other than a military dictator was his selection as vice-presidential running mate of the popular, if ineffective and ailing, Tran Van Huong, whom he had eased out of power as prime minister in mid-1969.

For all these gestures, Thieu's attitude was quite clear. He did not even bother to comment on passage by the Senate on September 2, by a vote of 28 to 3, of a resolution urging him to postpone the election. More significant than the vote itself was that twenty-nine of the sixty senators did not participate. Analysts could note, with some justification, that those who abstained were afraid to reveal their opposition to the election. Another explanation may have been that they did not wish to appear to *favor* the single candidacy, although basically they remained conservative and opposed to change and would probably have voted against the resolution. The Senate did not yet seem to pose a serious threat to Thieu, as would happen during the furor the following spring on his "emergency powers" bill. Still, the Senate vote did offer an insight into the scope of political forces that might some day coalesce against him.

In the meantime, the real source of Thieu's power lay not in political backing among Saigon politicians but in his ability to control the armed forces. A month before the election, Prime Minister Khiem went on a leave of absence, a move widely interpreted as indicating his personal opposition to the single candidacy. The real reason for the leave, however, was to give Khiem an opportunity to travel around the country sounding out the position of the four regional commanders as well as the commanding officers of some of the major army divisions. Khiem returned to Saigon with assurances that none of the commanders opposed Thieu—even though none of them, for political reasons, thought it advisable to issue public statements affirming support. During his trip, Khiem also coordinated preparations to insure that military, police, provincial, and municipal officials obtained a maximum voter turnout.

The supremacy of the armed forces over internal, civil affairs was the inevitable result of four years of close collaboration between American and Vietnamese military authorities in a period of escalating warfare. Despite rather haphazard efforts to project the image of a democratic leader, Thieu always knew his capacity to survive a crisis, military or political, would depend on the strength and loyalty of the military establishment. His order to the national police on September 29 to "shoot to kill" those who set fire to property or otherwise "upset the people's normal life" seemed to symbolize his reliance on armed force for the security and longevity of his regime. If he still was opposed openly by sophisticated citizens in major cities, he was certain peasants in the villages and hamlets beyond the main centers would dutifully comply with instructions from local officials to cast ballots for him. Thieu's closest advisers in the palace, Lieutenant General Dang Van Quang, confidant on security and military affairs, and Hoang Duc Nha, the president's second cousin and official palace spokesman, both believed a high voter turnout would solidify his position even though he faced no opposition.

Thus, all regions of Vietnam reported heavy balloting on October 3. Final reports stated a total of 6,327,631 persons, or 87.9 percent of those registered, went to the polls. Among those who voted, 94.3 percent cast their ballots for Thieu, while the remainder left theirs blank or mutilated them. It was extremely difficult to determine if the figures were exaggerated, but firsthand reports from the field indicated that most of the adult populace did indeed file through the polling place in village schools and offices. Loudspeakers squawked out pleas reminding people to vote, while police and civilian officials in many cases went from door to door urging them to fulfill their "national duty." It was significant that relatively low percentages were reported in major cities, where hordes of policemen and soldiers were deployed to prevent students' and veterans' groups from upsetting the voting. In Hue only 67.2 percent of the electorate was reported as voting, while 76 percent cast ballots in Danang. A total of

76.5 percent voted in Saigon, 77.3 percent in the mountain town of Dalat, and 82.2 percent in the coastal city of Vung Tau—all noted for antigovernment dissent among intellectuals and politicians.[9]

In the cities, moreover, accounts of ballot box stuffing by police and election officials appeared quite credible. Observers in Hue and Danang, in particular, questioned if the numbers going to the polls were nearly so high as the government alleged. The reluctance of urban Vietnamese to vote in an election many regarded as pointless, if not farcical, provided another indication of possible negative effects of the single candidacy long after the voting was done. At the same time, in order for Thieu's opponents to pose a major challenge again, they would have to find new leaders. On the day before the election, in a final attempt to assert himself, Ky held a meeting of a new amalgam called "The People's Force to Oppose Dictatorship." It seemed somehow symbolic of the weakness of the organization that a steady drizzle should disrupt its first—and last—public meeting, held outside the Government Guest House. Minh, who did not attend, contented himself with a final statement alleging the regime would "cease to have a democratic and legal basis" and would "lose all credit in the eyes of the world" if it held the election as scheduled.

Whatever it was, however, the 1971 election was not "meaningless," as some of its critics contended. It was a complicated struggle for power in which President Thieu, to all outward appearances, seemed to have maintained his position and his strength. Indeed, the election at first seemed to have enhanced his stature in Vietnam, if not internationally. Both Ky and Minh avoided public appearances or commentaries until the opening of the 1972 offensive. Ky in particular appeared to have lost any chance of regaining the prestige he had as premier. Living in his home at Tan Son Nhut airbase, he continued to see old military companions but showed no sign of returning to the political arena. There were persistent rumors that Thieu might elevate him to the honorific post of "adviser" to the chairman of the Joint General Staff. As time wore on the possibility seemed increasingly remote. Perhaps Thieu preferred to let his old rival fade into obscurity rather than try to "save face" for him with a conciliatory gesture.

The case of Minh was somewhat different. Like most opposition politicians, he remained silent during the first phase of the offensive but then began to comment to journalists who called on him at his residence. "It is amply demonstrated now more than ever that we cannot solve our problems by military means," he told a reporter at the beginning of June. "It is quite clear that President Thieu cannot win the war militarily and does not have the support of the people to win the peace. This is why the other side refuses to negotiate with him." Harking back to the election, Minh reiterated the view of most of those in favor of reconciliation. "We lost a golden opportunity," he said. "Anyone who was freely elected could have settled the war by now. But things cannot be solved without the support of the people. President

Thieu wants to solve them without the Vietnamese. He keeps all the information secret to himself so no one else can judge the situation." [10]

The tone of Minh's remarks indicated that Thieu's opponents were still waiting for the first chance to replace him. By handily solidifying his power through the machinations surrounding the election, Thieu had put the core of his opposition, the An Quang Buddhists, in league with sympathetic politicians from other organizations, on the defensive. As a result of the North Vietnamese thrust, however, some of them perceived an opportunity, through negotiations, to achieve their aim of overthrowing the existing regime and ending the war through coalition with the enemy. "You know Mr. Thieu does not have great support," said Tran Van Tuyen, a Saigon attorney who had defended some of Thieu's opponents at trials before military courts. "There are so many rumors about Thieu stepping down." Tuyen, a leader of the Vietnam Quoc Dan Dang, the Vietnamese National party, an old if badly splintered organization, predicted a "cease-fire" in the near future. "There will be some separate peace between North Vietnam and Washington," said Tuyen, in an interview with the writer in June 1972. Tuyen, elected to the Lower House of the Assembly from Saigon, predicted President Nixon "would do something" perhaps in the form of a "political move that could lead to a cease-fire."

It was in response to such sentiments, as well as to pressures of the offensive itself, that Thieu's advisers urged him to obtain "emergency powers" and curb public criticism. Basically, the attitude of the palace toward its critics was one of contempt mingled with vague apprehension. "They can speak," said Hoang Duc Nha, perhaps the most influential figure on Thieu's staff, "but it's another thing for them to carry out what they want." Nha admitted that a united "opposition front" would "give us a lot of trouble." Implicit in his words and tone was the sense that Thieu's opponents were too weak and diffused to pose more than a thorny police problem. Indeed, it was partly because of renewed confidence in the strength of the government, after the first shock of the offensive, that Nha consented to see reporters at all. Despite his official title of "press secretary," he refused to talk to the foreign press from the beginning of the offensive in April until the middle of June, when this writer finally obtained an interview.

If the palace and its critics shared one common view it was the realization that a major change in America's Vietnam policy was first required to undermine the government. "The whole system is based on American aid," observed Tran Van Tuyen in an interview before the offensive. "Militarily, Thieu's election campaign seemed successful, but the army will have to thin its defenses as the Americans withdraw. Perhaps the communists will launch big attacks in 1972 when the Americans are not numerous and our economic problems deepen." Tuyen's analysis of the prospects proved startlingly accurate in some respects, but all Vietnamese politicians and leaders were puzzled in assessing effects of the offensive on American support. Even President Nixon's address on May 9, in which he announced the mining of North Vietnamese harbors, was deliberately ambiguous, in the view of Saigon political analysts. As soon as the North Vietnamese returned American prisoners of war and agreed to "an internationally supervised cease-fire throughout Indochina," said Nixon, "we will stop all acts of force" and "proceed with a complete withdrawal of all American forces from Vietnam within four months."

Since Nixon did not require withdrawal of communist troops from areas they occupied, Saigon leaders believed he would settle for a "cease-fire in place," or de facto concession to the enemy of the territory gained in the offensive. Thus, it may also have been in response to the threat of such a settlement that Thieu attempted during the offensive to increase his personal power and then to regain lost ground. On June 19, Armed Forces Day, Thieu proclaimed "a new phase to last during the three coming months." Said Thieu: "Take advantage of our victories to attack and recapture the lost territory. From there we will kick the communist aggressors out of South Vietnam forever and restore Peace in Happiness for the entire nation."[11] Supported by record numbers of American air and naval gunfire strikes, South Vietnamese troops drove the North Vietnamese from large areas of Binh Dinh and Quang Tri Provinces, two of the worst hit in the offensive. They could not regain permanent control over much of Quang Tri and showed no signs of expelling the enemy "forever," as Thieu had vowed. As had so often been the case in the Vietnam War, the impact of the counteroffensive, like that of the initial offensive, was subject to wide interpretation.

"We have very good collaboration with Ambassador Bunker and close contact with the White House," Nha assured me during our palace talk, but fear of "sellout" and "betrayal" persisted. The secret negotiations in Paris between Henry Kissinger and Hanoi's Le Duc Tho, in August 1972, only deepened suspicion that the United States was prepared to make a "deal" with the enemy before the American presidential election. No Vietnamese politician could possibly forget that President Johnson, two days before the 1968 election, had shocked the Thieu regime by ordering a halt to all bombing of North Vietnam and agreeing to enter into full-scale peace talks with the enemy. The possibility of a stopgap "cease-fire," pending a political settlement, panicked the Saigon government—and heartened its opponents. Without American backing, Thieu would desperately need genuine political appeal among the populace. If he had enhanced his power through the 1971 election, he had missed the chance to win real admiration of his war-weary, often disillusioned countrymen. The failure of the president to enlarge his base of popular, as opposed to military, support, coupled with Washington's declining interest in prosecuting the war, might yet provide his critics with opportunity to gain power through coalition with the Front and the North Vietnamese.

Notes

1. *The New York Times*, April 2, 1972.
2. *Saigon Post*, May 13, 1972.
3. John E. Woodruff, *Baltimore Sun*, June 3, 1972.
4. *Tieng Vang*, September 6, "Two Contradictory Opinions."
5. Ibid.
6. Francois Nivolon, Interview with General Nguyen Van Thieu, *Far Eastern Economic Review*, June 8, 1967.
7. Arthur Dommen, who covered Vietnamese politics for *The Los Angeles Times*, provided the writer with valuable insights on this aspect of the campaign.
8. Chicago *Daily News*, September 17, 1971.
9. Figures supplied by the Central Election Information Center, Saigon, on October 4, 1971, the day after the voting.
10. Laurence Stern, *The Washington Post*, published in *Pacific Stars & Stripes*, Tokyo, June 6, 1972. Political allies of Minh in late May began circulating a petition urging Thieu to resign. At least eighty persons signed the secret document, which accused Thieu of having failed politically, economically, and militarily and asked Minh to assume authority in order to "save the country." Despite its tone, the petition had little effect and was criticized as "premature" by some of Minh's advisers.
11. Order of the Day of the President of the Republic of Vietnam to the Armed Forces of the Republic of Vietnam on Armed Forces Day, June 19, 1972, official English language text.

5 Power Towards the People: Local Development in Vietnam, 1968-71
Stephen B. Young

Many have concluded that Vietnam has been a great American mistake. Yet with the failure of the massive North Vietnamese 1972 invasion it became clear that South Vietnam has considerable resilience. Furthermore, the lack of adequate Viet Cong assistance within South Vietnam during the invasion indicates profound changes have occurred in rural Vietnam to the advantage of the nationalist government. Thus, a critical analysis of rural development in Vietnam since 1968 reveals fundamental social changes that have reversed terms of struggle between non-communist nationalists and communists. Conditions and events prior to 1968 heavily influenced the outcome, but beginning that year, efforts at rural pacification and development were made on an unprecedented scale to carry out long desired radical measures in rural South Vietnam. Americans were deeply involved in bringing these changes about, and lessons applied to Vietnam from 1969 on came from deep within American experience. Furthermore, what happened to change rural Vietnam for the better is by no means irrelevant for the modernization of other nations.

Inauguration of multilevel elections and decentralization of power away from elites in the national capital have begun to knit Vietnam together into a strong polity and to overcome the cleavages that make revolution possible. Many little steps have been taken where a big jump might have been more dramatic and attracted more notice from the press. And changes have been at a low level, far from usual haunts of American journalists. Nonetheless, Vietnam's political structure has at last been profoundly changed—though for how long no one can say.

Two interrelated processes have occurred: elections at hamlet, village, province, and national levels and transfer of political power away from central ministries and military officers. Simultaneously, rural economic power of the landlord class has been crippled. As power flows down and out to new councils and elected officials, men of ability present themselves for election, the people see direct benefit in political participation, and the councils have immediate effect in political, economic, and social realities. The entire process generates myriad cross-cutting ties as men in political life become brokers between different groups and separate interests. They become brokers for the same reason that the people now participate and men run for office: it is in their interest to do so.

A man who can link many Hoa Hao with Progressive National Movement votes in Vinh Long Province can not only guarantee himself a provincial council seat but becomes for the first time in Vietnamese politics a man sought after by Saigon politicians running for the Senate and Lower House. Village and provincial councils now have significant development funds to allocate: hamlet and village chiefs have power to control local police and militia. Members of the Senate and Lower House receive substantial salaries and have shaped basic acts such as the land reform law, the General Mobilization Act, and the economic stabilization program. Spreading of power creates new interests, and holding elections opens up new potentials for those interests.

This description of Vietnam's progress sounds as if it had been sanctified by the holy writ of the American Way, and new programs introduced with the Pacification and Development Plan of 1969 did draw on basic American lessons of local democracy and decentralization. But more importantly, they were demanded by leading nationalist elements within the Vietnamese government. Local elections and decentralization had long been discussed and advocated by many familiar with Vietnam, but mostly they were offered as alternatives to the major thrust of official policy. It was only in 1968 that they received first priority and vast fiscal support from both American and Vietnamese governments.

By late 1965, following the decay of the Diem regime and a turnstile succession of constable governments by generals, the Americans finally sought a political solution for Vietnam in constitutional democracy. Legitimacy for the nationalist struggle was to be achieved through elections.

This resolve strengthened during 1966, and prodded by the so-called Buddhist Crisis that year, we firmly nudged the ruling generals over to the road of constitutional development. But it wasn't until after Tet in 1968 that our senior officials came to realize the fundamental importance of building a low-level structure to support an electoral system. Previously, rural programs sought to impose government authority on villagers or else to "win their hearts and minds" by doing good. Neither approach gave the people a share of power and decision making. Until 1968 we had watched as largely formal exercises the election of a constituent assembly, drafting of a constitution, and election of a Senate, Lower House, and president. Some village elections were also held in 1967, and province councils were re-elected in 1966. That initial effort to hold village elections did recognize the importance and legal position of the villages. This was the first significant break with the centralized, autocratic past. But power was still held by central agencies and the military, and although many fine things were said about the village elections of 1967, in fact there was little change in terms of village political realities.

While our initial policy of democratic development was not thought through with sophistication or executed with any great thoroughness, its acceptance by the Vietnamese marked the first major turning point in the political struggle against the North. For the first time non-communists had a common platform for their political future, a platform that was also a present, unfolding reality,

not merely a distant vision. This gave the South a *chinh nghia*, a righteous
cause. The elements of the cause—democracy, elections, civilian rule—have
always been meaningful "goods" in Vietnamese tradition, where merit, virtue,
and the people's welfare have high values. The generals had to accept this constitutional departure, for it was a basic condition for our military support. The
politicians and public were not overly hopeful initially but welcomed the development as a significant improvement over the recent past. So Vietnam's experiment in democracy began largely under the thrust of a vague American policy
that had not yet given serious consideration to the underlying fabric of Vietnamese life.

All this and much more changed, for Americans and for Vietnamese, after
the Tet and May offensives of 1968. Senior officials on both sides saw that
though the communists had just suffered massive losses and tactical military
defeats, there was as yet no basic success in resisting a "people's war" concept.
The NVA-VC had come through the "secure" countryside to attack cities,
eliminating government control over many areas of the countryside. By June
1968, Vice-President Nguyen Cao Ky's influence over the government had
been curtailed and the new leadership group of President Nguyen Van Thieu,
Prime Minister Tran Van Huong, and Deputy Prime Minister for Pacification
Tran Thien Khiem decided on a massive new effort in the rural areas. On the
American side, Robert Komer, who was responsible for the pacification program (CORDS), suggested the outlines of the first integrated, comprehensive
pacification program. After modifications, the Vietnamese government
accepted it as policy for 1969.

The program was complicated, ramifying into pacification councils at district, province, regional, and national levels, but two objectives were paramount:
security and politics. Improved physical security would frustrate and then
extinguish National Liberation Front (NLF) and North Vietnamese Army
(PAVN) military threats, while new politics was to create a viable system
embracing the people and the government. The previous division of military
activity into "main force" and "other" was abandoned, and all military and
civilian program assets were combined in one operations plan. Haphazard efforts
by individuals, ministries, province chiefs, and military units were replaced with
coordinated efforts to achieve eight goals broken down into specific limited
targets. Rural security was to be achieved primarily through a massive increase
in local village and province forces under the General Mobilization Act, creation
of the People's Self-Defense Force (PSDF), and expansion of police and intelligence work. Main force tactics were changed from "search and destroy" to
"breaking up the enemy's system," by General Creighton Abrams, clearing the
way for pacification. Better security, of course, could only insure military
occupation of rural areas. Then the political thrust of the program was to
transpose occupation into popular participation.

And it had finally been accepted as doctrine that security must both precede politics and then remain constant. Pacification forces would now enter a village to stay, not to pacify and depart when "pacification" was complete. Top Americans and Vietnamese now understood pacification was not just a short-run program of military operations and handing out a few "goodies" from U.S. aid funds. Rather, it was the permanent task of sustaining a political community.

This perception of pacification as community building is held most clearly by the Tan Dai Viet political party. This party is primarily the southern branch of the old Dai Viet nationalist party and is today the most potent of all nationalist parties. Tan Dai Viets established the first Ministry of Pacification in 1964, only to be removed by Generals Nguyen Khanh and Nguyen Cao Ky. But in the new pacification efforts starting in 1968, they or their close associates have held leadership positions and continued to exercise a controlling influence. Their importance lies in their origination of concepts and programs for pacification and development and their mobilization of political power on behalf of new approaches. It is believed Thieu brought Khiem back from exile to run the pacification program, in part at least, because of his close ties with the Tan Dai Viets. (Khiem is from Long An Province, a Tan Dai Viet stronghold.)

Like all nationalists, the Tan Dai Viets find their political cause and theory in Vietnamese tradition. The Dai Viets were among the most xenophobic of nationalists and never cooperated as a party with the French or the Chinese in the forties and fifties. Their original leader, Truong Tu Anh, a young law student, was murdered by the Viet Minh in 1946. Knowing that the key to Vietnamese tradition is the village, their conception of pacification starts with the idea of building a healthy society up from the village, not down from the central administration. They are also deeply influenced by other elements in tradition calling for decent, effective civilian government. The concept of pacification, or establishing a legitimate mandate to rule, is ancient in Sino-Vietnamese tradition. The party has also now adopted democracy as the preferred route toward modernity without sacrificing the essential quality of Vietnamese life as they see it. A coalition, the Progressive Nationalist Movement (Phong Trao Cap Tien Quoc Gia), has been organized around a Tan Dai Viet core, and old Tan Dai Viets now call themselves Cap Tien or Progressives. As a result, a critical political force in modern Vietnam, the key impetus behind rural programs, had its own uniquely Vietnamese reasons for embracing the American-proposed pacification program. Crucial to the program's success has also been support of President Thieu, who personally knocked elements in the military other than the Tan Dai Viets into line. His motives for this were murky as always, but in 1971 the program's results were acknowledged as his success by the people.

The dramatic new element in the pacification effort of 1969 was the political element. Security was to be established through much more of the same: more men, more guns, more outposts, more small-unit operations. But on the political side there was a departure: building a program around decentralization of power and local elections. The slogan was "power to village government with the people's participation in that government." Two goals were set: real power for village officials and as much popular participation as possible in the exercise of that power. Old programs were redesigned to further these aims. Our theory was that the people, if offered power to manage their own community affairs, would come forward to take advantage of that power and, by doing so, would support the political structure giving them such opportunity. We wanted to turn the "people's war" concept against the communists and foreclose their support in rural areas after a mantle of security had been laid down.

This new political response to the problem of rural insurgency was no more than recognition of need for political modernization. The essence of insurgency in Vietnam has been neither the use of military force nor solely the spirited attraction to the oppressed of a new social order, but the competition of two political communities, one based in the cities and the other in rural areas. The urban political community organized by the government did not include large segments of the population in rural areas and was easily cut off from the countryside. The insurgent community was physically closer to the people and protected by that gap between the government and rural society. Thus, the problem was to bridge the gap in the political community by extending the government's community outward so as to incorporate new people, in other words, to accomplish popular mobilization and participation associated with political modernization.

In Vietnam, the gap in political community resulted primarily from three interrelated factors. First, those who had influence on state power were largely confined to one class, the wealthy and the educated, the landlords and the Catholics. The majority had no great stake in the government and so could easily do without it.

In my experience as chief of the Local Government Branch, CORDS, from 1969 to 1970—it was not that people were alienated from government in an active ferment, though they had grievances, but rather that they were not included in political participation. They were not pushing for revolution, contrary to much superficial Western comment on Vietnam; they were only unattached and open for mobilization. In numerous villages, government and VC alternated in control without unduly upsetting local affairs. The image of Vietnamese farmers as exploited and oppressed is largely false. Failure of successive Saigon regimes was not in driving the people away, though that did happen too many times to be excused, but in failing to attract them and give them a role to play in shaping the nation's destiny.

Second, points of formal access to the government were few. Local officials were limited in number and had little power. Decisions always had to be referred upward. The system would function only if people came to it and waited around for some reaction. In a fundamental sense, the people were outside the system, which was nearly a closed corporate entity. Under successive challenges of a war for independence and then insurgency, the government corporation closed further in upon itself, widening the gap between it and the rural people.

Third, the physical presence of the government was weak. One village of several thousand would have one policeman and a half-dozen militia, armed with a few pistols or old rifles at most. Government at its outer fringe, where it interacted with village populations, was in no position to counter a physical challenge to its authority. In 1959 and 1960 assassination of two or three officials could effectively terminate government authority in a village.

Pacification planning in 1968 attempted to overcome the third cause of the gap through security in depth and provision for adequate forces in each village in turn as the program was expanded outward from secure areas. The first and second causes of the gap would be tackled through the politics of the village strategy. Through elections of hamlet chiefs, village councils, and village chiefs and participation in a new development program, the number of people who could improve their lives by involvement with government was given a quantum jump. The less-well-to-do would have new hope for a meaningful relationship with local government, though they would continue to suffer a relative disadvantage vis-à-vis the rich. We knew the program would succeed only if such hopes were justified in the particular circumstances of each of 2100 villages. Thus, we had to insure that the people's access to officials was easy and frequent and that local officials had sufficient power to take final action in resolution of popular concerns. By the end of 1969, the new program's first year, we were confident that the combination of security, elections, and decentralization was actually bringing rural people into the desired political community with the government under the Constitution.

The outline of the village strategy was presented in a memo from Robert Komer to his staff in July 1968, which suggested that village chiefs should be given considerably more authority and should receive help in the matter of land taxes. Previous pacification efforts had taken the hamlet as the basic organizational entity because Diem and later leaders were from central Vietnam, where the hamlet was usually a distinct physical entity surrounded by a hedge. However, since the origin of the Viet peoples in South China several thousand years ago, the village, with its shrine and committee of elders, had been the focal point of rural life above the level of family. In the Constitution of 1967, provinces and villages are given independent authority to have their own budgets and executive councils. So it was at the village rather than hamlet level that the critical role of elections and participation could be carried out. The work of Ben Ferguson in 1967 in helping a few villages organize around their problems had helped to direct attention towards the village unit.

A critical decision was to give the elected village chief authority over military forces, police, and cadres stationed in his village, as well as over self-help projects. In theory he was tied to the village council and the people through his election. Thus, law enforcement was expected to become more respectful of the citizens. The people no longer needed to go to the district and confront bureaucrats behind desks to have troop misbehavior brought under control, for hamlet chief or village council member working through the village chief now could take action. Suddenly the entire play of community relationships—friendships, kin ties, power of social status—could bear upon one's treatment by government. Nearly everyone in a village is related to a village councillor or has a claim on the attention of someone who has a claim on a councillor. Over time the local village government would become enmeshed with local social structure, solidifying village political community. And local government would have sufficient power to meet community needs and maintain community prerogatives.

One aspect of local control over security matters had profound political implications. This was creation of the People's Self-Defense Force (PSDF), which placed the duty of national defense upon every citizen, male and female. Weapons were distributed to citizen units, which were given training and actual tactical responsibilities. The PSDF, with no ties to higher levels for pay or promotion, was directly responsive to hamlet and village leadership. It would shoot it out with more regular troops occasionally, including those of the national army, to protect villagers or their property. Here was a massive transfer of raw physical power to please the most radical populist. The theory was that if a man accepted a weapon to defend himself, family, or community against the NLF-PAVN he was an asset, even if he did not particularly like the central government; he was making a tentative commitment to the nationalist cause on the basis of which a more permanent relationship could grow.

A second critical decision of the village strategy was to give each village a development budget under its control. Prior to 1969, American aid had bought cement, steel, and tin roofing sheets to build the good works that would win the "hearts and minds" of the rural folk. Each hamlet designated for pacification received one school, one market, three cement pigsties, etc. But the people had little or no influence on the nature or location of the project. Although district officials gathered people for meetings to discuss projects, officials did all the talking. Materials were easily diverted by contractors hired by district officials to erect buildings, and there was little quality control. Many "white elephant" projects were built and stood unused. But in 1969 each village was given a budget and allowed to allocate its own development resources. Popular assemblies were held to determine projects, groups of interested citizens were formed by village officials to carry out projects. Villagers could choose either construction projects, like schools and markets, or profit-making undertakings, like pig raising, buying Rototillers, or introducing "miracle" rice. In effect, a central government subsidy replaced absurdly low and generally uncollected local taxes.

There was some opposition to this program from traditional Agency for International Development advisers who felt village leaders could not be trusted with money or that they first should be taught fiscal responsibility through tax collection. We in CORDS replied that if they could not trust the villages, they could not trust anybody in this war, and it would be more politic to show people what government could do for them before asking for their taxes. Special financial procedures were decreed to remove this new village development program from the usual red tape of the ministries. Villages with elected councils were given $VN1,000,000, and those without $VN400,000, to encourage holding elections. Instead of going up to the province level to draw funds, villages now had special extra-budget accounts and checkbooks (though province administration had some technical say over large construction projects).

Then, to expand popular participation, the village self-development program encouraged formation of People's Common Activity Groups (PCAGS) to create new links within a rural community. The idea was that a group would oversee implementation of a project and then maintain it upon completion. If it were for profit, the group would establish rules for distribution of rewards. If it were a public service venture, the group was expected to provide for future maintenance. We later saw more advantages in loans than group grants to achieve development goals, but only when we could assure community rather than individual or family selection of projects.

In addition to holding village and hamlet elections throughout 1969 and turning over military and economic power to local officials, this village strategy also featured special training courses for 15,000 village and hamlet officials. It was designed to be motivational rather than technical in order that local officials clearly understood they were backed by the highest government leadership and should stand up to minor district and provincial officials. We expected resistance to the new programs from those latter officials, especially military officers accustomed to monopolies of power in their little domains, but all significant flouting of the village strategy was slapped down by Thieu or Prime Minister Khiem. Still, in the first year the actual degree of independence exercised by village leaders and quality of popular participation left much to be desired. Our objective, however, was not to reverse overnight the authoritarian heritage of centuries but to set up new relationships that would be self-sustaining and grow in importance over time. Steady emphasis on decentralization and refinement of program details would build a new momentum in local government. As elected officials at higher levels grew in power and influence, they would assist and protect interests of elected village government, for their political futures depended on support from the village level.

As one reason for the gap between government and rural people was a heavy bias stemming from government ties to the landlord class, another major effort, not specifically part of the pacification program, was stressed: the land to the tiller program. Consequently, the landlord class in Vietnam was dispossessed in law by March 1970. Landlords now had claims on government for compensation but none on tenants. Land reform is a complicated story which is relevant here mainly in two aspects: landlords as a class had their power over rural life largely punctured in 1970, and village government was given the major role in carrying out the program. Local officials knew former landlords would be less involved in community affairs in the future, so landlord influence began to wane. Village officials simultaneously became vitally important to the tenant, for they accepted his application for land and processed his title.

Land reform was a corollary of the village strategy in breaking down centralized economic power over land and by reinforcing the power of village government. The issue was not primarily redistributing wealth from rich to poor. It was more subtle and complicated. The primary problem of rural Vietnam was lack of political community, of a bond between rural populace and government, not the fact that some were rich and some were poor. Discrepancies in wealth, status, and power exist in all nations, but only some undergo protracted insurgencies. The issue is ultimately political and not economic. Perhaps it is the fixation of American society on the importance of property that has led so many commentators to interpret the Vietnam War as a struggle by the poor to get the rich. Economic motives do play an important role, but they are affected by a flux of political and social forces. For example, to the extent government was bound to the strengths and weaknesses of one class, the landlords, it was limited in building a community that could share power with persons whose interests opposed those of the landlords. Splitting the government from the landlords was *the* critical consequence of land reform, a political one at that.

The village strategy, which began in April 1969, increased village government staffs as well as legally mandating the village chief's control over military and paramilitary forces in the village. The minimum cash expenditure a village could make on its own authority was rai̇s. '. And during 1969 the relationship between rural people and government began to change radically. Under the later emperors, the French, and then Diem, there had been a tendency to centralize power away from the village. Now power was flowing in the other direction back down towards the people. By the end of 1969 the people, the village, and hamlet officials, and the bureaucracy were beginning to adjust to these new ripples in the pattern of power. There was also more power added to the system, more resources over which decisions could be made, more points of decision on the old matters, and more individuals with a say in decisions.

A parallel departure was made at the provincial level, where each province chief could submit projects to the National Pacification Council for speedy approval. Freed from ministry delays and formalities, execution could proceed more rapidly, so the gap between promise and performance was shrunk to reasonable limits, narrower, in fact, than that typical of New York City.

At that time I personally was very excited at the massive break with tradition. Now the problem became one of institutionalizing the new approach so it would not fade or be casually abandoned, the fate of so many earlier programs. It was also necessary to correct program deficiencies. So for 1970 I obtained, against demands from field officials for sheer continuity, agreement that the village strategy would be modified to begin institutionalization and to remedy mistakes.

There were program weaknesses we regarded as inevitable: many local elections had not yet drawn out the best talent in the villages, or many district or provincial officials exercised too rigid a control over candidates. Many of the best men would not risk holding government office until they felt certain the NLF would not return and that the power promised them was real. Two or three cycles of elections would have to be run through before the advantages of officeholding were seen clearly and the disadvantages outweighed. Also, political manipulations of higher administrative officials were accepted in part as the initial price for the elite's acquiescence to the reform. And at least now they had to manipulate downward as well as upward and pay attention to local politics. Then, too, we knew just about every village had some son or nephew or grandson in a position of considerable influence in the army, administration, or a religious-political group. Since these individuals could usually be expected to stand up for the interest of their village (*gue huong*, or native place), the village always turned to them to intercede with Saigon if a higher official became too harsh. And finally, we had our advisers in the field apprise us of any gross deviation from law, so that appropriate central-level action could be taken.

The major program weakness we could correct was too little popular participation in the development program. Elections had been held on schedule as area security had expanded, officials had been trained, and new powers gradually put to use, but the desired degree of popular control over self-help project selection was lacking. I felt the failure was due largely to the information program; people could not participate if they did not know what was going on. Also, village chiefs were given only a short deadline to submit project decisions, a consequence of our unfortunate reporting phobia. Thus, many villages I knew best had project groups formed by village leaders on a "you, you and you: volunteer!" basis, and 1969 projects showed a high percentage of participation by friends and neighbors of village officials. Many of the village assemblies required to guarantee popular control came to nothing when word did not get out that they were being held. Furthermore, the Ministry of Rural Development's suggestions of possible projects listed pig raising first, and eventually thousands of projects were drawn up to include group pigsties. But while Vietnamese farmers do many things in common, raising pigs is not one of them, and most of these projects failed. (The AID auditors began to get very worried. We could not show specific results in each of twenty-thousand-odd projects, and if each did not make money or build a bridge, we were in trouble with Congress. This was only another difficulty we had with traditional foreign aid specialists who could not see that even if all the pigs died, the program might be successful in the sense that people had started to come together to make decisions and carry them out. Something important was happening and would grow stronger if reinforced, but unfortunately it was nothing that could be well measured quantitatively.)

The major modifications for the 1970 program were to extend the deadline for projection decisions, allocate funds to villages according to population, and use a household survey form. This survey form was suggested by Ben Ferguson and his team. Each household in the village was asked to list projects most wanted and how much they were willing to contribute. An open village assembly then would select from the hamlet priority lists projects to be financed. If a project cost under $VN100,000, the village could begin work on it immediately. More expensive projects required technical consultation with province officials, who could take a maximum of one month to reach this judgment. Families requesting a selected project were invited to join the common activity group carrying it out. Both the chairman of the village council and the village chief had to cooperate in the financial procedure, so neither part of village government was given a monopoly of power (though the village chief had more through his responsibility for security and administration).

The one weakness we really wanted to overcome was lack of an adequate information program. The Ministry of Information was controlled by men interested in resurrecting some form of the old Diemist party, the Can Lao. In particular they feared and opposed the Tan Dai Viets. They still held to the Catholic mandarin rule from the top that had failed under Diem, and they saw the Tan Dai Viets as "too" nationalistic. Therefore, there was not even minimal cooperation between the Ministry of Information and the Ministry of Rural Development, so that the latter had to dip into its own funds to print guidance pamphlets on the program. We drafted our own materials and then spent the rest of the year trying to get them published. Under pressure from the Prime Minister's Office, the Ministry of Information did print a few hundred thousand pamphlets—for a rural population of 10 million. American psychological warfare experts were dropping billions of pieces of paper on the jungles to induce PAVN soldiers to rally, but there was too little support for a political program designed to correct the relationship between government and the people.

Still, we were pleased with what was accomplished in 1969. A new dimension was added to village government, and now local officials could work directly with the people to meet economic and social needs. Local government had become more than law enforcement and administrative routine of birth certificates and identify cards. Village officials now were more than the lowest rung of an administration; they were a government in their own right. In contrast to previous programs, the village development program built more classrooms, more bridges over canals, more pigpens, and built them quicker. The program brought new miracle rice seeds and fertilizers to many more families than ever contemplated by the Ministry of Agriculture's agricultural extension program. Village self-development elicited meaningful contributions from people in the form of cash and labor inputs. The program would fund a water pump, and families would buy new rice and fertilizer. The pump would be rotated among families, and a second crop could be produced for the first time ever. The program was a great incentive to buy Rototillers, small generators for electricity, and even small rice mills, which posed such a challenge to the big mills monopolizing rice milling and thereby controlling prices that they unsuccessfully pressed high officials to choke off use of the small machines. Investment in such new technology allowed people to test new opportunities at reduced risk, and other farmers would buy machines when they saw they were profitable.

The process of institutionalization necessary to realize permanently the promise of the village strategy thus revolved around finances. Something becomes institutionalized when it becomes so meshed in the fabric of people's lives that its basic existence is unquestioned; an organization that remains, even though its purposes or leaders change, is an institution. Here, village development had to become self-sustaining, independent of nonvillage funding, and local power had to be protected from higher, potentially hostile levels in the power structure. If left alone, the local communities would develop the program's potential to its maximum. To maintain the thrust of development on this basis of self-sustaining interest, we fixed on a rural credit program under some form of village control and then on increased village taxation. To protect local power, our theory was that electoral system development would bring patron-client relationships binding the national leadership to village constituencies through Lower House Deputies and Provincial Councillors. As the Lower House was already functioning, we focused on the provincial level. This conceptual framework and focus for policy was the profound contribution of Ambassador William Colby, the pacification program's second head.

Subsequent progress of the village strategy in 1970 was slow. By the end of 1969 we had recognized the specific efforts needed for institutionalization. The Vietnamese leadership let me know informally that they were eager to start detailed planning, but first we had to win support within the American Mission for a new tax program (from the Public Administration Division) and rural credit (from three other offices: the Agricultural Directorate, the Program Directorate, and the Directorate of Economic Affairs). Provincial development and encouragement of provincial councils was within Colby's responsibility, so less delay was involved there.

In November 1969 the Public Administration Division replied to our suggestions for new tax laws and village powers by proposing a Vietnamese government committee study the matter and make recommendations. The Public Administration technicians felt villages should be made to levy all taxes on the books before receiving additional powers. We argued that tax levels had been absurdly low by recent inflation, and thus, to ask a village chief to perform an unpopular task for only a pittance in return was asking too much. More important, taxes should not be increased until the village had clear power to use them for public good. Provincial controls on village budgets had to be removed first. The taxes should go up only when the public benefits derived would also increase directly. We took this position after discussions with our district level advisers and many village officials. Villages only collected some 600 million piastres in revenue, the largest component of this being market taxes. Rates were out of date, assessments decades in arrears. But one single rice crop in the Delta that year would produce net revenue to farmers of about 100 billion piastres, for with the new security, farmers were no longer paying one-third to one-half of their crop to the NLF, and they paid few other taxes to the government. Thus, it was absurd to continue a 10-billion-piastre drain on the national budget for local government subsidies, especially when use of subsidies would maintain a top-heavy administration inconsistent with the decentralization already embarked on. As the English gentry and Parliament discovered in their struggles against royal power, the power of the purse is the power that counts. Villages had to have independent finances if local government were to work and elections have significance.

Six months later, after the government committee made its report, recommending essentially that it be instructed to proceed with further action, we achieved some revision of village fiscal powers. The Vietnamese Director General of Budget and Foreign Aid agreed to a new budget for villages giving them greater flexibility in "development." Each village was given its account in the province treasury, so province officials had minimal control over the deposit and withdrawal of tax monies. The procedures of accounting responsibility and contracting pioneered in the village self-development program were adapted for the regular village budget. In 1971 the development program could be integrated into the village council's regular budget. Giving the council more direct power was one of our subsidiary aims, as we felt it needed strengthening vis-à-vis the village chief. The next step was to raise taxes, but that required legislative approval, and no official was eager to present a bill to tax farmers. Furthermore, the land reform program, guided by the older theory of "winning hearts and minds by giving out goodies" had provided for a tax moratorium on all land distributed. Farmers were to be given free titles and not taxed for an additional year.

More progress, however, was made in the area of rural credit, for by fall 1970 we had a program funded and ready for action. Colby, whose concern was for institutionalization of village power as well as the short-term political benefits of easier credit, in July 1970 promised 400 million piastres from the pacification contingency fund if the AID mission, the Agricultural Bank and the Ministry for Rural Development could agree on a program. In 1969–70 the village self-development program had given grants for income-earning projects on the theory that interest would be reinvested by the group implementing the project. By mid-1970 we felt that putting income-producing projects on a loan basis would better perpetuate the program and come closer to achieving our basic political objective. AID and the Bank were most concerned that a soft loan program would never be repaid, echoing the experience of the Diem regime's rural credit effort. The economists were worried that more credit would fuel further inflation. However, by the fall of 1970 a compromise program was worked out providing that the provincial branches of the Agricultural Bank would establish accounts for each village and have a veto on each loan under the program. The village would form a credit committee composed of the village chief, chairman of the village council, the village cultural commissioner, and several citizens. That committee would recommend individuals for loans up to $VN50,000. If the loans were defaulted on by borrowers, the bank would make them up out of the village's repaid loan fund.

There was also a multiplier principle applicable to any money contributed to the program by a village over and above the government grant. Thus, if a village added a certain amount of its own funds and had no defaults during the year, in the next year it could lend out whatever was in the account plus twice that amount in a line of credit from the bank for a total loan fund of three times the hard assets. We hoped this incentive to building up the funds would insure that village credit committees would use sound economic calculations in making loans and that borrowers would feel more obliged to repay. Since a default deprived the village of three similar loans next year, this should generate community pressures to which borrowers would be responsive.

At the village level the most exciting event of 1970 was the re-election of about one-half the village governments, those which held their first elections in 1967. While most village chiefs were returned to office (they were first elected to their village councils and then were selected by the councils to be chiefs), over half the old council members were voted out. On balance we found the new councils to be younger and more active. Also, there was considerable effort by political-religious groups, particularly the Tan Dai Viets in the Delta, to get their men elected. In northern provinces, where the village structure dates back to the fifteenth century, elders who had achieved social status outside government seemed favored for council seats. But in the Delta, settled in the eighteenth and nineteenth centuries, most candidates seemed to be younger men coming from village administration or the military to seek the higher status accorded elective community officials. Successful candidates invariably were identified as representing a bloc of votes: a Hoa Hao faction, the My Thanh hamlet vote, the military-administrative vote, etc. The number of candidates was larger than in 1967, and their quality also appeared better. When questioned, people explained this improvement as a result of better security (community leaders were less fearful of NLF retaliation for holding office) and more power available to village government. You could now become somebody in the eyes of your community through election.

By 1970 the top and the bottom framework of the nationalist political strategy was in place. The Constitution provided a law of the land, and the village strategy was building solid rural communities within the constitutional framework. It remained to tie them together into a system. So 1970 also saw new programs begun at the provincial level, the nexus where village politics could have an impact and national leadership would remain involved. Pending legislative approval of a basic law for all local governments, the government issued several decrees to strengthen province council powers, gave substantial salaries to councilmen, and held new elections in June 1970. To encourage rapid emergence of constituency ties, councilmen would be elected from districts rather than at large as previously. This shifted control of the councils away from the populous province capitals to rural areas and gave more power to political-religious groups with organized followings in several constituencies, just as it guaranteed any sizable but geographically confined group some minimal representation. Colby offered further supporting funds to give the new councils their own project budgets so they would not have to request funds from either the province chief, a senior military officer, or the ministries in Saigon. The province council fund was the counterpart to the development fund already given to the province chief in 1969 to free province administration from the ministerial stranglehold.

The provincial council elections added another dimension to the political system. Candidates were not only numerous but could be found in villages wheeling and dealing with local factions and power-brokers. Many military officers ran to develop a base for future political careers or just to get out of the service. In many cases, after the election, a lieutenant colonel serving as province chief found himself with a lieutenant colonel elected as chairman of the provincial council and several majors or captains as members. The military alumni on the council were not likely to take strong opposition to their former military associate, the province chief, but the obstruction he could throw up against the council was restricted. On balance, councils represented a new source of power which the military hierarchy could not ignore. The emergence of a province-level political link between village politics and national affairs will not solve Vietnam's problem, nor will it blossom immediately into a powerful check on national leadership. It is only a beginning, but as such it is a considerable accomplishment.

Each of the major national political groups elected some followers to various provincial councils. The Hoa Hao, Cao Dai, Catholics, An Quang Buddhists, Montagnards, Tan Dai Viets, Farmer-Worker party, and other larger blocs strengthened their respective bases in rural areas by placing followers on the councils. Interest in provincial elections was heightened by expectations that success there would help in subsequent Senate and Lower House elections. Since many of these local leaders had direct ties to national political figures, province chiefs began to treat the local men with some care. Heads of ministerial services at the province level, formerly powerful bureaucrats in frequent collision with the people's interest, now had to respond to councilmen or risk inquiries at the ministry in Saigon. Of course, important village political figures knew that the higher officials they now could see about their problems had some interest in them and capacity to help them. And after the provincial elections, province council funds were quickly allocated in various villages to substantial public interest projects, like large generators, which were beyond the scope of village development plans and not included in tight ministry budgets. Province councillors were quick to exploit these opportunities to build support.

Then, too, in 1970 an experiment in development planning was begun. To prepare for 1971 budget allocations, each village and province was asked to formulate desired development expenditures for that community. Each province was informed of its planned allocation from pacification funds as well as from ministry budgets. The province then informed each village of its subtotal. First the village and then the province would list priorities as to how that total should be spent. The province council had final approval of the province list, thereby exercising control over the province chief's development fund and the services' budget requests. This was merely another phase in the policy based on the assumption that the local areas knew their needs better than Saigon bureaucrats and that elected local officials knew best of all.

By the end of 1970 the skeleton village program of 1969 had put on muscle and had begun to move of its own accord. Village projects were better in quality and fewer in quantity; there were few pig projects. Participation was up; 80 percent of rural people surveyed now knew about the program and 25 percent recorded themselves as having participated directly. They also indicated program decisions were made by village or hamlet elders or officials. Village and provincial elections brought out new and better men tied to one another in a new vertical dimension of the political system. The province government could reinforce this subsystem, having received some real autonomy from Saigon. The prescription for 1971 was more of the same. The village self-development program was merged with the new village budget; income-producing projects were placed in the village credit program; province councils again received their own funds just as province chiefs were given their development budgets. Another effort would be made in Saigon to increase rates for local revenues. And national elections for the Lower House, president, and vice-president were to be held.

There was, however, one new program element for 1971: "People's Organization." The thinking behind this on the American side was strictly Tocqueville, while the Vietnamese leadership was moved by a strategy of winning popular allegiance indirectly. Both sides wanted to extend the new decentralization and local participation. We held that if an electoral system were to be meaningful, organized groups had to exist between the individual and the formal structure of elections and administrators to shape the generally inchoate demands of the citizenry into specific political objectives.

The groups we wanted to encourage were not formal political organizations such as those organized under the Political Party Law, but associations of individuals for many purposes, associations that linked individuals with each other and forged private interests into social forces. In the pluralistic Vietnamese society, there has been an abundance of private, nonpolitical groupings, but few have had coherence or permanence. We sought a program removing heavy administrative control from organized group activity and creating incentives to reward and sustain group involvement.

The Vietnamese government formally broke with the authoritarian policy of organization used in the North and under Diem whereby the masses were coerced into "mass movements" guided by official cadre for government purposes. Again Tan Dai Viets were a key to this change. The plan for 1971 stated: "the free and democratic regime of the Republic of Vietnam cannot adopt an autocratic policy to force organization of the people as in countries with dictatorships. On the contrary, we must encourage the people to organize themselves on a voluntary basis." To avoid a Pandora's box of petty conflict and some not so petty, no religious group or political party was considered a people's organization for this plan. Each province council would reserve 25 percent of its development fund to support projects or operating expenses of people's organizations. This was the carrot to encourage group activity. We also relied on the natural attraction of elected representatives to voting blocs needing favors. I argued for some specific targets in a few organizational areas, such as PTAs, culture, and sports, but I was overruled out of concern that any mention of targets would trigger the administrator's instinct to order people out to participate, thus defeating what we had in mind. I still regard this group element as not only the crux of the political program but the most subtle and sophisticated part. When people are organized for political purposes into groups based on emotional, political, or economic interest there can be a connection of social and political forces capable over time of furthering great diversity, flexibility, and continuity in government.

The solid accomplishment of 1971 was to decentralize legal organization away from the prime minister of the interior to the province chief. Under the old law, drafted by the French for Bao Dai in 1950, any private group, even a village charity, to obtain legal permission to operate (i.e., avoid arrest as subversive) needed approval from at least a minister and likely as not the prime minister. Under this law private group activities languished. In other ways, too, the new program was disappointing. Again public information was minimal. Funds went largely to pre-existing groups and did not expand the political process very much. Then the 1971 communist strategy of reversion to phase II warfare, emphasizing political and guerilla activity, meant they were redoubling efforts to create legal undercover cadres and to penetrate legal groups. As the impact of this became more evident, the government began to back away from initial interest in people's organizations. Finally, repeal of Bao Dai's law required significant legislative action considered impossible in a presidential election year because it would bring out efforts by many political and religious groups to advance their interests at the expense of others, precipitating excessive conflict.

But 1971 did bring us closer to solving the problem of inadequate finances for local government. The prime minister established a special committee to increase village and province revenues as much as possible. This committee informed all provinces and villages of what taxes were on the books but not applied, and instructed them to collect all taxes at the maximum rates for 1972. Several new fees not requiring legislative approval were proposed for Rototillers, Honda motorbikes, and small-boat motors, which had been imported in vast numbers. For the first time the Ministry of Finance took seriously the problem of local government taxation and began to consider a new land tax law to generate billions of piastres and permit further decentralization by allowing transfer of services from ministries to local government. The ministry proposed that the prime minister give each village authority to levy a development "fee" to pay for the village's contribution to the development and rural credit programs.

The 1971 plan also took the first tough step towards village fiscal autonomy. High-income villages were told their central government subsidy would be reduced 100, 50 or 25 percent depending on the level of village income. All villages were put on notice that the development burden increasingly would be shifted to them along with increasing power over the program. This was expected to improve program implementation while allowing ministries to do a better job of planning and policy making. Senior officials in the Ministry of Education would no longer need to sign pay vouchers for hamlet teachers and could be more concerned with hamlet school curriculum. Real decentralization of administrative authority began as province budget requests were sent to Saigon accompanied by a profile of the potential tax base.

When I left Vietnam in September 1971 the only basic foundation block of the new political changes *not* in place was adequate local taxation. Otherwise the old political system of top-down administration by an elite was in the process of being turned on its head. The old autocratic system and its military subsystem were still there, but at the bottom between it and the people was a new layer of village government growing in strength. And parallel to the old hierarchy but sprouting up from the village and hamlet governments was a new vertical structure of elected officials, having many points of horizontal access to the bureaucracy.

Permanent results of all this effort do not yet speak for themselves and may not for a long time, but several trends can be pointed out. First, solidarity of subgroups was strengthened as the political system opened to more influence from outside the formal administration and rewards were easily achieved by effective political organization. As local interests gained more coherence and vitality through access to central resources, they developed more of a stake in that central system. Decentralization generated direct support for the nationalist government. People began to regard the administration not as a rival and hostile power, but as merely another force in an expanding political system, more of a first among equals rather than the sole "equal." Second, within the village the issue of rich versus poor, or the class confrontation necessary for a communist movement to recruit and nourish its core cadres, was mitigated. The rich still existed, but local government was no longer their exclusive preserve, while land reform limited their economic predominance. Today the idea of organizing villagers to throw out rich elders ruling through the guns of a foreign power no longer makes sense to people. Village leadership now depends on political skills in local and even, to some extent, district and provincial politics, not naked repression. Third, elected positions have brought out more able and energetic people. Regime opponents find attractive the possibility of winning elections and gaining access to resources for building interest-oriented support. Bureaucrats now give more than lip service to group or community problems, so the machinery of government becomes more effective. Bribery of senior officials is no longer a sure road to success if performance cannot be demonstrated.

Our role as allies in all this has not been complex. We had certain views of various policies and programs which in our judgment would strengthen the government and the society and further our objective of a free and independent, self-sufficient South Vietnam. In the main, and especially after June of 1968, Vietnamese leadership agreed with our assessment and recommendations, though the record is by no means one of consistent agreement in detail. First, however, it was essential to success that we insisted on a constitutional framework and provided combat military support when the Vietnamese under corrupt military leadership were at their nadir. Second, we added power to the entire system of politics so new departures were slices of the proverbial larger pie instead of hard choices between smaller slices of a pie whose size was rigidly fixed. With high aid levels we enabled prosperity for urban and rural sectors, so the level of poverty was far lower than could be expected for a country torn by war for most of twenty-five years. Urban prosperity based on imports provided a new source of wealth and power for the old landlord elite, which still composed most of the administration and officer corps. Thus, they no longer had a vested interest to protect in the villages and no selfish reason to oppose the new pacification strategy. Further, we provided budgets for the councils so that they could produce results and develop constituency ties without either raising taxes or drawing from the regular administrative budgets. Third, we provided a consistent series of recommendations, each one more or less mutually reinforcing the others, so that new sources of power all had a thrust in the same direction. While each program by itself might have been insufficient, together they were a massive water buffalo powering social change—slow, but steady and irreversible.

Many argue that such interference in another's society is none of our

business or somehow immoral. What hubris to act as if we know best! And see
what a mess our Vietnam policy has sunk us in. In fact, the thinking of critics
seems to be: We are in a predicament; therefore it was none of our business in
the first place! But since normal men's moral judgments of an action are so
highly colored by the practical results, moral repugnance over Vietnam is premature.

To my mind, mistakes in Vietnam were ones of comparative excess, not of
extreme hubris, but if we do ultimately witness a tragedy of Greek proportions,
I will have been wrong. I have no difficulty ascribing intellectual honesty to
those who oppose *all* wars and *all* forms of foreign involvement as immoral.
At the other extreme are those who hold for universal involvement on behalf
of some moral cause. But those who seek to distinguish between some involve-
ments and not others must retreat to a mixed world, where moral purpose and
practical fact must be balanced. And since it is impossible to hold conclusively
that the game in Vietnam has been won or lost, it is foolish to argue against all
U.S. foreign involvement by pointing to the Vietnam experience. Valuable
lessons have been learned in Vietnam, such as that massive intervention is
unnecessary and counterproductive. Others concern political development,
and our development policies in South Vietnam were consistent with the Title
IX legislation on foreign aid in which Congress called for promotion of democratic forms and popular participation in aid. Our experience here in Vietnam
was that directly aiding local governments, along with measures of popular
involvement, promoted more social change than did most rural health, agricultural extension, and other technical projects.

It seems clear from our experience that participatory programs cannot
succeed as mere adjuncts to technical programs. Providing for elections of
boards, committees, or councils that lack the power to allocate resources is
futile whether in Vietnam, Thailand, Brazil, or Bedford-Stuyvesant. Meaningful participation flows to and from power. In this profound sense technical
assistance, a dominant component of our foreign aid, is limited in development
impact, since it does little to change the relationship between classes or between
citizens and their government. In Vietnam a few years of political decentralization made progress where years of money, technicians, and "goodies" had hardly
any effect. If decentralization and participation can reverse a difficult situation,
they might do very well indeed in a more normal one. I am certain Thailand
could attain in this way what ten years of "counterinsurgency" have yet to
bring under control. I suspect the succession problems of Haile Selassie and
other autocratic regimes would be eased by building a political community
in rural areas by a meaningful sharing of power.

Another truth can be gleaned: If power goes low enough and wide enough
in community affairs, it poses no immediate threat to the central regime; but
giving power to the next subordinate layer may generate a potent threat to the
dispenser. This is because local communities usually only impinge on national

politics as a last resort when pressures for change are bottled up by the inter-mediate layers. Politicians just under the level of central power usually aspire for the throne; giving them power from the top puts them in a position to challenge the national government. Local politicians, frankly, play a different game, one less dangerous to the central authorities.

Third, the easy way to attain general system stability within which tensions interact to grind out qualitative improvements is to add power to the old system in order that hitherto denied persons or groups may share in it. And in this case, which is probably relevant to others, this involved politico-economic decen-tralization around new taxes. As soon as a potential tax base is discerned, a government body and a participatory process can be fostered to utilize it for control of certain programs important to that community. Where the tax base is limited, matching grants or loans from higher levels are most appropriate.

In conclusion, others must interpret and analyze what we tried to do and what we accomplished in encouraging political democracy in Vietnam. Our efforts arose from themes deeply bisecting the American past and present, growing out of the experience of our people. Yet I believe they contain a very valid truth: Society is just to the extent it allows its citizens a reasonable chance to improve their lot. If Americans have died assisting the Vietnamese towards this end, to me they did not die in vain.

6 Elections and Political Mobilization: Prospects for Party Development and More Significant Competition

Nguyen Ngoc Huy

In a democratic country elections provide opportunities for all citizens to participate in the management of all levels of national life. Political parties are the vehicles to mobilize the citizenry for such political activity. Yet for a democratic system to work harmoniously, there must be a favorable legal framework, a high sense of civic responsibility among the people, and well-organized parties.

At present, South Vietnam has an acceptable legal framework. The political system established by the Constitution of 1967 is a presidential system. Delegates to the Constitutional Assembly chose the presidential over the parliamentary form, which some had demanded. Experience shows that the parliamentary system works best in those nations with a strong two-party system, such as England. In nations with many parties or which have yet to develop parties, the parliamentary system usually leads to political disorder. Under the Third and Fourth French Republics the government was frequently overturned, and the average cabinet lasted only six months. Under a presidential system, the administrative agencies are more stable, whether there are two strong parties, many parties and political groups, or no parties. Vietnam is now in the position of having many parties without any party being strong. Because of this only a presidential system can avoid political chaos.

Furthermore, according to some political scientists, the parliamentary system does not afford the best protection for individual liberties, assuming control of the administration by the parliament. For under the parliamentary system a government with an absolute majority in the parliament can pass any law to oppress the opposition and increase its own power unfairly. We have seen the Menderes government in Turkey use just these techniques to set up a real dictatorship until it was overthrown by the army. Thus, the absence of a supreme court to pass on the constitutionality of laws and the lack of independence of the executive and legislative branches in a parliamentary system makes that system less able than the presidential system to protect basic freedoms.

The Constitution of 1967 established a more progressive political system than the first Constitution of 1956 because the Supreme Court legally became the equal of the legislative and executive branches. Nevertheless, the current Vietnamese presidential system has various defects.

1. Supreme Court justices are selected by the legislature for a term of six years from a list prepared by a group of lawyers and judges. The term of office restricts the freedom of judicial decisions from legislative or executive

interference, because the necessity for re-election makes judges dependent on the legislature or even the president, if he has significant influence in the legislature. Further, since the justices must be nominated by lawyers and judges under their authority before they can be re-elected, they are obligated to those elements and cannot maintain an independent position toward them.

2. The president has excessive power in the legislative process. With his constitutional power of revision, he can alter laws of the National Assembly to conform to his own wishes unless an absolute majority of the total of all senators and Lower House deputies can be mobilized to reject his counterproposal revising the assembly's measure. Such a majority is difficult to achieve, given the fragmented party structure in Vietnam, so that the power of legislating frequently passes from the National Assembly to the president. Thus, the Assembly has lost much of its weight in dealing with the president.

The idea of formal constitutional reform, however, is premature, because the main features of the 1967 Constitution are perfectly acceptable. For example, under the Constitution the people vote directly for the president, vice-president, senators, deputies, mayors, and province chiefs. There is also direct election for councillors of Saigon, the provinces, autonomous cities and the villages, and, by extension, the village chiefs. All of these elections have been carried out, with the exception of those for province chiefs and mayors of Saigon and the autonomous cities. The Constitution also recognizes the vital role of political parties in a democratic regime and grants freedom of party formation within the rule of law (Article 99). The Constitution emphasizes the establishment of political opposition to the government (Article 101) and encourages movement towards a system of broad coalition parties.

On the other hand, the election laws passed by the National Assembly have required that voting for president, vice-president, and senators be from a single, nationwide constituency. Senate candidates must run in slates of ten each, and each voter may cast his ballot for three slates. The constituencies of deputies in the Lower House are geographical units within provinces and autonomous cities. Cities and provinces having less than 75,000 voters elect only one deputy each. Most cities and provinces elect several deputies and if the voting population of a constituency is over 225,000 people, five deputies can be elected. However, each candidate runs independently. Voters may cast ballots for the total number of deputies to be elected from that constituency. A similar process, with the district as the electoral unit, applies for Saigon, provincial, and autonomous city council elections. The same procedure is used for village council elections, with the village as the constituency. In each case the voter places in the ballot box a number of votes not exceeding the number of representatives to be elected from the voting unit.

Because some electoral units are very large, the candidates' transportation expenses are heavy. But the experience of the First Republic showed that when electoral units were small single-member constituencies, the government could easily manipulate the voters to win a majority of seats. Now, despite the expense of the present system, there is more security for opposition candidates running in large constituencies.

Thus, the present legal structure of the Republic of Vietnam offers real opportunities for movement towards a democratic political system. People can choose among different local political figures for members of the village, city, province councils, for mayors and province chiefs, and for deputies to the Lower House. Presidents and senators may be chosen from among men with national reputations, including representatives of various organizations with branches throughout the country.

Considering the widespread use of such plebiscites, if the formal constitutional structure were to evolve smoothly, Vietnam could have an exciting political life at all levels of the political system. At the bottom, there would be many alternatives offered in response to the particular needs of each locality. But at the national level, political forces would be under natural pressure to combine with one another to participate effectively in presidential and senate elections, where competition would be stiffer.

It is likely that such cooperation among political forces will lead to a system of broad coalition parties: there might be one government party and one opposition party; or one government party and two opposition parties, with one a loyal opposition and one more extreme; or one opposition of the right and one of the left. If this materializes, then the parties will alternate in holding power to provide the vital essence of a democratic polity. Even if followers of the NLF decided to exchange their guns for participation in elections conducted fairly under law, the above development of parties probably still would occur.

Political Party Organizational and
Electoral Problems

Reality in Vietnam is never as perfect as our ideals. Furthermore, the people of Vietnam do not have a tradition of democracy. Too many citizens do not realize the value of their vote. Many vote merely to get their voting card stamped to show that they have participated, thus avoiding the kinds of complications with the government they experienced under the First Republic. Many voters know nothing about the candidates, so they follow blindly the orders and suggestions of their religious leaders, the advice of their friends or, out of fear, the word of officials. In short, voters are usually indifferent to politics or reluctant to become involved. On the other hand, those who want to experiment with elections and participate fully usually do so with an excess of zeal, so that they become impatient and frustrated and return to their initial resentment. This is likely if, for example, the candidate they worked for is not elected or if their candidate, for one reason or another, does not keep his campaign promises after the election.

In such a psychological environment, political parties cannot fulfill their role of organizing elections for themselves and their candidates, and the excessive number of parties forces them to lose frequently. Also, personal antagonisms, disagreements from the past, and differences on basic notions prevent coalescence into stronger political organizations with greater capacities for large-scale efforts. Many older political parties, caught in obsolete ways of operation, are becoming weaker and do not have much of a future.

A number of more modern parties are now making appropriate efforts to organize themselves. They are confronted by numerous difficulties. The General Mobilization (draft) Law has removed young and active members who could become good cadres for an effective organization. Those exempted from the draft are civil servants or cadres for the government and lack time for party activity. Another major difficulty for the parties is finance. In democratic countries political parties of the right survive mostly on contributions from big firms and the well-to-do, who desire governments with economic policies beneficial to their enterprises; parties of the left, striving to realize widespread social aspirations, survive thanks to the small but consistent membership dues from a large number of followers. But in Vietnam the wealthy make their money through deals and speculation, which require bending to the existing administration. They see no advantage in financing a political party. On the other hand, it is very hard to collect regular fees from party members, because followers who are civil servants or workers have seen their real salaries shrink owing to the war-induced inflation. And farmers who become party members are reluctant to make regular payments, even small ones, because they are just getting used to living in a monetized economy. Lacking funds, the progressive parties cannot provide the professionals the support necessary for an effective and stable organization capable of mobilizing people behind the party.

Besides numerous problems of organization, political parties in Vietnam must face elections that become constantly more competitive and more expensive. For example, in insecure areas, village council members formerly were priority targets for the communists. Few were willing to run for office, and officials had to strive to find the minimal number of candidates for the elections (at least one more than the seats to be filled). Officials sometimes promised those with prestige in the village that they would *not* be elected if they ran, in order to get them to agree to become candidates. Ironically, that was the golden era for older political parties with followers in the villages, because anyone willing to run could be elected.

But as the communist threat receded, the advantages of holding office became more apparent. Many young men from families of means or influence who had just graduated from college were pushed by their parents to run for positions on village, city, or provincial councils. This development increased the quality of local government and improved the low-level political structure. On the other hand, the number of candidates greatly increased, and the elections were more intensely fought.

The elections for the two halves of the National Assembly have developed along similar lines. Campaigning for elections has become more difficult, and campaign costs have been rising astronomically to figures far beyond the income of ordinary people. Inflation and the geographical extent of each constituency, combined with the increased number of candidates and the need for hard campaigning, have produced severe financial burdens. In the 1971 election for the Lower House some candidates spent tens of millions of piastres on their campaigns, though most of the independent candidates could only afford around three or four million. A Lower House deputy's salary is four times higher than the top civil service salary, but over his four-year term still amounts to only 6 million piastres. Thus, the campaigns deplete the financial assets of most elected deputies. Except for those few candidates with some commitment to political ideals, the only men who run either seek the special privileges given a deputy or desire to exploit the position for illicit personal profit.

Parties with a serious and upright political program have great difficulty in putting up candidates. Even though the candidate of a party spends less than independent candidates, because the party can offer the assistance of many campaign workers, he still usually needs one or two million piastres depending on the constituency and a minimum of 300,000 piastres for a small, single-member constituency. Even the most dedicated and energetic supporters lack the ability to raise these sums. Consequently, political parties are forced to back as their own candidates those party members who can provide their own funds, even though such candidates may be less-bound to the common enterprise or may not even be party members but only wealthy sympathizers.

To increase his chance of election, each candidate will usually ask for the assistance of the local administration or religious groups. Not only independent candidates but also party candidates seek such support in those areas where the party itself is not yet strong or well organized. But if the elected candidate owes his victory more to the local administration or to a religious group than to his party, then his loyalty to the party's bloc in the assembly may be weakened or at least his party discipline and activity less pronounced. Thus, political parties suffer a disadvantage as against the government and the religious groups.

So although one might say that the mechanisms of democracy have begun to function, Vietnamese political parties have encountered difficulties. The Progressive Nationalist Movement (PNM, Phong Trao Cap Tien Quoc Gia) has the most elected deputies of any political party, with twenty party members elected to the Lower House in 1971 and with ten additional deputies as symphathizers. But the party is only very strong in a few provinces in Military

Regions III and IV. Even though the PNM is active in other provinces, its development has been very slow. Other political parties have been less successful than the PNM, electing under ten deputies each. To improve their prospects, Vietnamese political parties must struggle for many years to come. One of their major objectives must be civic education for the populace so that voters leave behind old attitudes and overcome their fear of the government in power. They must learn to distinguish between the demands of religion *per se* and the tasks of civic life.

Today the Vietnamese have received the basic freedoms. Just by glancing at the front pages of the dozens of Saigon daily newspapers we can see that freedom of the press has some real substance and is not a charade.[a] Complete honesty in elections, however, has not been achieved, for local administrations sometimes exert pressure to insure the election of government candidates and to exclude the opposition. In the Lower House elections of 1971, both Vietnamese and foreign correspondents publicized incidents of this kind in Vinh Binh and Bac Lieu. But that is not to say that the authorities have used coercion in every election and in every district. Government candidates might win sometimes on the strength of their platform. And most of the deputies elected from Military Region I have followed the lead of the An Quang Buddhists to oppose fiercely the incumbent government. They were not elected thanks to any government favors. In several southern provinces, such as Long An and Hau Nghia, PNM candidates were harassed but were still elected. If the opposition is organized and strong enough, the government cannot exclude it even when it tries. Thus, elections in Vietnam, though not perfect, are still of great significance.

Obviously, there are frictions in this situation. In a stable democracy there is a steady dialogue between government and opposition. In Vietnam, government and opposition have never had a period of such respectful dialogue. Each demand that the war against a brutal and ruthless enemy imposes on the government conflicts with the ardent desire of the opposition for a speedy resolution of the war to improve life in general. Thus, conflicting demands adversely affect the political atmosphere among the non-communists, leaving them fragmented and suspicious of one another. Opposition politicians can easily launch off into demagoguery, and government leaders can just as easily fall into the excessive and unnecessary use of force. The political dialogue in Vietnam often has become an argument, shown every sign of becoming a fistfight, and then concluded in a monologue by the government.

In this frantic political scramble, minority pressure groups play a more important role than political parties. Among the strongest pressure groups are

---

[a]This was greatly restricted in 1972-73, after Professor Huy's paper had been written—Eds.

the religions, especially the organized Buddhists and the Catholics. These can mobilize large parts of the population and are important campaign forces with greater impact than the parties. These groups have won Senate seats when political parties have achieved only meager results. Will the religious groups maintain this electoral power? We can answer for the present but not for the future.

In 1967 the Catholics were very successful; most of the senators elected belonged to one of the Catholic slates. But in 1970 the Catholics did not do as well. Two of the three winning Senate slates contained candidates with ties to many other political forces as well. Other slates receiving Catholic financial support were defeated. The decline of the Catholics was confirmed in the Lower House elections of 1971, when many candidates of this faith were defeated. The falloff resulted from gains by the Buddhists. But the earlier success had also planted the seeds of later failure. Because the Catholics had done so well in 1967, many Catholics came out for office in 1970 and 1971, splitting the Catholic vote and reducing their chance of success. These recent defeats have caused the Catholics to reappraise their strategy. But they will be unable to arrive at an effective solution, because the only religious leaders who can effectively direct the voting of the faithful are at the parish level, and these parish priests do not cooperate with each other. Their superiors have difficulty in acting as mediators, because the bishops cannot use their authority to compel obedience in temporal matters.

The situation of the Buddhists is different because senior religious leaders do give political instructions to their followers. The Senate election of 1970 signaled their success: the Buddhist slate was elected with the highest number of votes. In the Lower House election of 1971, the An Quang Buddhists elected over twenty deputies. Almost all of the deputies' seats for Military Region I were won by the Buddhists.

To generalize, even though the religious groups have considerable ability to motivate important segments of the population, participation by religious leaders in elections is not without danger for the prestige (*uy tin*) of the religious organization itself. Whenever a candidate presented by religious leaders does not act responsibly, the followers speak out in protest, and some of them develop a more independent attitude, no longer closing their eyes and following unquestioningly the direction of the religion's leaders. This dilemma can be avoided only if people learn to divorce politics from religion and the followers of each large religion establish political parties led by laymen. The Catholics are trying to do just that, but without success as yet. Many Catholic parties have been established and frequently have merged. But up to now all alliances and united fronts have failed.[b] And each of their political parties has yet to establish direct

---

[b]As the last two chapters of this book describe, a Catholic party coalition was organized in 1973 in response to highly restrictive government policies toward the parties.

influence over the voters. They still depend on the priests too much. Each day that the priests fail to transfer their political power to lay leaders delays the emergence of effective Catholic political parties.

As for the Buddhists, the establishment of a Buddhist political party has been repeatedly rumored, but this plan—if it exists—has not materialized. Senior leaders of that religion continue to resolve political problems and issue political instructions to their followers.

The religious groups, for their own interests, cannot ignore the problem of political mobilization of people for elections. The political parties of religious affiliation as well as the other parties are not yet ready to replace the religions, especially under present circumstances. We must continue to search for solutions here.

The Future for South Vietnam's Political Parties

What will be the future structure of Vietnamese politics? To recapitulate, we can say that the Republic of Vietnam emerged from a dictatorial system with the overthrow of Ngo Dinh Diem but has not yet entered a regime of full democratic freedom under the Constitution of 1967. In the future, Vietnam may continue to progress along the democratic road, but on the other hand it may turn back to the path of dictatorship.

To be frank, many conditions favorable to the emergence of a fascist viewpoint exist in Vietnamese politics: a spirit of ethnic pride that has been deeply wounded by the actions of the great powers, economic adversity, a central government ineffective and unable to resolve national problems, and the violent activities of extremist elements, including the communists. All these factors create strong parallels between the present situation in Vietnam and the situation in Italy in 1922. The major difference is that in Vietnam the Americans had a military presence and continue to provide important economic aid. Even though those who most desire an ideal democracy for Vietnam have criticized the American presence, it has been a strong barrier against the forces of fascism. On the day when decreased American economic aid leaves the Americans without effective pressure over the Vietnamese government, those people unalterably opposed to the communists, if faced with confusion, chaos, and loss of mandate within the nation and the demagoguery of extreme oppositionists, easily could be led into overthrowing the constitutional government and restricting all freedoms. It is by no means certain that those fervent anti-communists would be able to hold the government for long, but their plots might well lead to further chaos, benefiting only the communists. In the event of a coup by extreme anti-communists, the mobilization of the people for politics, if any, could not be carried out through real elections but only through the proforma voting we find in most authoritarian regimes, whether fascist or communist.

Under the most favorable conditions, political mobilization of the people through political parties competing for elections can only be realized if President Nguyen Van Thieu decides to establish a government political party and approaches this task with energy and concern. If he becomes more open and frank in order to cooperate with various political leaders of ability and prestige among the people, he could form a progressive political party. With the plentiful resources available to a government party, it could energetically carry out constructive politicization while also implementing a program of national reconstruction and development. The natural predilections of the people would lead them to vote heavily for such a government party as well as giving it more than a little emotional support. In this way the government party could follow the present pattern of the UDR in France.[c] It possibly could hold power for a long time without alienating the people of Vietnam. The opposition would continue to be weak and divided, but if it had freedom to operate, it could gradually become stronger in preparation for future replacement of the government party in power. That would be a later and higher development for which we could hope.

But President Thieu also could possibly construct a government party with a narrow and limited viewpoint, composed of men now already within the government machinery. Such a party would be unable to do anything more than the government has done to the present day. It could obtain power for itself through force and pressure, and the opposition would be oppressed more severely and more effectively. The opposition could be expected to remain fragmented, but would react strongly. This difficult situation might culminate in a return to dictatorship.

In the event that President Thieu does not establish a government party, the present political arrangement will continue indefinitely. The basic freedoms now enjoyed by the Vietnamese will continue, but the general structure of politics will not change. No matter what, the structure of coalition parties that the writers of the 1967 Constitution sought to erect will be long in arriving. Like the problem of democratization, the problem of establishing coalition parties is a question of generations, not of months and years.

When we established the Progressive Nationalist Movement, the late Professor Nguyen Van Bong and I had before us the example of the English Labour party. This party was founded in 1900, but it was not until after the First World War that it participated in the government, and even then it did not have complete power, though its leader, Ramsay MacDonald, was prime minister. The party had to wait until after the Second World War before it could carry out policies with Clement Attlee as prime minister and a firm majority of members in Parliament supporting him.

---

[c]The UDR was the *Union pour la defense de la Republique* in the French 1968 election. Its name was changed to *Union des democrates pour la Republique* later that year—Eds.

The slowness of progress toward democratic development is very regrettable. But a lack of understanding exemplified by observations and criticisms of foreigners make the development even more difficult. They anger and frustrate those trying to achieve progress while exciting unrealistic hopes in the idealists, impelling the latter to irresponsible, irrelevant, and damaging acts.

Throughout world history nations that have suffered as has Vietnam have not succeeded in the task of building a perfect democracy. People should not demand such an accomplishment from the Vietnamese when all others have failed. At present the best we can do is to persevere through the difficulties and obstacles of our long struggle and to realize that political development will require an even longer effort.

7

The Possible Role of Elections in a Political Settlement with the NLF
Douglas Pike

Within the context of future South Vietnamese political development, what role could the franchise play in arranging a political settlement between the NLF[a] and the government of South Vietnam (GVN)?

The consideration is narrow, and one is tempted to state flatly that the answer is "none" and be done with it. However, as with most things Vietnamese, the matter cannot be that easily settled, particularly if one assumes an election is symbolic of, if not instrumental to, the imperative social and political change that will come, sooner, or later, in South Vietnam.

By 1971-72 the NLF found itself in a dynamic condition of flux and change. It was beleaguered as never before. It found itself shunted aside, perhaps only momentarily, by forces of big-unit war in which it played little or no part. The military standoff that developed between armed forces of the North and South Vietnamese (marked by something of a political stalemate between NLF and GVN nonmilitary elements) had driven the North Vietnamese, in the spring of 1972, to seek a decisive end to the impasse. The high-technology warfare launched by North Vietnam, the so-called Easter offensive in April 1972, did not particularly involve the NLF and consequently had surprisingly little effect on it. Nothing much changed in the GVN-NLF relationship and the outlook for the future. Had the Easter offensive been decisive, it would have radically altered the NLF-GVN relationship. Because it was not decisive, the question of political arrangement between the GVN and the NLF returned to the forefront.

The Franchise, the NLF, and the True Believer

We are concerned here with South Vietnamese political accommodation via the franchise as part of a broader political development process. The NLF true believer does not use these terms nor the conceptual framework from

---

[a]The abbreviation NLF (for National Liberation Front) is used throughout this paper as a verbal shorthand for all of the organizations opposing the Government of South Vietnam; the National Liberation Front, the People's Revolutionary Party (PRP), the PRP Youth League, the Alliance of National Democratic and Peace Forces, and the Provisional Revolutionary Government (PRG). It also includes the NLF's military force, the People's Liberation Armed Force (PLAF), formerly the Liberation Army—in short, all the organizations popularly lumped together as Viet Cong. It does not include North Vietnamese elements, either the Democratic Republic of Vietnam (DRV) or the North Vietnamese armed force, the People's Army of Vietnam (PAVN).

which they are drawn. Some extrapolation therefore is required. But given this concept of political development, probably the NLF true believer would make these general observations:

1. He has little respect for the franchise, either because he is a Marxist or a thoroughgoing Vietnamese. In the first instance, he would deny the idea, fundamental to elections, of loyal opposition in government. In the second instance, his political heritage of clandestinism has never included the ballot box. In any event—and this would extend to other Vietnamese—he holds little faith even in the theory of the franchise, the notion that the best way of dividing up political power or adjudicating political disputes is to have everyone go into a little room and stuff pieces of paper in a box.

2. He had a distinct definition of political accommodation. It is not seen as a fair-share arrangement and in fact is not a sharing process at all in the sense that each side accepts self-imposed limitations. The NLF true believer regards himself as the possessor of a monopoly of virtue. To share power with the devil would be immoral. Further, he would regard it as illegal, since the NLF (to quote its slogan) is the sole legitimate representative of the South Vietnamese people. He would define accommodation as attending to the desires of his enemy (or opposition), a matter of taking them into consideration, but not as sharing power. Power is reserved for sole legitimate representatives. Being realists, however, the NLF leadership knows it faces opposition by large, well-intrenched elements (the 1.7 million Catholics are perhaps the best single example), which are too large to digest or conquer and therefore must be accommodated. But accommodated NLF style. What the NLF stands ready to do—and this has been its position for ten years—is to establish a governing arrangement in which such opposition groups as Catholics would be represented, i.e., their voices heard in council. There would be genuine deference to their wishes (since otherwise the scheme could not possibly work) but no power sharing. This arrangement would exclude the present GVN or at least higher-level officials of the GVN, with whom there would be no accommodation of any sort. Since this is hardly acceptable either to Catholics or to the GVN cabinet, understandably the NLF accommodation offer has never been accepted.

The NLF's definition of enemy, that is, the list of those in the GVN ranks with whom it would never do business, tends to expand and contract with the fortunes of war. Its 1967 program stated it would not associate itself with those "forces" which have not "contributed to the cause of the national liberation" but there was no further definition of the words employed. The PRG in the Paris talks from time to time intimates provocatively that it defines enemy as cabinet level and above in the present GVN, but has never stated this formally; in the July 1971 PRG Seven-Point Statement, the PRG defined its hard-core enemy as "the bellicose group headed by Nguyen Van Thieu at present in office in Saigon." NLF followers in South Vietnam are given to understand that the definition of enemy is much broader.

In any event there is no evidence I am aware of to indicate the NLF would be willing to *arrive* at a political settlement by means of elections. Repeatedly it has stated in public pronouncements concerning elections that they must come *after*, not *before*, the new government is established. PRG Deputy Chairman Thich Don Hau, who makes most NLF statements on election matters, reiterated this stand in 1971:

> Question: Reverend Superior, the Saigon puppet administration is hectically preparing the elections of the "lower house" and "president." Would you tell us your view on these elections?
>
> Answer: The coming elections cannot reflect the people's aspiration and will for independence and peace. Only when all U.S. troops pull out, the diehard and warlike clique headed by Thieu is overthrown, and a government for restoring peace is set up to discuss with the PRG the formation of a government of national concord will the election provide conditions for our people in South Vietnam to faithfully express their will and aspirations."[1]

Externally the NLF dissembles on the matter of elections. For example in the PRG Seven Point Statement (Paris talks, July 1971) the issue of whether elections might be used to establish a governing arrangement in a political settlement was evaded by employing the term *means* rather than *elections* or something more precise. Point Two of the Seven Points said, "The political, social and religious forces in South Vietnam aspiring to peace and national concord will use various means to form a new administration."

The NLF position, which appears firm, is that the order of things, the scenario if you will, must be: (1) complete U.S.-Allied withdrawal; (2) abolition of the present South Vietnamese government; (3) formation of a caretaker or managerial government of South Vietnam which would (4) meet with the NLF (i.e., PRG) to negotiate organizational structure and the list of individuals to compose the new government (with NLF elements monopolizing political power, as detailed above?), after which could come (5) elections and the opportunity by the populace to endorse, or presumably disapprove, the new government now ruling it. In short, voting as a referendum is acceptable, but voting as a formative act is not. Ruled out therefore would be an election to choose a body of constituent assemblymen to write a new constitution or a National Assembly-presidential election to choose an entirely new slate of officials under the present governmental structure.

Would the NLF leadership's position on this become more reasonable if the NLF political condition deteriorated and there were no real prospect for victory by means of revolutionary war? Probably not, but there is no way to be certain, because of the dynamics of the situation. Is the NLF true believer as rigid on the subject? Generally, not as rigid as his leaders. He favors political development. He knows and accepts the idea of political development in the sense of political modernization, is a modernist, antitraditional. He stands for government that is rational, efficient, honest, and one that, if not totally acceptable to the populace, is made palatable by persuasion.

Magnitude of the NLF

We are unfortunately involved, when considering the NLF true believer, with an affective characterization. It is not possible to develop a statistical definition of the true believer, and in fact the available data are too few and too unreliable even to permit a quantified statement of the NLF as a political force. As a sort of gross parameter, for working purposes of this paper, I would offer this:

The NLF has influence over about 10 percent of the South Vietnamese population. Total population currently is estimated at about 19 million and its mean age is eighteen. This means the NLF has influence over about one million adults. Of the one million, about 20 percent, or 200,000, can be called true believers. These true believers are not spread uniformly across the country but tend to be concentrated in about six province-sized areas.

This control or influence is here defined in noncoercive terms, excluding those over whom the NLF can assert itself by sheer physical presence and force. By late 1971 the NLF actually had physical control over far less than 10 percent of the population. By the criteria set down in the GVN-U.S. Hamlet Evaluation Survey (HES) system, a complicated method of attempting to quantify GVN vs. NLF control, the E-D hamlet total (those under firm NLF control) amounted to about 3 percent of the total population. This 3 percent figure rose sharply in April-July of 1972 as ARVN troops were pulled out of pacification duty and sent to the three frontal areas in Quang Tri province, Kontum-Binh Dinh Provinces, and northern Binh Long Province. At one point fourteen districts of South Vietnam were entirely under military control of PAVN forces pressing forward in these three frontal sectors. But this sort of military occupation and the control it provides is largely irrelevant to this article, which seeks to treat the NLF and its allied forces in terms of voluntarily offered support, influence that comes through social organization and other nonmilitary activity, and which largely (but not entirely) is immune to countermilitary or even pacification efforts by the GVN.

The True Believer

It is with the true believer, even those in detention camps, with whom we are chiefly concerned in this paper. A true believer is so for one or more of these reasons:

1. Organizational. He lives in a social system under NLF control which

generates social pressures in the normal way, through social organization, caus-
ing him to support and believe in the system. Social pressure of course is the
strongest force in any society. The NLF harnesses this social pressure through
the mechanism of various social movements of which the true believer is part,
to sustain and reinforce his belief.

2. Familial. He is related by marriage or blood, directly or through the
extended clan, to a true believer. Thus, his belief, largely unarticulated, is a
matter of familial loyalty.

3. Reflexive, or what might be called traditional. He lives in a village that
has been under a non-GVN government (that is, NLF and before that Viet Minh)
control for so long that he considers the NLF the norm. He believes in the NLF
in his village for the same reason most people everywhere believe in their local
government, because they inherited it. His village is the most totally NLF. The
social control here is largely internal and self-generating unlike that in the first
category above, which is the result of steady application of outside NLF effort.

4. Ideological. He understands and embraces the programs and the philosophy of the NLF and is hostile to the system represented by the GVN. The
ideologue is the least common of the NLF true believers.

Both the NLF true believer and follower see their organization (as the
organization also depicts itself) as an example or a direct continuation of a
very traditional kind of Vietnamese social movement, the mutual interest association. The NLF is regarded, to use sociological jargon, as a traditional undifferentiated social movement, one unlimited in its interest in the individual
member. It is concerned with his whole life from cradle to grave, his economic
well-being, his religious and philosophic outlook, his social life, his child rear-
ing, etc. (as opposed to the modern or differentiated social movement, for
example a trade union or PTA, which is concerned with only a single or narrow
aspect of the member's life). As such, the NLF is commonplace in South Vietnam. The political scene (and in fact the political unit) is the undifferentiated
social movement, each of which can be located more or less geographically,
making claim of total loyalty on the member and, in turn, seen by him as the
highest order of allegiance.[2]

Condition of the NLF

The central fact of the NLF's condition by the time of the 1972 offensive
was its diminished significance, its loss of both status and power.

The North Vietnamese Politburo never did trust indigenous NLF leadership
and over the years sought constantly to fix controls on its influence. With the
war's escalation and deepening involvement of the DRV, beginning in 1965,
the NLF steadily dropped in relative importance. To maintain momentum of
the war, the DRV was forced to assume an ever larger burden of the struggle.

By 1970 the war was largely in its hands; for example, 80 percent of the day-to-day combat was by PAVN soldiers, uniformed North Vietnamese troops, the remaining 20 percent being conducted by the full military and paramilitary forces of the PLAF, the armed force of the NLF. This shifting of the military burden had several consequences, the major one being a shift of strategic objective. When the PLAF had carried the war, backed by the DRV, there had been a pursuit of dual objectives: the NLF objective of political power and the DRV objective of unification; parallel objectives but obviously not identical. When the DRV and PAVN assumed the burden of the war, there was a consequent shift to almost exclusive pursuit of the DRV objective of unification.

As the war intensified and the NLF weakened, the DRV grew increasingly blunt in word and deed, indicating that it felt the NLF was undependable and that it would make no sacrifice of its objective for sake of the NLF. NLF true believers came to realize—and this was a cause for many defections in the 1965-67 period—that what the DRV wanted was what counted in strategy, diplomatic activity in Paris, and resource allocation.

This basic condition of NLF-DRV relations explains one of the most puzzling aspects of the 1972 PAVN military offensive: the lack of significant role by the NLF. The offensive made full use of PAVN troops, in fact all fourteen of the PAVN combat infantry divisions at one point were outside North Vietnam (not all in South Vietnam; some were in Laos and Cambodia) while the PLAF elements, including the deadly sapper units that the leadership had been so carefully constructing throughout 1971, simply sat out the battles. Admittedly the PLAF had declined in military prowess, but it had not declined that much. It still represented a striking force. Yet it was not used, an exact reverse of the 1968 Tet offensive, in which the entire PLAF force was thrown into combat while the PAVN elements sat on the sidelines and watched.

The all-PAVN nature of the 1972 attack is explainable in one of two ways: either the PLAF was being held in reserve to be used at the opportune moment (which never came) or Hanoi's evaluation of the potential contribution and general reliability of the NLF and PLAF was so low that it was decided to use only the PAVN forces. The NLF did use this period in spring and summer of 1972 to do some rebuilding of its local-level apparat; how successful it was could be determined only later and would depend on subsequent GVN action or inaction.

Areas of Organizational Weapon Application

The NLF leadership, of course, is fully aware of its situation and has not been idle. During 1971 it quietly but intensively focused its still impressive organizational prowess into three major spheres, possibly a fourth.

Organizational Overhaul

First the leadership attempted to revitalize and streamline the whole organizational structure, not only the NLF but the PRP, the PRP Youth League, the Alliance, and the PRG. Organizations were formed, merged, or eliminated. Consolidation of administrative units was common. The revolutionary committee concept, introduced in early 1968, moved to the forefront and possibly may replace the front or mass organizations, that is, the various liberation associations, as the basic NLF institution. The leadership recognized it was overextended and cut its activities ruthlessly. Quotas set for cadres—in recruitment, tax collection, organizing struggle movements, etc.—repeatedly were lowered as the leadership strove to keep "assignment of missions" within the realm of reality and avoid what always is a major danger in revolutionary war planning, the temptation to be seduced by the grandiose. It is apparent that NLF leaders retain full faith in the organizational weapon that previously served them so well. The heart of the effort remains the village of the liberated area. The incantation continues: organize, organize, organize.

The social changes the NLF wrought in its organization and its villages may have significant, even profound, bearing on any possible future integration in a political settlement. Unfortunately for us, this is an imponderable, so gross is our ignorance of the social, economic, and political systems operating in the longtime NLF area. Undoubtedly there has been change, but the question is how much? and how deep? Some Vietnamese maintain the NLF has effected fundamental social change, in village management, rice marketing, child-parent relations, adjudication of disputes, and other change, mostly in the direction of collectivization. As a result, NLF villages are so different from their non-NLF neighbors they could not mesh into the larger society even if they wanted to. Other Vietnamese insist differences in the two villages are fewer, that most change is superficial. The fact is, we don't know, nor will we until some intensive research has been completed. It could well be that South Vietnam now is pocketed with patches of a highly alien subsociety creating still more roadblocks—mechanical rather than ideological, but still highly frustrating—to creation of a single sociopolitical arena in South Vietnam.

Neoguerrilla War

Second, by 1971 the NLF had nearly completed transformation of the PLAF from a supportive element of PAVN in regular force strategy, or big-unit warfare, into an independent, self-contained, but not yet logistically self-supporting guerrilla force. The chief activity in this effort was innumerable retraining sessions for PLAF members. One has the impression that the NLF camp by the 1970s had become one gigantic classroom. Manuals on basic tactics of guerrilla war, not seen since the early 1960s, were dusted off and put back into use. Courses offered: How to Make a Booby Trap from a Dud Bomb; the Rifle Against the Helicopter; Technique of Firing at an Armored Vehicle; How to Lay an Ambush During an Enemy Sweep Operation; and How to Grow Vegetables (PLAF troops by then were expected to be 60 percent self supporting with respect to food). Even more ubiquitous, if possible, were the political reorientation courses, which assessed the situation and explained enemy and NLF strategies. Political re-education courses also were common; these were only for deviants and unreliables, deserters, for example, who had been captured and returned or those who had mutilated themselves in order to avoid combat (apparently fairly common in PLAF ranks).

Equipment, particularly for elite units such as the sapper teams, is the finest the communist bloc can provide. Gone is the image of the guerrilla in ragged black pajamas fighting with a homemade shotgun from his mangrove swamp lair. It was replaced by the image of the fully trained guerrilla using complex weapons and explosive devices, communicating with highly sophisticated radios, in his way equal or superior in technology to his enemy.

The strategic target in this neoguerrilla war, which of course is still revolutionary war, was not ARVN *per se* but the pacification programs. Lesson plans and indoctrination material indicated the kind of war for which the PLAF was being prepared. There was a high cast of defensiveness, and indeed it was termed a "large-scale resistance movement." The NLF intention was that the vast majority of day-to-day guerrilla attacks, beyond the occasional spectacular foray into Saigon or other major enemy lair for psychological purposes, would be directed against roads and canals, the arteries into the hinterland. The second most common type of action, judging by force-training plans, was the well-prepared set-piece ambush, off the highway in inaccessible areas, under conditions most favorable to the ambusher. The goal was to make ARVN military operations costly and dangerous. If ARVN could be discouraged, then full attention could be paid to the more strategic targets, the GVN villages and village militia. For the time being the objective was not to gain ground militarily but to develop and sustain quasi-political pressure.

Clearly the NLF leadership's object during all 1971 and in early 1972 was to field a high-technology guerrilla-force. Press reports during the period termed this "creation of the super guerrilla," "equipped by Mission Impossible." While somewhat hyperbolic, the terms are not inaccurate.

Then came the PAVN offensive in April, and it was anything but guerrilla war. The scene was dominated by the image of a juggernaut: divisions of tank-riding, cannon-firing troops smashing southward, deliberately employing a Panzer-like assault to induce trauma. Had the assault been accompanied by coordinated strikes of the "super guerrilla" sapper teams, all would have been understandable. Instead, the PLAF forces sat out the offensive. The reasons are not clear; the fact is beyond dispute. PLAF potency was there, but it was not used.

A final assessment of the nature and future of neorevolutionary guerrilla war, as far as NLF plans and directives are concerned, cannot yet be made. Quite possibly the DRV-launched Easter offensive will be set down by future historians as a mere interlude in the struggle, an aberration even, after which the war resumed as a neoguerrilla struggle. Certainly nothing happened during 1971 and the first half of 1972 to disprove the essential soundness of the concept as it had been worked out by NLF theoreticians. It remains to be tested.

Quality Control Through the Party

The third sphere of activity was to concentrate even greater authority and responsibility in the Communist party (that is, the People's Revolutionary party, or PRP cadres) if that is possible, considering the party's centrality since at least 1964.

A steady stream of directives went to party members stressing that on their shoulders rested success of the cause. The party must lift itself by its bootstraps or all would be lost. Party members were harangued "to analyze accurately and correctly evaluate our successes and failures, consolidate party organizations, improve efficiency, apply correctly the strategic guidelines sent down [from higher headquarters] . . . . work out realistic resolutions to various problems, keep abreast of the political situation in [your] area." Above all there was the urgent demand that party leadership be improved by improving quality of members, most of whom, of course, were cadres.

This theme—for a better party, get better men—dominated major PRP pronouncements. It is difficult to measure its significance, because there was about it a high quality of God-give-us-men, that universal assertion by all of us when our world is in trouble that what we need is great leaders followed by great men (the difficulty being that having made a call for greatness, one has not said very much of practical use). The unanswered, and largely unanswerable question, therefore, is whether the NLF leadership actually believed it would fail unless there was a marked improvement in cadre quality, or whether its summons to greatness was more or less routine.

The leadership correctly diagnosed poor quality cadres as the NLF's single greatest danger. Indeed, if the NLF does fade and die in the next generation, it will be for this reason. More than other systems, NLF effectiveness rests almost entirely on its cadres. Virtually superhuman performance is expected of them. When the system works it works very well. The central, vital role played by the cadre simply cannot be exaggerated.

The NLF in its reporting systems, particularly those required from agitprop cadres, makes a strong effort to distinguish among levels of commitment of its followers, true believers, and cadres. Criteria employed often are vague. One of the most durable is the tabulating of those who are considered to be "close to the Revolution," meaning faithful come-what-may, or what could be termed the true believer (that term of course is not used by the NLF).

Good cadres are hard to come by at all times; never has the NLF enjoyed a surplus, and since 1967 there has been a staggering if not catastrophic drop in cadre quality, partially because the DRV siphoned off better cadres and incorporated them into its own ranks. Another cause was normal revolutionary war attrition: good cadres take more risks, have a higher casualty rate, and the war has been long.

That NLF would do better with better men there can be no doubt. Unfortunately, leaders in the foreseeable future will be obliged to depend on what they now have, a cadre structure largely composed of second-raters and bright but inexperienced teenagers. The leadership is striving desperately to recruit better raw material and provide these recruits with far better and more intensive training. Its success in recruitment largely will depend on GVN actions and reactions. The broader-based and the more enlightened the GVN, the less success the NLF will have in recruiting. Even if good recruits are obtained, the quality level will rise only slowly. A first-rate cadre above all is a product of lengthy experience. There is no way to create instant first-rate cadres, not even by importing them from North Vietnam.

The 1971 Elections

There was a fourth sphere of NLF activity not comparable in magnitude to the above three. Although its significance remains unclear, it is a fact that the NLF took unusual interest in the 1971 GVN elections, particularly those for the National Assembly Lower House.

In previous GVN elections, the NLF attitude had been essentially standoffish. It had sought to denigrate them as fraudulent and meaningless and to disrupt them if this could be done without much risk or expense. Clearly its past attitude was that GVN elections were important enough to try to spoil, but not at the cost of high casualties or even the expenditure of much time, money, or manpower.

This view was the practical result of the NLF's grand strategy of revolutionary war. The imperative demand in that strategy, which the agitprop cadres played like a single-note symphony, was that victory could come only through the three-pronged struggle techniques (armed struggle, political struggle, and proselytizing efforts) of revolutionary war. There was no other road to victory, not through the talks in Paris, not via political settlement (with or without elections) in South Vietnam. To suggest any other route was to undercut this basic contention. If an NLF follower came to believe victory could be achieved by other means—for example, through elections—obviously he would be less willing to sacrifice himself to the strategy of revolutionary war. Hence, the agitprop cadre tried to disabuse him of the notion that any elections, even totally honest ones supervised by disinterested outsiders, could assist the cause. Psychologically the soundest way to do this was to ignore GVN elections, to dismiss them briefly when they could not be ignored, and at no time to confer importance on them by excessive denunciation or spoiling efforts. Of course, in the interest of its external image, in the Paris talks for example, the NLF could not afford so stark an anti-election posture. Abroad it dissembled. In its own private councils the NLF leadership did not treat an approaching GVN election with disinterest. Here it was evaluated for possible utility to NLF goals and strategy. But the decision in each case in the past decade was that involvement was not worth allocation of many resources.

This changed with the 1971 elections. The NLF sought to insinuate itself into both the National Assembly elections and, initially, into the presidential election. It issued directives to cadres, established special election organizations, and encouraged NLF members to politick.

The NLF policy of involvement contrasted notably with Hanoi's opinion. The DRV position was rock-hard negative. The elections not only were farcical but were illegal, therefore invalid. The NLF line was far softer. It echoed the DRV farce theme, but distinctly toned down the illegality theme. And by distinguishing between "progressive" and "reactionary" candidates for the National Assembly, it conferred legitimacy on that election.

The GVN presidential election was a more complex matter for the NLF. The NLF's original calculation apparently was that by proper involvement it could exacerbate in a major way the already extensive divisiveness in the Saigon political establishment. In June and July, when it appeared three slates might be on the ballot (Nguyen Van Thieu, Nguyen Cao Ky, and Duong Van Minh), the NLF issued highly ambitious orders to agitprop cadres calling for maximum effort in special village meetings and other media to denigrate the election and to pull support away from whichever candidate was strongest in the cadre's immediate area. It was a campaign against the campaign and against the front-runner, who in most areas was Nguyen Van Thieu.

NLF leaflet and bandarole slogans most commonly used in the campaign to indicate the nature of the NLF public appeal were:

a.   While Thieu is in Power There Will be War
b.   Thieu: Peace, Not Serving Americans
c.   Peace Comes Only With U.S. Troop Withdrawal, Thieu Overthrow
d.   All Support to General Minh (Central Vietnam)

As pre-election maneuvers became more complicated and the outcome less certain, NLF policy became confused. Then orders went out to curtail much of the anti-election activity. Finally, when it became clear that Thieu's slate would be unopposed, the NLF abandoned its special campaign and fell back on a standard vilification effort of about the same intensity as in previous GVN elections. The question remains, what would have been the NLF instructions had the presidential election been a two- or three-way competition.

After wading through all the NLF verbiage on the 1971 GVN elections, one is left with the impression that NLF leaders were slow to conclude what involvement really meant, or should have been, or whether it was worth while. In view of the fact that two-thirds of incumbent deputies in the National Assembly Lower House were defeated in bids for re-election (which certainly indicates the election was anything but a farce, at least as far as *they* were concerned), it is interesting to speculate whether the NLF leadership believes it contributed significantly to this overthrow. As the presidential campaign was ending, agitprop cadres, largely because of conflicting directives, were attempting to have things both ways. They were spending much time and energy in activities dealing with the elections and at the same time asserting the elections were without significance.

It is probable the NLF leadership concluded that, given the rather inconclusive nature of the election itself (in which Thieu's opposition sought to hurt him politically by declining political engagement), nothing much of significance could be drawn from the elections.

The NLF and a Political Settlement

From this we can perhaps draw several tentative conclusions with respect to a political settlement between the NLF and the GVN, possibly through elections.

The first conclusion is that to the degree there is indigenous control of the NLF, which will increase in the next few years, there is more NLF interest in principle in a political settlement than in the past. Conversely, to the degree the DRV continues to maintain control, there will be no interest. The DRV objective is unification. It values the NLF in terms of the NLF's ability to contribute to this objective. The Politburo sees its goal of unification can be served in no important way through establishing even an NLF-GVN *modus vivendi* and can see several ways in which its interests could be betrayed by such an arrangement. Barring a major change of composition of the Politburo, therefore, there is no prospect the DRV will abandon its unremitting hostility toward accommodation of the NLF. Since the DRV controls the NLF now, this means there will be no accommodation now. The real question is whether the DRV will *want* to continue to control the NLF, whether it will be willing to pay the price for such control (continued presence of large numbers of North Vietnamese, materiel support, etc.) For reasons not clear, the DRV launched a high-technology kind of war, independent of the NLF, in the spring of 1972. The meaning of this campaign to the future of DRV-NLF relations is difficult to discern. Actually, the DRV throughout the first half of 1972 continued to Vietnamize (or Viet-Congize) the war; PAVN activities were in and of themselves not for the benefit of the NLF or PLAF.

In any event, as the 1972 PAVN offensive failed to crack ARVN and the GVN, the DRV has been thrown back on its original problem: what should be done, what *can* be done, with the NLF? It is possible the DRV may decide to write off the NLF on grounds that continued expenditures in the South in the name of the NLF would not be worth the few benefits received. Or what seems more likely to me, it could return to a fuller effort to halt the NLF deterioration. Had such been its calculation, however, it should have been integrated with the spring offensive. Even so, the DRV probably will continue to see utility to itself in the NLF and will continue to revitalize it or, more accurately, to get the NLF to revitalize itself.

The second conclusion is that a political settlement between the NLF and the GVN need not be formalized and need not come at the national level. Therefore, if there is a genuine political settlement, probably it will not be codified or formally negotiated in any way, and will be at the local rather than the national level.

Almost all Vietnamese, regardless of what they may think of the NLF, believe that eventually there will come some sort of arranged settlement involving the NLF. Vietnam has been torn or polarized for a decade by two more or less separate political processes. As long as this condition remains, government in South Vietnam will be unviable and society will be unstable. Obviously what must happen is creation of a single political decision-making arena. To this idea the NLF would subscribe. The problem is not to bring the NLF into this arena—it has been trying to enter since inception—but to do so in such a way that it is granted its rights to a share of political power, while denying its unreasonable demand for a monopoly of political power. In fact, this is what the struggle has been all about since 1954: Under what sort of arrangement will South Vietnam be governed?

In this process the GVN can treat the NLF as a single national entity, or it can deal with individual local NLF blocs. The problems in a national-level settlement, which of necessity would be legalistic and the product of lengthy private or public negotiations, are infinitely greater and more complex than accommodation at the local level on a piecemeal basis, which would be no simple matter either.

As a thesis we can offer the assumption that the NLF has a finite number of people, villages, and areas it can truly call its own in the social sense that its control there stems from allegiance rather than from repression. These areas are not as numerous or extensive as they once were. The earlier local accommodation idea presented by various observers in the mid-1960s, the so-called Swiss cantonment solution, was difficult to envision because of its sheer complexity, involving as it did at the time literally hundreds of NLF

areas. Probably the NLF social-control areas now are all or part of those six
(or nine) areas noted above; I say probably, because again we simply do not
have sufficient information about these areas to know what is their condition
or the attitudes of their people. In any event, local accommodation now
involves relatively fewer blocs, which if nothing else makes the problem more
manageable.

Not only is local piecemeal accommodation more likely, but I would argue
it is the essence at least theoretically, of the GVN's Doan Ket, or national
reconciliation, program. The philosophic approach of Doan Ket, as I understand it, is that the half million or so NLF members are to be accommodated
as individuals or members of small-sized local NLF blocs, but that this ought
not, and need not, require an over-all political settlement with the NLF as a
national organization. From the GVN standpoint, such an approach obviously
is easier, safer, and more satisfactory. Hence, the GVN probably will continue
to separate in its policy thinking the people of the NLF in local blocs from the
NLF as a national abstraction. It will continue to offer a policy which, in its
view, quite fairly tells the member in his local NLF bloc he is free and is
encouraged to seek what he always has said he wants—political power in South
Vietnam—but that he cannot seek it as part of his nationwide organization.

To be somewhat harshly simplistic, the GVN is asking the NLF National
Central Committee to disband, while offering local NLF elements the opportunity to accrue political power at the price of disestablishment. This option
is slightly more attractive to the member bloc than to the Central Committee.
For the individual NLF bloc, the offer is evaluated in terms of its prospect in
the event it accepts or rejects. Possibly acceptance would prove of benefit.
Its decision also, of course, depends on control the national leadership (and
the DRV) can continue to exercise over it. There is nothing for the National
Central Committee (or the DRV) in the Doan Ket program. It would never be
accepted by present leaders even if it were a matter of that or extinction.

The GVN's unwillingness to deal with the NLF as a national entity is not
a matter of ideology—the Vietnam War has never really turned on communism
or Marxism—but a function of its sense of insecurity. It fears strong organization. Once, when the GVN was weak and the NLF strong, this fear kept the
GVN from making even the most tentative gesture of political settlement. Once
it was stronger and the NLF weaker, there was less reluctance to sup with the
devil. Probably this reluctance will continue to diminish as the GVN's sense of
security increases, even possibly to the point where it will deal directly with
some future NLF Central Committee.

From all of this then must follow the general conclusion that a political
settlement is less rather than more likely, a local-level political settlement is
more likely than a national-level one, and elections in any event largely would
be ritualistic, putting the overt stamp of approval on arrangements already made
by other means.

Notes

1. Liberation Radio, August 8, 1971.
2. The major longtime NLF strongholds are:
    a. the area the Viet Minh called the Do Xa-Mang Kim, chiefly in Quang Ngai Province but also running down the inland spine of foothills and mountains, through Binh Dinh Province, and into Phu Yen Province;
    b. to Hap area in Khanh Hoa Province, behind Nha Trang city, also extending into southern Tuyen Duc and southeastern Darlac Provinces;
    c. Duong Minh Chau area of northern Tay Ninh Province adjacent to the Cambodian border;
    d. the so-called Phuoc-Binh-Thanh or Zone D area, chiefly in Binh Duong and Phuoc Thanh Provinces, probably also part of adjacent Binh Long Province;
    e. Ban O Qua area in southeastern Kien Hoa Province; and
    f. Kien Lam area along the eastern coast of the Ca Mau peninsula north of Quan Long in An Xuyen Province, probably extending northward into southern Kien Giang Province.
    Other areas of less NLF duration and firm social control are:
    g. the border strip opposite Cambodia of Kien Giang (above Ha Tien), Chau Doc, Kien Phong and Kien Tuong Provinces;
    h. The western edges of Quang Tri and Thua Thien Provinces in Central Vietnam adjacent to Laos; and
    i. an area in northern Ba Xuyen and southern Phong Dinh Provinces.

8

Elections and Political Party Constraints Following the 1972 Offensive
Ta Van Tai and Jerry Mark Silverman

President Nguyen Van Thieu has developed a strategy of presidential leadership and electoral process that integrates the often contradictory requirements arising from political competition with both the National Liberation Front[a] and nationalist opposition groups. This strategy has required that the actual application of its constituent parts be phased over time as circumstances and opportunities presented themselves. However, the fundamental structural characteristics of that strategy have been adhered to consistently since 1970.

The constituent parts of that strategy continue to be characterized by attempts to accomplish the following:

1. The co-optation of national-level power brokers (notably the Army leadership) and regional, but strongly anti-communist, religious groups.[1]

2. The isolation of the Saigon-centered political opposition elites (notably the intellectual leaders of individual political parties and factions) and the regional religious opposition elites. This characteristic represents the major shift in Thieu's strategy since he assumed the national leadership. Prior to 1970, he had apparently hoped that he could build his political organization on a foundation provided by at least some of the already existing political party structures. Thus, in 1969 he announced the creation of a National Socialist Revolutionary Alliance, consisting of six pre-existing parties. This policy of co-opting, rather than isolating, the Saigon-centered political elite was apparently based on his desire to assume the Gaullist role of the President standing above partisan competition. However, in 1970 the Alliance collapsed, as individual party leaders began to disagree on the designation of candidates as members of the slates to run in the 1970 Senate election.

3. The development of a political apparatus rooted in the administrative and cadre structures of the government to serve as direct links between presidential authority and anticipated popular support. This provided the political

---

[a]To avoid monotony in the text, we will use the terms National Liberation Front, Provisional Revolutionary Government and, occasionally, communists interchangeably in these pages. However, we acknowledge that not all who recognize the authority of the Provisional Revolutionary Government are members of the National Liberation Front nor are communists to be found among all persons, other than the functional leadership, who support either of these two groups.

motivation for the village self-development program and, more recently, the "Administrative Revolution," which intends to transfer the political powers of the individual ministries to the province chiefs in their political role as Thieu's representatives.

The forms through which these characteristics have been apparent in the past as regards the electoral process have been described elsewhere.[2] The purpose of this paper is to carry these analyses further into 1973. Since Henry Kissinger's announcement on October 26, 1972 that a cease-fire in Vietnam was imminent, four events have affected the electoral process in South Vietnam: the promulgation by President Thieu of a new decree on party organization (Decree 060—December 27, 1972); the Paris Agreements (January 27, 1973); the Senate Election Law (June 1973); and the Senate elections (August 26, 1973).

As one result of the public announcements by both the Democratic Republic of Vietnam (DRV) and U.S. spokesman Henry Kissinger during October 1972, it was anticipated (correctly) by many national opinion leaders in Saigon that a suspension of the conventional main force military conflict in South Vietnam was imminent. Although opinions differed as to what mechanisms ought to be established for participation of all indigenous political groups in a nonviolent political process in South Vietnam, there was general agreement that such mechanisms should include an electoral component. Alternatively, there was the general expectation that without agreement between the two sides concerning some set of elections, a return to the pre-1965 mode of rural-based insurgency was inevitable. This would ultimately lead to a renewal of large-scale military conflict between the DRV and the Government of the Republic of Vietnam (GVN).[3]

Although the anticipated agreement was not signed until January 27, 1973, its main features regarding the future electoral process were known in Saigon by December. The final documents initialed in Paris contained five articles that referred to future elections in South Vietnam: three in the agreement and two in the protocol concerning the International Commission of Control and Supervision (ICCS). The two most important articles are in the main body of the agreement itself: Article 9(b) states, "The South Vietnamese people shall decide themselves the political future of South Viet-Nam through genuinely free and democratic general elections under international supervision." However, Article 12(b) defers to future consultations between the "two South Vietnamese Parties" in all decisions concerning the specific "institutions for which the general elections are to be held" and gives the National Council of National Reconciliation and Concord the responsibility for all decisions as to "the procedures and modalities of such local elections as the two South Vietnamese parties agree upon."

In effect, the agreement avoided the political issues separating the RVN from both the DRV and the Provisional Revolutionary Government (PRG).

As Henry Kissinger admitted at the outset, "While the agreement provided that the two South Vietnamese parties should settle their dispute in an atmosphere of national reconciliation and concord . . . they have not yet quite reached that point; indeed . . . they have not yet been prepared to recognize each other's existence."[4] Thus, although the agreement provided for the establishment of a mechanism whereby other procedures could subsequently be established for the conduct of national elections, the specification of the modalities of such elections (constituency boundaries and election laws regarding voter and candidacy qualifications; single or multimember districts or election by plurality or majority), and the institutions to be created or maintained by them were unspecified. However, it was recognized by the Nguyen Van Thieu government that it would eventually have to meet with the NLF and others in face-to-face electoral competition. In preparation for such an eventuality, President Thieu promulgated a new degree on party organization on December 27, 1972, the *final day* of the six-month term previously granted to him by the National Assembly for the exercise of emergency powers in the fields of security, defense, economics, and finance.[5] This new Decree 060 amended Decree 009, dated June 19, 1969, in a number of respects, as presented in Table 8-1.

The major change required by the new decree is the limitation of participation in the electoral system to broadly based and publicly known political *parties*. The Vietnamese political system has been noted for its fragmentation, not only among political parties, but also among politicized religious, regional, and ethnic groups.[6] These groups frequently emerge in public as nonparty political associations and national fronts, the formal designations of which often change. They are characterized by urban-centered intellectual leaders whose base of support rests not in the general public, but rather on networks of personal interrelationships with middle-level leaders of communal groups. Indeed, beyond claims to the loyalty of all members of specific communal groups, and with the exception of the formal leaders themselves, information as to the number and specific identities of a group's membership normally remains secret.

As in most electoral systems characterized by competition between associational interest groups that are not organized in the form of political parties, whose interests extend beyond secular political concerns, and whose strength is a function of the needs and desires of individual communal groups, candidates for election to public office in South Vietnam most often present themselves as *independent,* although their affiliations are well known to the opinion leaders within relevant communities. Thus, the requirement that in the future all candidates for national elections must be nominated by a political party that meets the increasingly stringent membership and electoral success criteria of Decree 060 forces individual communal groups to either enter publicly into effective and lasting coalitions with others or to withdraw from any attempt to participate *directly* in the institutionalized arena of national decision making through the electoral process.

Table 8-1

Political Party Organization Laws: Decrees 009 (June 19, 1969) and 060
(December 27, 1972)

Pre-existing Requirements Decree 009	New Requirements Decree 060
I. *Location of Party Headquarters* No requirement for central head-quarters, but a "liaison office" must be located in Saigon.	I. *Location of Party Headquarters* Central headquarters must be located in Saigon.
II. *Numbers and Distribution of Membership* A. "Committee Executive Boards" must exist in at least 15 provinces and/or autonomous cities with committees of at least 500 members in each place. *or* B. Have such boards in at least five provinces and/or autonomous cities, with committees of at least 500 members and at least 10 declared members of the National Assembly.	II. *Numbers and Distribution of Membership* A. Must establish and maintain local "headquarters" in at least half of the 44 provinces and/or 10 autonomous cities and in each of those provinces or cities must establish and maintain branch headquarters in at least 25 percent of the total city wards or rural villages. B. Must have a total membership of no less than 5 percent of the total electorate, defined with reference to the last election for the Lower House, in each of the provinces or cities in which local headquarters are established, plus Saigon.
III. *Participation in Elections* No requirement.	III. *Participation in Elections* A. A party is *required* to nominate candidates in every National Assembly election (Lower House and Senate). B. A party is *not* required to nominate candidates in presidential elections. C. Only legally recognized parties have the right to designate candidates in national elections. Candidates cannot stand for election as independents.
IV. *Dissolution* In addition to provisions for voluntary dissolution, a party will be automatically dissolved if it fails to meet any of the above requirements.	IV. *Dissolution* In addition to provisions for voluntary dissolution, a party will be automatically dissolved if it fails to meet any of the above requirements. In addition, a party will be dissolved if: A. it fails to win at least 20 percent of the total seats in any Lower House election; B. it fails to receive votes equal to at least 20 percent of the total number of voters casting ballots in a Senate election (if a party fields more than one slate, the computation will be based on the slate receiving the highest vote); or C. having voluntarily nominated candidates for president and vice-president, it fails to receive votes equal to at least 20 percent of the total number of voters casting ballots.

Having failed in his prior attempt during 1969 to create an effective and lasting progovernment alliance from among six pre-existing political parties, President Thieu was prepared this time to meet the requirements he had himself developed, by creating a new political party with himself as chairman. The new Dang Dan Chu, or Democracy party, was granted legal recognition on March 24, and the inaugural meeting of its village, provincial, and national leadership was held on March 29, 1973.

During remarks presented at this meeting, President Thieu explained his views on the role of political parties in general and the Democracy party in particular. He stressed the need for political parties to promote the "masses' political activities" and to have "national dimensions." They should include one "ruling party," and Thieu made it clear that the Democracy party would serve as the political arm of the government. Thus, among other things, he said:

> The Party will *control the administration* in order to achieve maximum efficiency of the state apparatus. Thus, for the first time in our country, a *ruling party and the administration* assume responsibility before history. . . .
>
> An administration is not really strong without popular support, which can only be effectively won through political parties. An administration is regarded as truly democratic only when it accepts a political opposition. The opposition and ruling parties must be strong to maintain the stability of democratic national political activities. This can only be achieved when the bipartisan party system succeeds in taking deep roots among the people and organizing broad masses of the people. . . .
>
> As this government has been formed in a special historic situation without stemming from a political party, it is necessary to organize a ruling party so that the government can actually spread its roots among the people. . . . Now that there is a ruling party, the opposition parties will feel all the more strongly the need to unite and develop rapidly to control the government in an effective manner.[7]

Opponents of the Thieu regime viewed Decree 060 as a mechanism for their exclusion, rather than as a catalyst for their effective participation through an aggregation of marginally different splinter groups into a smaller number of political coalitions. Thus, negative reactions to Decree 060 ranged from reluctant acceptance to outright opposition.

Reluctant acceptance of the presidential decree was expressed by Senate President Nguyen Van Huyen and other Catholic leaders in and outside the Senate on behalf of the People's Common Progress Bloc (Khoi Quoc Dan Dong Tien), and by Tran Quoc Buu, chairman of the Worker-Farmer party

(Dang Cong Nong). Huyen and leaders of various Catholic-oriented parties, such as the Humanist (or Personalist) Socialist Revolutionary Party (Nhan Xa Cach) Mang Dang, commonly called the Nhan Xa) and Greater Solidarity Force (Luc Luong Dai Doan Ket), announced the formation of the Freedom (Tu Do) party and began to organize party chapters with the hope that the Catholic electorate would coalesce. However, the Saigon press reported on January 9, 1973 that the Vietnam Council of Bishops had issued a declaration that the Church would not participate in partisan secular politics. The council reminded Catholic priests in Vietnam not to accept any positions within political parties. These moves were followed by denials from a source close to the Saigon archbishop that the Freedom party had any connection with the Catholic Church. Thus, the party was faced with the necessity of building its organization without the *official* support of the Church.

Tran Quoc Buu reacted to the promulgation of the new party law by expressing publicly his confidence that the Worker-Farmer party would meet the new requirements and continue to operate. He even went so far as to argue that the new law was necessary for the consolidation of political forces in the South in order to fight against the communists.[8] However, after the Worker-Farmer party had tried vainly for several months to comply with the requirements, it found it necessary to join with six other parties in the creation of the Democratic Socialist Alliance (Lien Minh Dan Chu Xa Hoi).[9] This new party did qualify for registration with the government, but its seven original components no longer have any legal status as individual parties.

Among those declaring outright opposition to the new law were leaders of the Revolutionary Dai Viet, or Dai Viet Cach Mang; the southern section of the Viet Nam Quoc Dan Dang (VNQDD or Vietnamese Kuomintang); the Progressive Nationalist Movement, or Phong Trao Cap Tien Quoc Gia; and the An Quang Buddhists. Revolutionary Dai Viet leader Ha Thuc Ky, earlier a strong supporter of President Thieu,[10] pledged that his party would "fight with the people and other friendly organizations to the last ditch." Others, including Senator Hoang Xuan Tuu and Lawyer Tran Van Tuyen, maintained that those parties that could not meet the official requirements should continue to operate clandestinely in the manner of traditional secret societies.[11]

One of the most vocal critics of Decree 060 was Senator Vu Van Mau, a member of the Buddhist Lotus slate, which had placed first in the Senate elections of 1970. In a speech of March 21, 1973, Senator Mau condemned the new party law's "harsh requirements" and in another speech on April 24, he charged that Thieu would be able to "fill the power vacuum" with his Democracy party through an "abuse of the government's administrative apparatus from central to local levels." Thieu had "purposely issued a death certificate to the political parties . . . so that the Democracy party would profit" and " in many places local governments threaten that anybody unwilling to join the Dan Chu party, the bulwark of anti-communism, will be blacklisted as pro-communist."

The political parties' arguments against the new decree-law and the government's rebuttal are summarized in the Addendum to this chapter. The information and most of the *language* in it are based on a memorandum prepared by Nguyen Ngoc Huy, leader of the Progressive National Movement and a subsequent memorandum from the Office of the President. Huy's memorandum stressed the harshness of requirements for parties to be legally authorized, the time and energy demanded for registration and other administrative details which would detract from party political activities, and the degree to which the new regulations made it appear the government was attempting to control and restrict open political party activity. Denying these accusations, the government's memorandum argued that the new decree-law forced parties to mobilize the masses and to form coalitions, thereby making party activity more responsible and eliminating the confusing proliferation of small parties, which have been predominant in South Vietnam in the past.

To implement the new party law, the Ministry of Interior issued decrees on May 16, 1973 dissolving twenty-six parties previously chartered under the 1969 decree 009.[12] Thus, as of October 1973, only three political parties were authorized to participate in national elections: the Democracy and Freedom parties and the Social Democratic Alliance. (As late as October 1973, however, there were reports that a fourth, the Republican party or Cong Hoa was also being organized.)

Although critics continued to attack Decree 060, most people agreed with government supporters that elections were unlikely to be held under the requirements of 060. After the Paris Agreements, opposition leaders began to ask whether the National Liberation Front would be required to abide by the new party law in order to participate in the elections anticipated by these agreements. As Senator Mau pointed out at a meeting between President Thieu and party leaders and legislators on February 17, 1973, the communists would be extremely unlikely to agree to participate in elections under conditions requiring them to expose the members of their political infrastructure to the government police prior to the victory of one side or the other. Thus, many political leaders, although still publicly debating the merits of the new party law, privately expected it would simply be abolished as part of the implementation of the Paris Agreements.

However, in anticipation of the Senate election of August 1973, a Senate election law consonant with the party law was passed by the Lower House. When it was sent to the Senate in April, opposition senators succeeded in amending it to reduce the deposit required of each Senate slate from 15 to 1 million piastres, (the U.S. dollar varied in value during 1973 from $VN420 to $VN550), to omit the requirement that candidates be nominated by a legally registered party as required by 060, and to cut a stipulation written into the

Lower House version that communists and "pro-communist neutralists" should be barred from candidacy.

The amended version was approved by the Lower House and forwarded to the president. Thieu promptly vetoed it, and as is possible in this system, added his own amendments to it before sending it to both houses sitting in joint session. In this forum, the deputies and senators can override the president's veto by a vote of two-thirds of their total membership. There are 60 Senate seats and 159 Lower House seats, so the vote required to override is 146 of the total 219 seats. If the override succeeds, the previously vetoed version of the legislation becomes law. However, if the effort to override fails, the *president's version becomes law.* It is important to note that the required vote is two-thirds of the total authorized membership and not two-thirds of those present and constituting a quorum or actual current membership strength of the two houses. Because there are no provisions for by-elections for the Senate, a seat becoming vacant for any reason (death, resignation, appointment to the cabinet) automatically becomes, in effect, a vote for the president in any attempt by legislators to override a veto. Thieu has contributed to this phenomenon by appointing legislators to positions in the government, thus vacating some seats and, at crucial times, sending mildly "opposition" deputies and senators on short trips abroad to represent South Vietnam in one forum or another.

In this case, the president's veto was accompanied by his own alternative provisions: Senate candidates must be neither communists nor "pro-communist neutralists"; they must stand for election on tickets of fifteen men each (with a sixteenth as an alternate); and they must be nominated by political parties authorized under Decree 060. However, Thieu yielded on two other points: the deposit required of each slate would be only 2 million piastres, and the requirement that Senate candidates be members of and nominated by political parties would not take effect until the 1976 Senate election.

When the votes were cast on June 8, only 109 of the legislators were present, 37 short of the minimum number required to override the president's veto, and of the 109 present, only 29 voted against the president. Thieu's version of the Senate election regulations thus became law. But the provisions of Decree 060 requiring a connection between candidates and political parties were waived until 1976.

By the time the new Senate election law was promulgated, the candidates had only four days to file their applications. Potential candidates might have been expected to be prepared for this in advance, but only the candidates on four progovernment slates did file by the deadline. Opposition candidates failed to do so for one or more reasons: they did not really expect that a Senate election under the 1967 Constitution would ever be held; they chose not to contest the election; and/or they were not able to form adequate slates of candidates.

Given the short time between the promulgation of the Senate election law and the final date for filing, accusations and counteraccusations flew between opposition political leaders and the government. The opposition charged that the delay in promulgating the law had been a deliberate government ploy, as four days simply had not been enough time for candidates to secure all the papers required for filing. For example, one of the papers required is a tax-clearance certificate, the issuance of which, as both authors of this paper can testify from personal experience, takes at least one week and often much longer. And if any one of the fifteen members of a slate fails to present his certificate or any other required document, he is disqualified and often the rest of his slate is, too, due to the lack of sufficient alternates.

However, the government was not without reasonable counteraccusations. It argued that the delay had resulted from the late passage of its version of the bill by the Senate and the required reconsideration by the Lower House and joint session. Government spokesmen claimed this was a deliberate attempt by Senate opposition leaders, among them Senate President Nguyen Van Huyen, to at least delay, if not defeat, the bill. Thus, the government contended, the opposition had expected that the June 1973 Paris Joint Communiqué, signed by the original parties to the January 1973 Paris Agreements and reaffirming their provisions, would set some new conditions for the elections stipulated in the original agreements which would nullify both 060 and any new Senate election law. If this had transpired, and if the National Council for National Reconciliation and Concord had been established and a date for new elections fixed, it would have been disadvantageous for the opposition to have nominated candidates to run under terms of the government's election law.

These disadvantages to the oppositionists were fairly obvious. First, if they failed to gain significant public support in the elections, the oppositionists' bargaining position with the government over future participation in the proposed council as part of the "third force" would be reduced. Second, it was feared that the Provisional Revolutionary Government or the NLF would deride them as "government lackeys" for participating in government-sponsored elections. Third, whatever benefits accrued to them by running in the elections would probably be short term, since new elections would most likely be required again, and the costs—financial, material and organizational—of the first set of elections would deplete the resources available for the second. Furthermore, the costs of abstention from the elections were not great. Two of the major opposition groups or sets of personalities, the Catholics and the An Quang Buddhists, would retain their representation in the Senate until their terms (which had begun in 1970) expired in 1976.

As in the United States, Senate terms are staggered so that only a certain number of seats are contested in any one election. Thus, one half of the Senate is re-elected to six-year terms every three years. Since the first election in 1967 elected the whole Senate of sixty members, three slates of ten each, selected by lot, served only three-year terms. Thus, during 1970, three more slates of ten

members each were elected to a six-year term, among them a strong Catholic
slate (slate 3) led by Senate President Huyen and another (slate 1) representing
the An Quang Buddhists. Thus, oppositionists were not faced with immediate
exclusion from that body in any event.

It is fair to say that both government and opposition were correct in this
debate. Both had an interest in delaying promulgation of the law. However,
by the time the June communiqué failed to mention elections, the opposition
realized the law would be passed anyway; but by then it was too late to
organize adequate slates of candidates.

Actually, the activist elements within the two major religious groups,
Buddhists and Catholics, did make last-minute attempts to organize joint
slates or an alliance of candidates. On the Catholic side, agreement on candidates could not be reached among the various factions, and there were also
serious divisions among the Buddhists. For example, the official head of the
Church, Thich Thien Minh, was being strongly accused of misconduct by Buddhist youth elements, and among the An Quang faithful, the youth provide the
operational strength for Buddhist *political* activities. So, when Thich Thien
Minh became aware that some Buddhist elements, including the youth, were
attempting to organize a slate of candidates and were supported in this by his
colleague Thich Tri Quang, he declared publicly that the Church would not
officially support any slate; and presumably he directed provincial organizations to stay neutral in the elections. And when it became evident that Buddhist candidates could not expect the full support of the Church, they gave up
the fight. Another reported reason for the abstention was inadequate financial resources.

Thus, by the time that campaign activity began for the August Senate
elections, it appeared that all opposition groups were boycotting them. The
one major surprise was that the Democratic Socialist Alliance, including the
Worker-Farmer party and the Progressive Nationalist Movement, did not enter
candidates. Although the reasons for this are not yet clear, two interrelated
factors seem to have been determinant: the inability to agree on candidates
and their financial resources. Consequently, only four slates competed, with
two to be elected. (In 1973 each slate consisted of sixteen candidates, one of
whom was an alternate, rather than ten candidates as had been the case in
1967 and 1970.)

There is evidence available that under the best of conditions the Vietnamese citizen has a very low level of interest in Senate elections as compared
to elections for village councils, the Lower House, and the presidency.[13] Given
the absence of a vigorous opposition and the generally uncertain political cli-
mate of 1973, interest among opinion leaders and citizens alike in the election
remained minimal. Furthermore, it was generally believed that all four slates
were sponsored by the government in order to avoid the appearances of an

unopposed election like that of President Thieu in 1971, which had damaged the government's credibility both at home and abroad.

Only two of the slates were clearly identified as government sponsored: the platforms of both slate 1, Dan Chu (Democracy), and slate 2, Bach Tuong (White Elephant), were identical with that of the Democracy party itself.[14] Both slates were headed by government ministers,[15] and the first carried the very name of the "ruling party" itself. The first slate also included three active progovernment incumbent senators, two former progovernment deputies,[16] and two incumbent progovernment chiefs of the most important city and province councils.[17] It also included younger specialists who had demonstrated strong loyalty to the government in professional or political work, such as lawyer Ngo Khac Tinh, brother of the minister of education and cousin of President Thieu. The second slate's assets included, besides Foreign Minister Tran Van Lam, another progovernment senator, two former deputies, and one province chief. However, most of the slate 2 men could be considered prominent only by comparison with the relatively obscure members of the third and fourth slates.

These did not include one candidate of national stature, and the members of the third were considerably younger than those of the other slates, averaging only thirty-eight.[18] Table 8-2 presents summary data on occupations of candidates by slates and shows a preponderant number of university graduates and civil or military members of the bureaucracy as members of the third slate. If we assume these candidates were sponsored by the government (and some members of all four slates assured the authors that the government did indeed finance all of them), the participation of the younger professional members of slates 3 and 4 might have been an exercise in preparation for future political roles on behalf of the Democracy party. By contrast, the higher ages of slate 4 candidates would indicate less likelihood that these men were being groomed for significant political activity. Their campaign literature emphasized their past service to the anti-communist nationalist cause, and the government support of their candidacies presumably was in recognition of that. (In contrast to the candidates of slates 1, 2, and 3, whose campaign leaflets did not specify their regional origins, such origins were given for seven of the sixteen candidates of slate 4: five were from the North and two from central Vietnam.)

As expected, all of the candidates' occupational profiles were generally consistent with those of candidates for national-level elections since that for the Constituent Assembly in 1966; they were almost completely "Westernized" and urban oriented. Except for three of the candidates (two on slate 4 and one on slate 2), all fell within the four categories of political officeholders (18.8 percent), career government officials (24.6 percent), professionals (32.8 percent), or businessmen and "free professionals" (23 percent).

About the only really competitive feature of the election campaign did not receive any public attention. For some reason, some members of slate 3 began to think they might have a chance of winning second place. As a result,

Table 8-2
Candidate Career Histories

Most Significant Occupation Up to and Including 1973	Slate 1	Slate 2	Slate 3	Slate 4	All Candidates
Current Member of Cabinet	1	1	0	0	2
Member of Previous Cabinets	2[a]	0	0	0	2
Current Member of National Assembly	0	1	0	0	1
Former Member of National or Constituent Assembly	3	2[b]	0	0	5
Member of Province or City Council	2	0	0	0	2
Subtotal: Political Office	8	4	0	0	12
Assistant Minister	0	1	0	0	1
Secretary-General, Director General, Province Chief, or Equivalent	1	5	1	1	8
Lower-Rank Civil Servant	0	0	2	1	3
Military Officer (other than one in position above)	1	0	1	1	3
Subtotal: Career Government Official	2	6	4	3	15
Educator	3	1	6	4	14
Judge, Lawyer	2	1	1[c]	2	6
Subtotal: Professionals	5	2	7	6	20
Journalist	0	1	0	3	4
Doctor, Dentist, Pharmacist	1	2	1	0	4
Economist, Engineer	0	0	3	0	3
Banker, Businessman	0	0	1[d]	2	3
Subtotal: Business and Free Professionals	1	3	5	5	14
Other	0	1[e]	0	1[f]	2
Unknown	0	0	0	1	1
TOTAL	16	16	16	16	64

[a]Both were incumbent senators in 1973.

[b]One also was current secretary of state for legislative liaison.

[c]Military magistrate.

[d]Also vice-chairman of Association of Ethnic Minorities of Southern Origin.

[e]Chairman of Hoa Hao Association in Kien Phong Province.

[f]An influential adviser to the Hoa Hao Religious Council.

some of them began to make private and personal appeals to Catholic, Buddhist, Cao Dai, and Hoa Hao leaders, journeyed to some provinces to canvass voters, and began to put up additional campaign posters. In addition, as described by one member of that slate after the election, they began to think the Americans might help them indirectly by forcing the president not to "rig" the elections.[19] None of this, however, had any significance for the electoral outcome which had been predicted by almost everyone who had a direct stake in it.

Actually, of course, slates 3 and 4 never had a chance. The formal campaign machinery itself is structured in such a manner that candidates for national election lacking an extensive network of previously organized support to supplement the officially granted facilities are doomed to failure—as, some would argue, should be the case. Each slate of candidates is limited to two government-provided appearances on radio and two on television, five mass meetings of all candidates with the electorate (one each in Danang, Nha Trang, Bien Hoa, Can Tho, and Saigon), and one joint press conference at the city hall in Saigon. In addition, the government prints thousands of campaign posters and handbills of a standard format for each slate, but it leaves to city, province, and district officials and party representatives in each locality the responsibility for posting them. The result of this system is that candidates lacking supporters throughout the country to mobilize voters on their behalf are losers from the start.

The official statistics on the August 26, 1973 Senate elections are reported in table 8-3.

Because of the basically noncompetitive and thus nonrepresentative nature of the 1973 Senate elections, it is clear that it had no more than meager significance as an event providing possible movement towards the creation of mechanisms for the integration of the communists into a competitive but peaceful electoral system; nor did it provide for the broadening of the government's base of support; nor did it result in meaningful participation on the part of the noncommunist opposition. The official returns showed such an apparently great magnitude of victory for the Democracy party that further analyses would seem to be superfluous. However, on closer inspection, statistics derived from those in table 8-4 are instructive concerning the more important question (given the realities of the current political system in the South) of the Democracy party's ability to *organize* voter turnout to *its own ends*, rather than the less important question of its relative *appeal*.

Unfortunately, since each voter was entitled to cast votes for two slates rather than just one, we cannot know for certain exactly what number of voters cast both of their votes for the two Democracy party slates. However, we can compute for each province and autonomous city the possible numerical range of such voters, i.e., the minimum and maximum number of voters who possibly cast both of their ballots for the two slates. In addition, we can determine the total maximum vote available for distribution among any two slates. Although, according to the data presented in table 8-4, the Democracy party

Table 8-3
Results of Senate Election by Provinces and Cities

Provinces and Cities	Number of Registered Voters	Percentage Voting	Vote Received As Percentage of Total Voters				Percentage of Voters Casting Only 1 Ballot
			Slate 1	Slate 2	Slate 3	Slate 4	
Hue	60,853	74.5	64.0	61.5	29.3	23.1	22.1
Danang	165,948	90.4	78.1	67.9	25.1	18.7	10.2
Quang Nam	238,265	91.4	85.4	76.0	12.1	10.2	16.3
Quang Ngai	226,072	98.2	89.9	78.4	7.9	6.7	17.2
Quang Tin	153,833	95.3	91.8	88.0	5.6	4.9	9.7
Quang Tri	30,197	96.9	75.6	75.1	18.3	17.0	14.0
Thua Thien	217,419	90.7	81.5	74.9	8.4	7.3	19.6
Qui Nhon	71,412	93.0	85.7	77.0	13.3	10.1	14.0
Nha Trang	85,906	82.6	60.5	52.8	29.1	21.7	35.9
Cam Ranh	47,343	94.7	76.6	71.5	17.7	15.2	19.0
Dalat	36,690	96.8	84.7	71.2	18.7	16.4	8.9
Binh Dinh	245,082	96.7	96.0	75.9	4.1	3.0	21.0
Binh Thuan	116,382	95.9	91.1	79.7	6.8	5.5	16.8
Darlac	96,309	95.2	83.4	79.4	12.5	10.5	13.5
Khanh Hoa	97,652	91.8	88.6	73.1	8.8	7.9	21.7
Kontum	40,052	100.4[a]	85.5	84.1	12.3	10.2	7.9
Lam Dong	37,575	97.3	93.9	83.9	8.9	4.9	8.3
Ninh Thuan	84,172	92.0	77.7	76.4	17.3	14.6	14.0
Phu Bon	29,512	94.6	91.6	71.3	12.8	10.6	13.7
Phu Yen	127,297	94.7	86.7	81.0	10.3	9.4	12.6
Pleiku	92,616	97.3	89.3	83.3	8.2	7.0	12.3
Quang Duc	16,547	97.7	90.2	74.9	8.5	6.5	20.0
Tuyen Duc	45,507	99.1	83.6	74.3	10.9	8.9	22.3
Saigon	611,947	81.1	55.0	54.5	29.4	27.0	34.0
Vung Tau	42,528	92.1	71.1	64.9	22.1	17.5	23.9
Bien Hoa	219,551	90.9	79.2	69.1	23.4	19.8	8.4
Binh Duong	118,519	93.6	74.8	64.6	19.4	17.2	24.0
Binh Long	19,525	98.0	84.3	72.3	13.6	13.0	16.8

Binh Tuy	35,564	99.7	91.4	60.2	9.1	7.5	31.9
Gia Dinh[d]	577,289	90.5	80.6	65.9	15.9	13.7	24.0
Hau Nghia	100,917	95.6	85.8	69.4	14.4	12.7	17.8
Long An	147,909	95.8	81.2	68.2	16.3	15.1	19.1
Long Khanh	76,993	97.6	83.0	76.6	14.7	12.9	12.9
Phuoc Long	21,986	99.4	93.9	85.2	6.4	6.1	8.3
Phuoc Tuy	59,024	93.5	77.9	65.9	21.7	18.8	15.7
Tay Ninh	161,955	93.7	78.7	66.4	17.4	15.2	22.4
My Tho	40,750	92.9	85.2	71.6	16.7	12.6	13.9
Can Tho	70,696	97.9	74.4	68.1	23.7	19.4	14.4
Rach Gia	34,402	96.5	67.3	66.2	28.7	24.8	13.0
An Giang	253,710	87.7	78.7	66.4	17.5	14.4	23.5
An Xuyen	78,426	94.9	91.2	82.6	8.6	8.6[c]	9.1
Ba Xuyen	175,067	91.7	89.7	80.0	7.8	5.4	17.0
Bac Lieu	117,524	97.5	94.4	90.6	6.0	4.8	9.0
Chau Doc	242,218	99.8	93.9[b]	78.2	7.7	8.0[c]	12.3[b]
Chuong Thien	92,383	98.0	92.5[b]	71.8	15.5	18.0[c]	2.2[b]
Dinh Tuong	186,205	97.5	80.9	67.8	18.4	13.5	19.4
Go Cong	75,552	99.3	93.6	72.5	8.0	7.0	18.8
Kien Giang	127,443	96.1	91.3	75.7	10.6	9.7	12.6
Kien Hoa	226,569	90.1	81.1	68.9	17.7	15.7	16.7
Kien Phong	150,652	90.3	83.3	69.5	14.1	13.0	20.1
Kien Tuong	21,697	98.0	90.0	75.0	13.5	8.1	13.4
Phong Dinh	138,349	96.5	81.8	73.2	15.3	13.0	16.7
Sa Dec	109,906	98.7	88.3	70.7	9.0	5.9	16.7
Vinh Binh	145,072	98.9	95.7	84.3	8.6	6.4	26.1
Vinh Long	217,058	91.9	82.2	75.1	13.8	12.5	5.1
TOTAL	7,060,027[e]	92.7	82.6	71.8	14.7	12.6	18.2

[a] Percentage based on error in reported registration figures.

[b] Percentage based on adjustment of the figure erroneously reported in the source.

[c] The only returns deviating from the pattern of each slate receiving more votes than the next in numerical sequence.

[d] Includes Con Son Island

[d] Total numbers from which percentages are calculated include spoiled ballots and/or missing envelopes.

Table 8-4
Democratic Party Performance

	Range as percent of possible voters casting ballots for both Democracy slates		Mean of range as percent of possible voters casting ballots for both Democracy slates	Percent of votes possible, cast for either or both Democracy slates
	High	Low		
REGION I				
Hue[a]	71	48	59	63
Danang[a]	75	56	65	73
Quang Nam	88	78	83	81
Quang Ngai	92	85	88	84
Quang Tin	94	89	91	90
Quang Tri	82	65	73	75
Thua Thien	92	84	88	82
REGION II				
Qui Nhon[a]	87	77	82	81
Nha Trang[a]	71	49	60	57
Cam Ranh[a]	82	67	74	74
Dalat[a]	81	65	73	78
Binh Dinh	96	93	92	86
Binh Thuan	93	88	90	86
Darlac	87	76	81	81
Khanh Hoa	91	83	87	81
Kontum	88	77	82	85
Lam Dong	91	86	88	89
Ninh Thuan	83	68	75	77
Phu Bon	87	76	81	82
Phu Yen	90	80	85	84
Pleiku	98	85	88	86
Quang Duc	91	85	88	83
Tuyen Duc	89	80	84	79
REGION III				
Saigon[a]	71	44	57	55
Vung Tau[a]	78	60	69	68
Bien Hoa	77	57	67	74
Binh Duong	81	63	72	70
Binh Long	86	73	79	78
Binh Tuy	91	83	87	76
Gia Dinh	84	70	77	73
Hau Nghia	85	73	79	78
Long An	84	69	76	75
Long Khanh	85	72	78	80
Phuoc Long	94	87	90	90
Phuoc Tuy	78	60	69	72
Tay Ninh	83	67	75	73

Table 8-4 (Continued)

	Range as percent of possible voters casting ballots for both Democracy slates		Mean of range as percent of possible voters casting ballots for both Democracy slates	Percent of votes possible, cast for either or both Democracy slates
	High	Low		
REGION IV				
My Tho[a]	83	71	77	78
Can Tho[a]	76	57	66	71
Rach Gia[a]	71	46	58	67
An Giang	82	68	75	73
An Xuyen	91	83	87	87
Ba Xuyen	92	87	89	85
Bac Lieu	94	89	91	93
Chau Doc	92	84	88	86
Chuong Thien[b]	82	67	74	83
Dinh Tuong	82	68	74	74
Go Cong	92	85	88	83
Kien Giang	89	80	84	84
Kien Hoa	82	67	74	75
Kien Phong	86	73	79	76
Kien Tuong	86	78	82	83
Phong Dinh	85	71	78	78
Sa Dec	91	85	88	80
Vinh Binh	91	85	88	90
Vinh Long	86	74	80	79
TOTAL	85	72	78	77

[a]Autonomous city

[b]Percentage based on adjustment of the figure erroneously reported in the source

was able to accomplish the task of convincing at least 72 percent (and perhaps as much as 85 percent) of the voters nationwide to cast both of their ballots for slates 1 and 2, they were not as successful in certain areas as would probably be necessary against a determined opposition. The returns from eleven of the sixteen urban centers in South Vietnam with a reported population in excess of 75,000 (as of 1971) for which we have data indicate that the ability of the party to deliver the votes there was not as impressive as we would have expected, given their prior advantages. Thus, among these eleven cities as a whole, the number of voters who cast ballots for both slates ranged from a possible low of only 48 percent in Hue (as compared to the possible low among *rural* provinces of 60 percent in Phuoc Tuy) to a maximum high of only 87 percent in Qui Nhon (as compared to the possible maximum among rural provinces of 98 percent in Pleiku).

Viewing from the other direction, we find essentially the same results. The data on the party's share of the total possible votes cast for either one or both of the first two slates indicate that the cities returned a significantly smaller percentage to the Democracy party than the countryside. Using this latter measure, the percentage of possible votes actually cast in these eleven cities ranged from a low of 63 percent in Hue to a high of 81 percent in Qui Nhon, as compared to a range in the other forty-four constituencies from a low of 70 percent in Binh Duong to a high of 93 percent in Bac Lieu. Table 8-5 presents the distribution of "voter support" (an index based on the percentage of possible votes cast for either one or both of slates 1 and 2) among the forty-four provinces and eleven cities of South Vietnam.

If we compare President Thieu's personal vote-winning ability as evidenced in the unopposed presidential election of 1971 with the Democracy party's ability to do so in a similarly noncompetitive election, the same pattern emerges. Table 8-6 compares the placement of fifty-three voting districts on a dichotomized scale of "Support" for Thieu's Democracy party. Forty of the fifty-three provinces and autonomous cities remain at the same end of the scale for both elections. Thus, only twelve provinces and one autonomous city (those included in the lower-left and upper-right cells on table 8-6) move from the "High Support" to the "Low Support" position or vice versa. It is also apparent that eight (40 percent) of the twenty consistently supportive voting districts are those with high ethnic minority populations, a full 75 percent of such provinces. On the

Table 8-5
Voter Support for Democracy Party

High			Low	
	Q1		Q2	Q3
1. Bac Lieu	Phu Yen	My Tho[a]	Cam Ranh[a]
2. Vinh Binh	Kien Giang	Binh Long	Gia Dinh
3. Quang Tin	Go Cong	Dalat[a]	Danang[a]
4. Phuoc Long	Kien Tuong	Hau Nghia	An Giang
5. Lam Dong	Quang Duc	Phong Dinh	Tay Ninh
6. An Xuyen	Thua Thien	Ninh Thuan	Phuoc Tuy
7. Pleiku	Chuong Thien	Kien Phong	Can Tho[a]
8. Chau Doc	Phu Bon	Binh Tuy	Binh Duong
9. Binh Dinh	Darlac	Quang Tin	Vung Tau[a]
10. Binh Thuan	Qui Nhon[a]	Kien Hoa	Rach Gia
11. Ba Xuyen	Khanh Hoa	Long An	Hue[a]
12. Kontum	Quang Nam	Dinh Tuong	Nha Trang[a]
13. Quang Ngai	Long Khanh	Bien Hoa	Saigon[a]

NOTE: We omit Sadec, Tuyen Duc, and Vinh Long, with scores centered on Q2, in order to divide into even quarters.

[a]Autonomous city

Table 8-6

1973 Voter Support

(for Slates 1 and 2, identified closely with Democracy party, read DOWN)

	High		Low	
	Sadec	Darlac[b]	Ninh Thuan[c]	Quang Tri
	Kontum[b]	Khanh Hoa	Can Tho[a]	Long An
H	Quang Duc[b]	Lam Dong[b]	Binh Tuy	Dinh Tuong
	Kien Giang[b]	Long Khanh[b]		
I	Quang Nam	Phuoc Long[b]		
	Phu Bon	Go Cong		
G	Chuong Thien	Vinh Binh[b]		
	Binh Dinh	Quang Tin		
H	An Xuyen	Qui Nhon[a]		
	Phu Yen			
VOTER SUPPORT 1971	Kien Tuong			
(read ACROSS)	Quang Ngai	Ba Xuyen[b]	Hue[a]	Hau Nghia
	Thua Thien	Bac Lieu[b]	Danang[a]	Phuoc Tuy
	Binh Thuan	Chau Doc	Cam Ranh[a]	Tay Ninh
L	Pleiku[b]		Dalat[a]	My Tho[a]
			Nha Trang[a]	Rach Gia[a]
O			Saigon[a]	An Giang
			Vung Tau[a]	Kien Hoa
W			Bien Hoa	Kien Phong
			Binh Duong	Vinh Long
			Binh Long[b]	Gia Dinh

NOTE: Tuyen Duc is the mode for 1973 and Phong Dinh is the mode for 1971; therefore they are omitted from this table.

[a]Autonomous cities

[b]Considerable percentage of ethnic minority population not including Chams

[c]Considerable percentage of Chams

other hand, of the eleven autonomous cities, a full 82 percent place in the "Low Support" cell for both elections as we would expect (the exceptions are Qui Nhon in the "High Support" cell in both elections and Can Tho in the "High Support" cell in 1971 but the "Low Support" cell in 1973).

However, the potential irony of the electoral system in South Vietnam is represented by two interrelated hypotheses: those provinces that appear to be the areas of Thieu's greatest strength actually represent his greatest future weakness, and measures such as Decree 060 potentially reinforce these weaknesses.[20] In other words, we suspect that high voter turnout combined with high vote percentages for Thieu is most often a function of voter apathy and, at least in some cases, vote fraud. If these assumptions are correct, President Thieu would probably find that the "support" he has in the past drawn from the rural areas and on which he relies to offset the lack of voter support in the cities would be eroded in an election that included the NLF, without compensating gains in the urban areas. If this were the case, measures such as Decree 060, by excluding from electoral politics the strong but regionally based noncommunist opposition, would likely provide a relative increase in the level of voter "support," in terms of votes cast, for the NLF. One would expect that in *any* election, voter turnout in urban areas would remain low, so the importance of the voter turnout in rural areas would be increased, even though population distribution in South Vietnam is becoming increasingly urban. Thus, the comparative ability of the Thieu government and the NLF to mobilize *rural* voters, many of whom have only minimal interest in the nature of political representation in Saigon, would become very important, indeed. In that event a strategy of co-opting regionally based "opposition" groups (e.g. An Quang) and providing for their participation in broadly inclusive elections would probably decrease the relative importance of the total votes cast for the NLF without substantially reducing the voter support that Thieu would in any event receive.

We do not intend to predict the outcome of any future national-level elections that might include the NLF. To do so would require detailed information about a large number of variables such as the offices for which elections were to be held (Constituent Assembly, Senate, or presidency), constituency boundaries, whether or not districts would be served by only one or more than one representative, whether candidates would stand as individuals or as members of slates, and whether winners would be determined on the basis of majority or plurality of votes cast or persons voting. However, President Thieu's apparent assumption that the exclusion of regionally strong political groups from electoral competition will benefit him rather than the NLF is still open to serious question.

Addendum: Arguments For and Against Decree 060

A. *Objections To 060*

1. Number of party members is too harsh compared with requirements in other countries, especially when military personnel and citizens under eighteen must stay out of party politics.

Government Rebuttal

1. The membership requirement is not designed to bar formal recognition, but to force parties to mobilize the masses, organize and lead them in political participation, thereby taking them away from the grip of the communists. Masses are like virgin lands, just waiting to be excavated by the most diligent tillers.

In most countries, political activities and elections are like sports competition, free from the threat of communist encroachment. In Vietnam, each election is a life-and-death struggle with the communists; therefore, the support of the masses is a most important requirement.

2. Conditions for formal recognition are too complicated, including the reporting of lists of party members in each village or subdistrict and requiring of members to have membership cards and residence cards. Formal recognition depends too much on local government officials.

2. This argument is unwarranted, as all these requirements were contained in the Political Party Law (009/69) of 1969 (see Article 10 of that law).

3. Dissolution of a party which no longer has enough members will force the parties to devote too much time to administrative matters, jeopardizing their capabilities for carrying on the political struggle.

3. This criticism points out exactly the purpose of Decree-Law No. 060: parties must devote attention to expanding their membership constantly, after formation and recognition as well as during those crucial stages. Parties must never permit their membership to drop below the minimum legal requirement.

4. Forcing the parties to propose candidates in elections and dissolving them if they fail to gain enough Lower House seats or enough votes may create doubt about the government's intention.

4. This criticism points out exactly the purpose of Decree-Law No. 060: parties in a democracy must seek power only through the electoral process, and if they cannot muster enough followers in elections, they are no longer capable of mobilizing the masses on a nationwide basis. Thus, they should be dissolved.

Moreover, the requirement that all candidates for elections must be nominated by parties consolidates the prestige of parties and eliminates excessively individualistic politicking.

5.   In practice, the government aims pursued will not be attained.

   a.   These conditions prevent the communists from nominating candidates under their own party banner but do not prevent them from planting their agents to recruit members rapidly.

   b.   Parties will simply lapse into clandestine activities.

6.   The immediate application of the decree-law is damaging to the nationalist cause. How can one go out and tell the population that the government is fighting for democracy when the survival of the parties is apparently threatened by the decree-law? If parties are too busy reorganizing themselves according to the new decree-law, who will be able to devote energy to appealing to the masses? The communists will move into the power vacuum created thereby.

5.   It is too early to predict the law's practical implications or results.

   However, it does not appear probable that parties will go underground, as clandestine activities will not attract a popular following. In open and legal activities, the parties have not been very successful; how can they hope to achieve popular support in the form of secret societies?

6.   This criticism is ill-founded. In recruiting new members from the masses, parties by the same token participate in the political struggle against the communists. Therefore, it is unreasonable to say that parties busy with recruitment will have no time for the political struggle. Parties must coalesce into opposition, independent or progovernment coalitions. Therefore those current, but temporary coalitions will no longer exist.

   Communists' propaganda about our killing of democracy cannot be taken too seriously, for they are always demanding the abolition of all our laws.

   We *have to fight to keep our laws or at least to use them as elements for negotiation.* Therefore it is not acceptable that we surrender a position immediately when the communists demand it. [Italics added]

B.   *The Parties' Proposals*

1.   *Respect the acquired rights of the formally recognized parties.* Do not apply Decree-Law 060 retroactively.

B.   *Rebuttal*

1.   This is not a logical proposal, as this would prolong the present multiparty system and the disunity within the present parties. Without some pressure for coalition, parties will

continue to be divided because of divergent interests or pride.

2. *Treat separately parties of national stature and small parties.*

2. This proposal would not be helpful because there would still be too many "national parties." There should be about three parties representing three political tendencies (i.e., the government, opposition, and independents). There should be an end to the present situation wherein many parties with the same ideology and program exist side by side. Also, there should be a stop to ephemeral coalitions because they create political instability. Coalition should be on the basis of the three political tendencies mentioned above.

Vis-à-vis the small parties which have not mustered enough strength to be recognized under Law 009/69, their continued existence is not useful to national political life. Parties that cannot operate in one-quarter of the subdistricts and villages cannot create sufficient organizational strength to be significant in the anti-communist fight. The lack of a minimum membership requirement would perpetuate them with all their weaknesses. Not forcing them to muster enough qualifications for recognition in a shorter time would leave them in their laziness and slowness, characteristics inappropriate to the urgent, impending political fight with the communists.

Notes

1. For a discussion of the strategy of cooptation and the difference between cooptation and accommodation in the Vietnamese context, refer to Jerry M. Silverman, "South Vietnam and the Elusive Peace," *Asian Survey* 13 (January 1973), pp. 37–41.

2. Especially Elizabeth Pond, "South Vietnamese Politics and the American Withdrawal," in Joseph J. Zasloff and Allan E. Goodman (eds.), *Indochina in Conflict; A Political Assessment* (Lexington, Mass.: Lexington Books, 1972), p. 1-24 and Donald Kirk, "The Thieu Presidential Campaign: Background and Consequences of the Single-Candidacy Phenomenon," *Asian Survey* 12 (July 1972).

3. For details, refer to Jerry M. Silverman, op. cit., pp. 36-38, 41-45.

4. Transcript of Henry Kissinger's Press Conference, January 24, 1973.

5. For a discussion of emergency powers as applied during 1972, refer to Jerry M. Silverman, op. cit., pp. 33-34.

6. See especially, Allan E. Goodman, "South Vietnam: Neither War Nor Peace," *Asian Survey* 10 (February 1970), p. 107-32 and Peter King, "The Political Balance in Saigon," *Pacific Affairs* 44 (Fall 1971), pp. 401-20.

7. Translated from a recording.

8. *Tien Tuyen*, January 19, 1973.

9. The Socialist Democratic Alliance (Lien Minh Dan Chu Xa Hoi) consists of the following seven parties previously chartered under the terms of Decree 009, 1969: Vietnam Social Democratic party (Vietnam Dan Chu Xa Hoi Dang); Social Republican party (Cong Hoa Xa Hoi); Hoa Hao Social Democratic Veterans' Group (Tap Doan Cuu Chien Si Hoa Hao Dan Xa); The People's Nation-Building Force (Luc Luong Nhan Dan Kien Quoc); Worker-Farmer party (Dang Cong Nong); Progressive Nationalist Movement (Phong Trao Cap Tien Quoc Gia); and Vietnam Unified Kuomintang (Viet Nam Quoc Dan Dang Thong Nhat).

10. Ha Thuc Ky had been a candidate for president in the 1967 election, joining a field of eleven, including Thieu. However, in 1969, he had taken the Revolutionary Dai Viet into the six-party National Socialist Revolutionary Alliance.

11. Song Than, June 27, 1973.

12. These parties were: Humanist (or Personalist) Socialist Revolutionary party (Nhan Xa Cach Mang Dang); Greater Unity Force (Luc Luong Dai Doan Ket); Progressive Nationalist Movement (Phong Trao Cap Tien Quoc Gia); Worker-Farmer party (Dang Cong Nong); Hoa Hao Social Democratic Veterans' Group (Tap Doan Cuu Chien Si Hoa Hao); Dai Viet Revolutionary party (Dai Viet Cach Mang Dang); Southern Section Kuomintang (VNQDD); National Salvation Front (Mat Tran Cuu Nguy Dan Toc); Vietnam Democratic party (Vietnam Dan Chu Xa Hoi Dang); League for Vietnam Reconstruction (Lien Minh Phuc Viet); New People's party (Dang Tan Dan); Democratic Freedom party (Dang Tu Do Dan Chu); Force for the Renaissance of the South (Luc Luong Phuc Hung Mien Nam); New Socialist party (Dang Tan Dan Xa); Unified Kuomintang (Quoc Dan Dang Thong Nhut); Vietnam Democratic party (Dang Dan Chu Vietnam); Vietnam

Buddhist Socialist Democratic party (Dang Dan Chu Xa Hoi Phat Giao Vietnam); Humanitarian Revolutionary party (Nhan Dan Cach Mang Dang); Republican Mass party (Dang Cong Hoa Dai Chung); Unified Social Democratic party (Dan Chu Xa Hoi Dang Thong Nhut); National Recovery party (Hung Quoc Dang); People's Nation-Building party (Dang Nhan Dan Kien Quoc); Force for the Unification of Vietnam Minority Ethnic Groups (Luc Luong Doan Ket Dan Thieu So Vietnam); Citizens' Rally (Tap Doan Cong Dan); Vietnam Quoc Dai party (Chanh Dang Vietnam Quoc Dai).

13. Howard R. Penniman, *Elections in South Vietnam* (Washington, D.C.: American Enterprise Institute for Public Policy Research, 1972), pp. 96-97; 111; in addition, as yet unreported data collected during 1972 and 1973 by the authors for separate studies of (1) candidates for the Lower House of the National Assembly by 1967 (sponsored by the Southeast Asia Development Advisory Group of the Asia Society) and (2) local village officials in eighteen villages of five provinces in central and South Vietnam.

14. Refer to Jerry M. Silverman, "South Vietnam: The Symbolic Nature of Election Campaign Appeals" *Journal of Southeast Asian Studies* 3 (March 1972), p. 44-62.

15. Minister of Health Tran Minh Tung (slate 1) and Minister of Foreign Affairs Tran Van Lam (slate 2).

16. Senators Le Van Dong, Pham Nhu Phien, and Tran Trung Dung and Deputies Phan Thong and Nguyen Van An.

17. Nguyen Van Dieu (Saigon) and Tran Tan Toan (Gia Dinh Province).

18. Although the youngest members of all slates were in their thirties (in order, from 1 to 4: 36, 35, 31, and 35 years of age), the oldest candidate in 3 was only 54, as compared with an average *oldest* age among the other three of 62. As compared with the average age of 38 for slate 3 (and indeed, 11 of its 16 members were 39 years of age or younger), those of slates 2 and 4 were both 48 years and that of slate 2 was 54.

19. Conclusive evidence that the central government intended and/or was able to successfully implement electoral fraud is not available to us. As in all national-level elections in South Vietnam, accusations of election fraud emanated from and were directed towards all participants.

20. For a full discussion, including aggregate analyses of four national elections during the period 1967 to 1973, refer to Jerry M. Silverman, "Political Presence and Electoral Support in South Vietnam," *Asian Survey* 14:5 (May 1974).

Prospects for Political Cohesion and Electoral Competition
John C. Donnell

In view of the authoritarian political tradition in the Republic of Vietnam, of which President Nguyen Van Thieu is just the latest practitioner, the reader has a right to ask whether the detailed attention given elections in this volume is relevant to the real distribution of power in the system. As Paul Mus cautioned Americans in 1965,

> Do not be hasty and do not believe that such a thing as the right to vote is the solution. It is the problem. It is a solution only in the long run. For the time being, you have the problem of convincing the Vietnamese that it is the solution.[1]

The contributors to the present volume generally would agree with Mus's statement. Professor Nguyen Ngoc Huy, for example, a practicing politician as well as a student of South Vietnamese politics, acknowledges that a certain amount of voting behavior here is pro-forma and/or coerced by government officials. But Professor Huy and the rest of the authors still consider the noncommunist political arena of South Vietnam to be relevant to the interplay of the major political forces, to be the locus of political change that has broadened political participation and the responsiveness of the political process.

In the present writer's view, some of the interpretations presented in this volume swing too far in the direction of claiming that the very occurrence of local and national elections on a regular schedule since 1967 proves that constitutional democracy has come to South Vietnam, particularly since some instances of genuine electoral competition can be cited. This kind of judgment is, of course, premature. An American writer who has regularly defended the South Vietnamese government's record has acknowledged that what has occurred is more aptly described as "predemocratic"—and there is no guarantee that it will necessarily develop beyond that.[2]

In contrast, some commentators consider a victory of the revolutionary forces so desirable, or at least inevitable, that they disdain studies of anti- and non-communist political forces and processes. Noting the exclusion of neutralist and pro-communist forces, the official, irregular pressures on electoral processes, and the obvious weaknesses of the non-communist groups, they dismiss much of the politics within the legal political arena of South Vietnam as of slight significance to the fate of the country.

A more reasonable approach lies between these two views. True, it must take into account that some of the old-line nationalist party factions are indeed relatively conservative and unreceptive to some of the strong contemporary demands for rapid political change; that many political "parties" are really only fragments or factions, based on tiny constituencies and clustered around leaders operating in highly personalistic style; and that many of the latter groups have not differed much from each other in terms of political ideals and programs, except sometimes in their regional focus. Thus, they have not really offered programmatic alternatives, and their political doctrines often have been based on a routine, often sterile anti-communism.

However, some wings of the older parties have become more forward looking under younger leadership in recent years, and they, along with some of the newer parties and new groups entering politics, such as the Buddhists and the comparatively liberal southern Catholics, have appeared to possess a new potential. This has led some observers to hope that a moderate, or "third force," group or alliance might develop a significant position on the political spectrum between Thieu's authoritarian, hard-line anti-communism on one hand and the communists on the other. Actually, "third force" is a misnomer here. The cohesion and strength denoted by the term *force* have been lacking and even the idea of a third political position has been somewhat erroneous because many of the groups loosely identified under this rubric actually have been in agreement with the Thieu government on goals and even many methods and disagreed only with the government's monopolizing of political power and shutting them out. It was hoped, however, that such a group might play a critical role in getting the two sides together and then helping to supply the political lubricant for a political settlement based on the principle of accommodation.

Events have turned out very differently. Fragmentation has persisted among the non-communist groups, and President Thieu has taken strong measures to mobilize electoral support under the banner of his new Democracy party and to force the already existing parties together into larger entities or out of existence. These policies have produced some new, unsteady amalgamations and left most of the moderate "oppositionists" dispirited. We will examine the impact of Thieu's policies on the political arena, with particular interest in the following questions: What are the prospects for greater cohesion among the non- and anti-communist groups and for more significant competition between them and the Democracy party?[3] Beyond this, what are the chances for directing some of the often lethal politico-military competition between communist and anti-communist forces into nonviolent institutional channels such as party competition and elections? Would the entry of the National Liberation Front-Provisional Revolutionary Government (NLF-PRG) into legal political participation in the arena controlled by the Republic of Vietnam be a disaster for the non-communist forces, including the moderates, or would it perhaps supply an impetus to cohesion among these groups?

Let us look first at the problem of fragmentation among the non-communist parties and specifically at the impact that might be produced on them by opening the legal arena to the NLF-PRG. Professor Nguyen Ngoc Huy theorizes about the possible coalescence of small anti-communist parties into broader "coalitions." At the time he prepared his paper, he believed the increasing role of elections would be conducive to the eventual emergence of a system of a government party and one or two opposition parties; if there were two of the latter, one would be relatively moderate and the other more leftist or "extreme." An earlier analysis by Huy had dealt more explicitly with the possible emergence of coalitions in the event of a political settlement that allowed overt NLF political participation. There he had predicted that the emergence in the legal arena of a left wing composed of the NLF and other "militant leftists" would stimulate anti-communist groups to unite, producing a sole party or league of them or perhaps two blocs: a right wing including "conservatives and ultra-rightists" and a center group of "radicals and moderates." The communists' possible resort to "murder and sabotage" would constitute a danger, but their participation in the open arena would provide a unique stimulus to non-communists to cooperate in the creation of larger political blocs and to gird themselves for the serious competition ahead by organization, planning, and programs.[4] So while

> the elimination of the communists from the political scene [would be] more reassuring for the future of the [non-communist] nationalists, it could retard the formation of large, well organized parties, especially if the leaders of pressure groups [attempted] to keep their members under their influence and prevent them from joining disciplined parties.[5]

This argument for legalizing the NLF as an opposition party had been espoused earlier, of course, and had a troubled history. The 1967 Constitution (Article 4) proscribed "every activity designed to publicize or carry out Communism," a blanket provision used by the government to take tough measures against oppositionists of various stripes along with those suspected of pro-communist activities. Truong Dinh Dzu, first runner-up in the presidential election of 1967, had been arrested that year (officially, for financial irregularities) after his campaign had called for negotiations with the communists, and he was rearrested in 1968 after telling foreign journalists he stood for legalization of the NLF as a party (and, implicitly at least, a coalition government).[6]

Then legal participation for the NLF was espoused most dramatically by a Thieu regime stalwart, Deputy Tran Ngoc Chau, an outstandingly successful province chief in the Delta and later leader of the government bloc in the Lower House. He was tried for antiregime activity in early 1970 and given a long prison sentence. The charges focused on his contacts with a brother working as a

North Vietnamese intelligence officer, but the government had been antagonized also by Chau's endorsement of negotiations with the communists and of admittance of the NLF to open political participation (though he opposed the idea of coalition government). Chau had predicted that if the Vietnamese government made certain concessions necessary to a negotiated settlement, the NLF would become "an open political party," whereupon the non-communist parties would be forced to reach agreements among themselves, "make mutual concessions and form an alliance to cope with it." This would bring "tense competition" between the two sides, but "precisely this competition" with "a serious adversary" would erase "all open or latent conflict due to religious and regional differences" among the non-communists. Chau predicted further, "In the new political struggle, the Army will no longer play the main [political] role, but the political parties, religions and the people will have to directly and totally resist the communists."[7]

This was extremely dangerous ground, for Thieu's intransigence toward communist legal participation was well-known. In July 1969 he had felt obliged by American pressure to offer the NLF electoral participation if they laid down their arms, but by 1970 he had formulated his "four no's," which now appear on signboards throughout the country, expressly rejecting such communist participation. These "four no's" are: no coalition with the communists, no neutralism (of a type dominated by the communists), no ceding of territory to the communists, and no open communist participation in the legal political system.

Curiously, Vice-President Nguyen Cao Ky, noted for his hawkishness but looking for possible sources of support in his intended candidacy in the presidential election of October 1971, told an American visitor that spring that he favored communist participation in the election, though he evidently did not attempt to publicize this view after reports of it were censored in the Saigon press. Ky was quoted as saying that if the communists "represent 10 or 15 percent of the people, then that's how much power they should get."[8]

However, international diplomatic exigencies were eroding Thieu's uncompromising position at least temporarily, as reflected by the January 25, 1972 joint announcement of the eight-point peace proposal by Presidents Nixon and Thieu. It urged that "all political forces in South Vietnam" be represented in an "independent body" to organize and run a new presidential election within six months of the agreement and that these forces be allowed to "participate in the election and present candidates" under international supervision. It also proposed that President Thieu and Vice-President Tran Van Huong resign one month before the election and turn authority over to a caretaker government, headed by the president of the Senate.

Thieu remained extremely sensitive about these points, and in the eventual cease-fire agreement signed a year later, all mention of his resignation was removed. With regard to NLF participation, there was simply a call for "genuinely free and democratic general elections" under international supervision to enable the "South Vietnamese people to decide themselves the political future of South Vietnam." The elections now were to be set up by a nonelective National Council of Reconciliation and Concord described only as comprising "three equal segments," presumably communist, anti-communist and neutralist, to be formed through consultations between the Saigon government and the communists.[9] In the sequel, of course, the two sides have failed to agree on establishing such a council, legal political participation has continued to be denied the communists, and the future of such elections appears hazier than when the cease-fire was signed.

The present writer was in South Vietnam in the period after the announcement of the Nixon-Thieu eight points of January 1972 and observed some interesting reactions in political circles there to this proposal for legalizing communist participation.[10] An optimistic, though tentative sense of new opportunity, tinged with anxiety, stirred among oppositionists, in contrast to the dread more common among government leaders (and becoming more widespread among politicians also after the communists launched their military offensive in late March).

In this changing atmosphere, various non-communist political groups began more systematic and determined efforts toward cooperation and merger. The Thieu government was not pleased with the talk about legalizing NLF participation, but for the time being it showed some forebearance, maintaining that now the people unavoidably must come to see that their own interests lay in supporting the government more strongly against the enemy.

The writer was able to query a couple of dozen Vietnamese politicians about their views on possible legalization of the NLF. Some of the answers were guarded and one was flatly negative, but the majority were positive. A prominent National Assembly figure with an earlier attachment to one of the old nationalist parties thought the non-communist parties still were too weak and fragmented to avoid destruction in competition with the NLF. Some active party leaders responded in such guarded, tentative ways as to indicate some doubt that they really believed their own basically positive statements. One well-known old-line party leader answered with such vibrant optimism, tinged with braggadocio, that it sounded like one of his periodic pep talks to his lower-level cadres instead of the more thoughtful, realistic analysis he might articulate to his higher-ranking confidants in the party. Another response was ominous: a leader of one of the old parties based in central Vietnam replied that yes, there would be an advantage in admitting NLF members to open political participation—it would make it easier for the anti-communists to mark them for extermination! Generally, though, this very small and unsystematic sounding of non-communist politicians revealed, along with varying degrees of anxiety, an expectedly great eagerness to see the kind of liberalization of Thieu government political controls that would be requisite to NLF participation and, along with this, a feeling that legal competition with the

NLF would provide them with opportunities for growth and be a real catalyst for cohesion among themselves.

In his paper in the present volume, Professor Huy has addressed an important aspect of the non-communists' potential for cohesion. He expressed the hope (as of late 1971) that President Thieu would proceed energetically to form a government party (as Thieu was preparing to do at the time) because Huy believed that broad-scale political mobilization of the people in preparation for electoral competition could be achieved only via this route. Huy's analysis of that period resembled that of Samuel P. Huntington, who had emphasized earlier that "where traditional political institutions are weak or non-existent, the prerequisite of stability is at least one highly institutionalized political party." Huntington, who stressed the need for concentrating on elite organizations before mass organizations, also said, "In modernizing systems, party institutionalization usually varies inversely with party competitiveness."[11] But Huy added the important qualification that Thieu would have to adopt a "franker, more open" stance of cooperation with able politicians if his party-building efforts were to draw popular support for a positive program of reconstruction and development. For if Thieu's party were narrow in outlook and composition, based only on the existing political leadership and the administrative bureaucracy, Huy predicted that it would use its power to coerce the opposition and would be politically ineffective.

Thieu's approach to the problem of building an anti-communist support base for electoral competition with the communists had centered originally on efforts to create an "alliance" or "front" of existing groups and, later, to lead a new political party of his own. Just after the 1968 Tet offensive, the first of a series of such alliances, the People's Front for National Salvation (Mat Tran Nhan Dan Cuu Nguy Dan Toc), was organized by Senator Tran Van Don and claimed to represent twenty-two political, religious, and professional groups.[12] Thieu was reported to have given it some support but its main thrust came from men who earlier had supported his principal political rival, Vice-President Nguyen Cao Ky.[13] The following month, March, Thieu's political-liaison specialist and secretary-general of the presidency, Nguyen Van Huong, launched a new party designed to generate mass support for Thieu, the Free Democratic Force (Luc Luong Tu Do va Dan Chu). In June, however, it was merged in a broader National Alliance for Social Revolution (Lien Minh Dan Toc Cach Mang Xa Hoi) also led by Nguyen Van Huong and including (and said by some to be led by) Senator Don's earlier People's Front for National Salvation.[14] Finally, in 1969, the most ambitious of these efforts occurred in an attempt at a six-party alliance, the National Social Democratic Front (Mat Tran Dan Chu Xa Hoi Quoc Gia), again led by Nguyen Van Huong and claiming to represent about 40 percent of the population on the basis of the 1967 election results.[15] It was given substantial government funds for its operations, but like the earlier formations, it suffered from internal squabbles, an ambivalent attitude toward it on the part of Thieu and the top leadership, and finally the fall from presidential favor of Nguyen Van Huong.[16]

During this period, Thieu also showed some sympathy to the organizing of two Catholic-led efforts to build neo-Can Lao parties, the Nhan Xa in 1968 and the Republican Mass in 1969, thereby arousing speculation that he might use them as mass-support vehicles.[17] However, he evidently considered them too limited in potential to suit his purposes, and some of their leaders evidently preferred not to become closely identified with Thieu.[18]

In the next period, which included the presidential campaign and election of 1971, Thieu did not try any further organizational experiments, preferring a more personal approach to the building of rural voting support for that election: he made helicopter visits to villages to preside over ceremonies for the distribution of aid items such as farm tools and machines, chatted with villagers about local problems, and addressed graduating classes of village officials at the Vung Tau training center. His organizational linkage with the peasantry continued to be confined to the bureaucracy.

After the cease-fire agreement was signed on January 27, 1973, signaling the onset of the "crunch" to mobilize the citizenry for participation in the eventual elections stipulated, Thieu assigned high priority to the building of a powerful government party, and very shortly he would deal forcefully with the plethora of existing parties. Now much began to be heard of the officially sponsored Democracy party (Dang Dan Chu), which had been projected since about late 1971 but had remained in the shadows, the subject of vague rumors. The new party would carry the regime's banner itself rather than constitute an amalgamation of previously existing parties, and it would adopt essentially the Ngo regime's Can Lao party strategy of recruiting government officials down through the administrative echelons all the way to the hamlet. Thieu had tried this briefly in 1968 on behalf of his Free Democratic Force, but now the government went all out. Officials claimed that membership was to be voluntary, so as to foster a dedicated, democratic spirit, but reports from the provinces described a mass recruitment campaign based on outright coercion and designed to enroll practically all civil servants and many military officers.

The prime movers of the party's organizational effort appeared to be the following officials in the presidency: Nguyen Van Ngan, who had succeeded the late Nguyen Cao Thang as Thieu's chief political agent for liaison and financial disbursements to politicians and National Assembly deputies; Hoang Duc Nha, a cousin and adopted nephew of Thieu's, who in 1972 gradually became his most trusted adviser (Nha was promoted that year from presidency press officer and personal secretary of the president to a cabinet-level post responsible for national press and communications matters); and Nguyen Van Ngai, charged with much of the actual party organizing, and who merged a minor party of his own, the Vietnam Democratic Force (Luc Luong Dan Chu Viet Nam), with the new one.

Recruiting had begun in earnest in early 1972. When the writer interviewed officials in the southern part of the country in that period, a considerable number said they had been told they must join the party or lose their jobs, so they were hurrying to comply. In central Vietnam, where the old nationalist parties were more firmly established, Democracy party expansion did not appear to put such immediate pressure on officials belonging to nonofficial parties.

Not long afterward, the government's political and administrative responses to the communist offensive of that spring began to impinge on political party activity and local elections. President Thieu proclaimed martial law on May 11, giving all civil authority to the military, and then got an emergency presidential powers bill through the Assembly by June 27, 1972, using manipulation and ruses, particularly against Lower House deputies, to obtain passage.[19]

On May 12, elections were temporarily suspended for province councils, village councils, and hamlet chiefs.[20] Province and district chiefs could now replace village and hamlet chiefs at their discretion, a measure described as counteracting increased NLF political activity in the villages attendant on the communist military offensive. All local officials were to be screened within two months, and any found "unqualified, negative" or lacking in "anti-communist achievements" would be removed."[21]

However, the government decided not long afterward that the communists' political inroads at the local level had not been so extensive after all and restored the village council elections in May 1973. Government spokesmen even claimed that candidates did not necessarily have to belong to the Democracy party. However, information on the nature of these candidacies since the resumption of elections is still scanty.[22] It is significant that Thieu government pressure on the electoral process at the local level had begun even before the spring 1972 offensive, when members of regular political parties unwilling to join the Democracy party were already complaining that government officials were rejecting their candidacies for village and hamlet elections.[23]

This period saw greatly stepped up recruiting for the Democracy party, and by the fall of 1972 district chiefs were pressing village and hamlet administrative staffs to sign the party rosters en masse even when the recruits seemed to know little about the party.[24]

Eventually, even the Revolutionary Development program conducted by cadre teams in the countryside was refocused on recruiting and organizing villagers for the Democracy party. Ordinarily assigned to help farmers in organizing self-help reconstruction projects and applying for government credit, the 22,000 RD cadres now were spending most of their time in recruitment, political indoctrination lectures, and compilation of surveys on probable voting tendencies among the rural population. This brought a revamping of the cadre training and even a shake-up of the top RD leadership: Colonel Nguyen Be, the Vung Tau camp commandant, who enjoyed wide prestige among the cadres and American and other observers, opposed this policy change and was fired, a change foreshadowed in April when one of the party's leading organizers had been named new Minister of Revolutionary Development.[25]

By this time, the party was said to have 700,000 members, and its mass recruitment campaigns in the rural areas swept in government personnel down to even the unpaid self-defense unit members in the villages. In at least some instances, villagers were reporting that failure to attend party activities could result in such punishment as confiscation of identity cards.[26]

Labor union leaders were coming under similar pressure, and after half a dozen leaders of small unions had been so detained in May, it was even alleged that the government was arresting and imprisoning some union leaders to accelerate party recruitment. One of the leaders died in prison under mysterious circumstances, possibly from the effects of torture.[27]

Clearly, the bulk of the party's burgeoning membership was made up of government jobholders and farmers subjected to heavy-handed recruiting. Civil servants and politicians joining in the capital included opportunists of a type described wryly by President Thieu's close adviser Hoang Duc Nha as trying to get in on the ground floor by "joining the politburo," as they jocularly referred to the party. Asked how he believed the party could avoid becoming dominated by routine-minded functionaries and self-seekers flocking in simply to protect their careers and use the party's assets to personal advantage, Nha replied cryptically that the government anticipated it probably would have to use a secret inner core of the most dedicated members to guard against such potential opportunism and corruption.[28]

This massive, often indiscriminate recruiting recalled the Ngo government's practices with its National Revolutionary Movement and, later, with its Republican Youth, but now the possibility arose that the Democracy party would attempt to become a combination of mass party and some kind of clandestine inner vanguard group, the equivalent of the Ngo mass organizations plus the semisecret Can Lao which was supposed to comprise more dedicated persons keeping tabs on the political loyalty and administrative efficiency of government employees, politicians, and others.[29] Thieu's thus became the first post-Ngo regime to return to the general outlines of the organizational model adapted by the Ngos from the Vietnamese communist system, with its complementary relationship of an elite vanguard party and mass organizations. The earlier governments after 1963 had disdained this model as too recently and negatively associated with the Ngos; and then, particularly from 1967 on, the growth of more spontaneous, unofficial political party activity had further strengthened the tendency away from such a concept. Interestingly enough, even the Democracy party's flag suggested this imitative process, for it used the flag design of the Democratic Republic of Vietnam in the North but reversed the colors to feature a red star on yellow field. Possibly the designers of the Democracy party flag calculated that it could bring in some votes for the government from relatively unsophisticated or confused citizens with pro-NLF sympathies in an eventual electoral competition with the communists. But too much importance should not be attributed to the flag design, because nationalist parties typically have featured stars of various colors on their party banners.

Rather than emphasize their debt to the communist organizational inspiration, two of Thieu's closest advisers stressed that the party system of South Korea appeared more appropriate to South Vietnam's needs than other models.[30] This was indicative of Thieu's interest in strengthening the Democracy party and decreasing the limited political competitiveness the nonofficial parties had enjoyed. For the South Korean is a dominant party system in which opposition parties never have challenged successfully the ruling party's monopoly of power.[31]

The Democracy party appeared to ride even more roughshod over existing citizen loyalties to other parties than had the Ngo regime's organizations and those of the earlier Thieu years by simply demanding that all members renounce previous affiliations. (The party law of June 1969 also had required this, but only on paper; considerable interlinkage of groups and of loose clusters of their members actually was tolerated unofficially.) This caused great anxiety among leaders of other parties and particularly the moderate Progressive National Movement (Phong Trao Cap Tien Quoc Gia), which was composed mainly of government officials, the prime recruitment target of the new party.

Then, on December 27, 1972, just before the expiration of his emergency powers, Thieu drastically compressed the political atmosphere by handing down Decree 060, which required parties to reorganize on a nationwide scale or be dissolved.[32] (In the same period, the government also decreed tighter regulations on almost all other kinds of associations.)[33] This brought strong protests from the existing parties and, through ancillary decrees of May 1973, the dissolution of twenty-six previously legal parties, leaving only the Democracy party plus two new amalgamations of older groups.

One of these new formations was Catholic, the Freedom party (Dang Tu Do), composed of the Nhan Xa, the Greater Solidarity Force, and others, and it was composed largely of politically conservative elements within the Catholic faith. The other new formation, the Democratic Socialist Alliance (Lien-Minh Dan-Chu Xa-Hoi), was constructed by seven former parties chartered under the 1969 party law.[34] Some two dozen political groups and factions thus were combined in the three new parties, but a number of others were left out in the cold (at least one of which promptly threatened to go underground).[35]

The Democratic Socialist Alliance was led by one of the seven groups ostensibly fused within it, the Worker-Farmer party, political arm of the largest labor union, the Vietnam Labor Confederation, or CVT. This party had been meeting regularly for a year in an attempt at merger with two other alliance components, the Progressive Nationalist Movement and the Revolutionary Dai Viet. In addition, the alliance also included a faction of the VNQDD and two factions of the Hoa Hao, three of which also had been meeting for over a year in efforts to get together. Thus, the new party law did seem to provide a final, forcible impetus to some of these groups to coalesce. However, among the parties divested of legal standing were some from the Hoa Hao, the badly fragmented Cao Dai and several factions of the VNQDD; and groups left unrepresented included the An Quang Buddhists and also ex-General Duong Van Minh and his associates. As Tai and Silverman note, efforts to form a fourth amalgamation of parties were continuing as they wrote in October 1973 but these have not borne fruit.

The loosely-knit Buddhists had tried to found a party, the present writer learned during field interviewing in March-April 1972, but were unable to produce one before the deadline. Some Buddhist leaders have claimed that they are able to exert a sufficient impact on politics without forming a party and indeed that they consider their direct sponsorship of a political party inappropriate for their religious movement. However, it appeared that the absence of a Buddhist-sponsored party from the scene was due chiefly to the more mundane difficulties of conciliating various leaders and factions and obtaining agreement on how such a party should be organized and led.

The Democracy party was inaugurated, with Thieu as chairman, on March 29, 1973, and Thieu emphasized that it would fill the need for a "ruling party" and would "control the administration." He formally acknowledged the role of political parties in developing political support, expressed the hope that a bipartisan party system would take root, and predicted that the formation of the government party would stimulate the opposition to unify itself further.[36]

Thieu sought to impose still further restrictions on parties in a new Senate election law drafted in the spirit of the party law, but the version finally passed on June 8 contained compromises between the president and Assembly softening and delaying its application until 1976. However, the bill then would require party endorsement for all slates running for the Senate and a 2 million piastre deposit from each slate filing for candidacy.[37]

Then, as Tai and Silverman relate, stratagems by the government and hesitancy and perhaps bumbling by the oppositionists resulted in a complete lack of opposition participation in the 1973 Senate election four days later. All four slates filing by the deadline were progovernment, and the platforms of the first two were even identical to that of the Democracy party.[38] The predictable result was that for the first time Thieu gained really firm control over the Senate, which, in contrast to the Lower House, had not been easily manipulable by a reliable majority of his own.[39] In this first election under the new party law, there was less competition between government and opposition than in any previous one since the Ngo era, but the reluctance of oppositionists to participate was due largely to the exceptional uncertainties injected into the situation by the June 13 Paris Joint Communiqué designed to make the January cease-fire agreement more effective. For the oppositionists anticipated that the communiqué might strengthen the January agreement's provisions for new general elections in ways negating the value of the scheduled Senate elections.

Furthermore, a number of oppositionists, especially from the An Quang and General Minh groups, hoped to become members of the neutralist segment of that three-way body to be formed to carry out those elections, the National Council for National Reconciliation and Concord.

The parties yielding to fusion in the new alliance had been anti-communist and therefore generally cooperative with the government, but they long had desired more political leeway. Many of their leaders and rank and file expressed resentment of the government's pressure on them to coalesce—but even as they did, they continued to deplore the chronic fragmentation of the non-communist parties, for they recognized their own weaknesses.

The Democratic Socialist Alliance appeared to be a particularly artificial political growth. Severely compressed within an arbitrary time span had been the vital incubation processes of exploratory negotiations between factions and parties and the preliminary testing of organizational links starting with coopera- tion in small projects to generate the beginnings of mutual trust. And the vital experience of expanding rudimentary cooperation through genuinely challeng- ing, at least somewhat competitive, ventures in the electoral arena did not appear to be in the offing at all.

The forces for cohesion were still weak or only latent among these groups, which languished, dispirited, in a state of impotence. A prominent Lower House Deputy, Tran Van Tuyen, remarked that the opposition was "not a third force. It is just a political position—a third segment—and a potential third force."[40] They felt a heightened sense of danger from the communists after the Paris accords, but not the kind of urgency that could knit them together. Not only were they weaker than before against Thieu's divide-and-control tactics, but ironically, some of them felt even more reluctant to challenge Thieu seriously. As the outspoken Catholic oppositionist deputy Ho Ngoc Nhuan put it, "Now we are facing the communists directly, so the opposition should be more cau- tious in its activities."[41]

A sense of urgency capable of inducing cohesion among the oppositionists could perhaps be generated by genuine prospects for winning power through cooperative effort within the anti-communist system controlled so firmly by Thieu. Another powerful motive for cohesion, as suggested earlier, would be that of survival in the face of impending competition with the tough and dis- ciplined NLF. And this competition, despite its obvious dangers, was viewed as desirable by many of these strongly anti-communist politicians, who there- fore wanted early execution of the Paris Accords provisions legally guarantee- ing it.[42]

But these two hypothetical incentives remained only remote possibilities. The oppositionists had had little enough chance to win power, and now that Thieu had further restricted the arena of competition by fiat, they were so subordinate as to be almost superfluous. As for political competition with the NLF, Thieu's approach still was mainly one of suppression, and the limited competition envisaged was to be pretty exclusively the domain of his own Democracy party. The way was clear for the party, with its huge, mostly indiscriminately enrolled "paper" membership led by civil servants and government agents to monopolize political participation, but the party was likely to exhibit the flimsiness of the Ngo regime's organizations, which had been similarly constructed.

Among the grave difficulties involved in Thieu's arbitrary course, a major one was the regime's self-deception in prolonging its own unpreparedness for real political competition particularly in the rural areas. As the Tai-Silverman analysis shows, it is precisely in the critical rural sector that the government has registered its greatest formal electoral strength while the NLF-PRG obviously has its greatest support here also. As for the urban areas, an election free enough to record actual political tendencies probably would be dominated by non-communists opposing both the government and NLF-PRG.[43]

South Vietnamese governments since 1954 have counted on major electoral support from the rural areas, in view of the lesser support they could expect from the cities and towns, where personal anonymity and individual freedom from political and administrative harassment is greater. In the 1973 Senate elections, as Tai and Silverman report, Thieu again was able to rack up large vote totals in these rural constituencies. However, as these authors suspect, such voting "support" masked considerable political indifference and, this writer believes, weak to moderate opposition, though the regime's electoral controls generally have been able to produce compliant voting behavior.

But how likely was the political competition between government and NLF-PRG to culminate in a national election free enough to register the actual strengths of such political forces, as stipulated by the Paris Accords? The two sides had taken opposing tacks on elections: the Republic government, after initial repulsion to the idea of elections, had swung around and demanded that a presidential election be held first and as soon as possible, considering its chances better to foreclose effective NLF participation under early rather than later elections; and the NLF wanted the first election to be for a Constituent Assembly that would draft a new constitution and proceed from there to reshape the government. The two sides were intransigent in holding to these conflicting demands, so it appeared that perhaps another large-scale military confrontation would occur before any further conciliation was possible.

The more likely form of political competition in the shorter run would be that of less spectacular, prolonged politicomilitary struggle. Both sides clearly were working to consolidate their authority in the rural areas, the NLF with more apparent effectiveness. It was aided in this by its widened access to those regions provided it by the 1972 communist offensives. The Thieu government's policy toward the unofficial political parties, especially in central Vietnam, amounted therefore to writing off as irrelevant or expendable some actual and potential allies in non-communist regional and local organizations that had demonstrated that in the contemporary, rudimentary stage of non-communist political organization they possessed some real, though limited, capacities to mobilize villagers. And these groups had the potential, given reasonable encouragement, to develop additional active support and swing it to the government side, despite their parochial, sometimes warlord-like tendencies, which bothered the Saigon government most.

This rural support of the anti-communist nationalist parties even had a military dimension, for such parties as the VNQDD had, since 1964-65, maintained a considerable military presence in some central Vietnam provinces by placing their cadres in the Regional Forces (RF, Dia Phuong Quan) and particularly in the Popular Forces (PF, Nghia Quan, also sometimes referred to as the militia). This was done mainly to protect party members and sympathizers from the kind of repression suffered earlier from the Ngos.[44] Some of these units had acquitted themselves surprisingly well during the 1972 communist offensives, even against North Vietnamese regulars. Now, however, there were signs that the discouragement felt by the nationalist parties because of aggressive Democracy party expansion was depressing military morale in these units as well.[45]

In conclusion, then, the government was not likely to strengthen its capabilities for political mobilization of rural and other support by organizing its official party or by attempting to produce cooperative, dynamic, political bedfellows within the surviving "opposition" parties. It was possible that some of the politicians whom the regime had succeeded in pushing into close quarters with one another might learn to subordinate some factional interests to broader ones and work out some limited modes of cooperation. But the regime clearly had restricted even further the range of political participants and of debatable political issues. This would increase the superficiality and irrelevance of much of the officially tolerated politics with regard to the important questions of war and peace. Legal political activity would tend even more to be the restricted, manipulated preserve of President Thieu and his military and other backers. And it would constitute essentially window dressing within the context of the larger South Vietnam political arena in which the conflict between the real political forces, including the communists, ground on outside institutionalized political channels at a murderous level of violence.

Notes

1.   Paul Mus, "Cultural Backgrounds of Present Problems," a fall 1965 lecture to the Asia Society, New York, published in *Asia*, no. 4 (Winter 1966). p. 12.

2.   Gerald L. Steibel, "The Presidential Election," *Focus on Vietnam*, New York: American Friends of Vietnam, Reprint No. 12, October 1971.

3. The problem of cohesion has been discussed extensively elsewhere. John T. McAlister, *Viet Nam, Origins of Revolution* (New York: Knopf, 1969) gives useful historical perspective on the problem. Some works dealing with more recent manifestations of it include Charles A. Joiner, "Patterns of Political Party Behavior in South Vietnam," *Journal of Southeast Asian History*, March 1967, pp. 83-98; Peter King, "The Political Balance in Saigon," *Pacific Affairs*, Fall 1971, pp. 401-20; Allan E. Goodman, *Politics in War, the Bases of Political Community in South Vietnam*, (Cambridge: Harvard Univ. Press, 1973); and the present writer's *Vietnam: The Politics of Manipulation*, forthcoming.

4. Nguyen Ngoc Huy, "Political Parties in Viet-Nam," *Viet-Nam Bulletin* (Republic of Vietnam Embassy, Washington, D.C.), 5:1 (January 4, 1971) pp. 1-7 (note especially pp. 6-7); *Les Partis Politiques au Viet Nam*, Saigon: Vietnamese Association for the Development of International Relations, n.d., 18 pp. (note especially pp. 11-14). These items are only slightly different versions (the second is more detailed) of a lecture to the Association on November 16, 1970. Huy emphasized very pointedly in the latter article the cohesive impact of this on the non-communist parties: "The officially authorized presence of the NLF will cause the nationalist parties to unite. The formation of blocs of parties thus will be greatly facilitated" (p. 13, trans. by the present writer).

5. Ibid., p. 14 (trans. by the present writer).

6. Keesing's Contemporary Archives, South Vietnam: *A Political History, 1954-1970*, New York: Scribners, 1970, pp. 134-35.

7. Chau's espousal of accommodation with the NLF, including election of a minority of NLF representatives to village and province councils and the National Assembly, freedom for NLF candidates to compete for other offices, and a general election for the reunification of North and South within ten years, is presented in U.S. Senate, Committee on Foreign Relations, *Vietnam: Policy and Prospects, 1970, Hearings on Civil Operations and Rural Support Program*, February and March 1970, pp. 369–70.

   Chau admitted having held a series of conversations with his communist brother from 1965 to 1969 but claimed he had reported these to the Vietnamese and American governments. Another factor in Thieu's hostility toward Chau was his sharp criticism of a presidential aide, Nguyen Cao Thang, for bribing national assemblymen.

8. *The Washington Evening Star* of April 29, 1971 carried an Associated Press report from Saigon that Ky had made this statement to Los Angeles businessman Harold Willens, member of a party headed by Congressman Paul McCloskey, which made a twelve-day visit to Vietnam. Ky appears to have been grasping desperately for issues and support at that time, and no further statements of this position were heard from him later.

9. For the eight-point proposal of the American and South Vietnamese govern-
ments and Hanoi's counteroffer of a nine-point proposal, see Henny Giniger,
"Hanoi Discloses Peace Proposals It Made in Paris," and "Hanoi Communi-
que Disclosing Peace Plans Offered at Private Sessions," *The New York
Times*, February 1, 1972. See also Bernard Gwertzman, "U.S. Plays Down
Reports of Discord with Saigon," ibid., February 9, 1972.

Terms of the January 27, 1973 "Agreement on Ending the War and
Restoring Peace in Vietnam" are contained in a U.S. Department of State,
Bureau of Public Affairs News Release of January 24, 1973.

It was revealed that the American and South Vietnamese governments
had offered their eight-point proposal to the North Vietnamese in Paris the
preceding July, and though Hanoi claimed there were some discrepancies
in the version presented it then and that disclosed by President Nixon on
January 25, 1972, the two versions agreed on the points focused upon here:
the participation of all political forces in new national elections and President Thieu's resignation one month before them. So Thieu had been under
pressure from Washington since at least July to accept the idea of legal
communist political participation.

10. The writer was studying non-communist political organizations on a grant
from the Southeast Asia Development Advisory Group (SEADAG) of the
Asia Society, New York, which, of course, is not responsible for the
author's views presented here. Systematic research findings will be published later.

11. Samuel P. Huntington, "Political Development and Political Decay," *World
Politics*, 17:3 (1965). Quotes are from pp. 25-27. Huntington added,
"Modernizing states with multiparty systems [and this would include
South Vietnam] are much more unstable and prone to military interven-
tion than modernizing states with one party, with one dominant party, or
with two parties" (loc. cit.).

Huntington saw fit to omit most of the last few pages of this article in
Chap. 1 (bearing the same title as the article) of his later book, *Political
Order in Changing Societies*, (New Haven: Yale University Press, 1968).
Hence, only the first of these three quotes appears there (p. 91).

12. Allan E. Goodman, "South Vietnam: Neither War nor Peace," *Asian
Survey*, 10:1 (February 1970), p. 128.

13. See, for instance, Peter King, "The Political Balance in Saigon," *Pacific
Affairs*, 44 (Fall 1971) p. 402.

14. Allan E. Goodman, op. cit.

15. Ibid.

16. Tai and Silverman note in their paper in this volume that it could not agree
on candidates to run in the 1970 Senate elections. Peter King points out
that there also were Hoa Hao defections from it in 1970 (King, loc. cit.).

17. The full names of these are, respectively, the Personalist (or Humanist) Socialist Revolutionary party (Nhan-Xa Cach Mang Dang), and the Republican Mass party (Dang Cong Hoa Dai Chung).

18. Elizabeth Pond, "The Fading of the Neo-Can Lao Party," New York: Alicia Patterson Fund, Newsletter EP-2, October 1969, p. 4. (The second party originally was called the Great Masses Force.)

19. Jerry M. Silverman, "South Vietnam and the Elusive Peace," *Asian Survey*, 13:1 (January 1973), pp. 32-34 describes some of the manipulation involved in securing passage of the bill, which gave Thieu extraordinary authority in the fields of defense, security, economics, and finance.

20. Ibid., p. 35. Village chiefs were still to be elected, but now this increasingly authoritative post would be diminished by the fact that the village council as well as the hamlet chiefs would be appointed by the province chief and all would be more completely dependent than ever on the province and district chief for financial and other support.

21 Craig R. Whitney, "Thieu Abolishes Democracy in Hamlets," New York Times News Service, *Rutland* (Vt.) *Herald*, Sept. 7, 1972. Government sources claimed that many hamlet chiefs had turned out to be communist agents aiding the enemy.

   The abolition of these elections was regularized by an August 22 decree reducing the number of village and hamlet officials (Jerry M. Silverman, loc. cit.).

   Actually, Thieu had indicated as early as August 1971 his preference for abolishing hamlet chief elections (ibid., p. 35) and the present writer had learned from the American Embassy in Saigon in February 1972 of his intention to do it soon.

22. Fox Butterfield, "Saigon Resuming Local Elections," *The New York Times*, March 17, 1973; "Saigon Sends 196 Back to Vietcong," ibid., May 8, 1973.

23. *Cap Tien*, February 27, 1972 and a two-part series by Minh Thao and Tran Can Nam, *"Tinh Trang Dang Phai O Lam Dong Khi Dang Tong Thong Thieu Banh Truong"* (Situation of the Political Parties in Lam Dong as President Thieu's Party Expands), *Song Than*, March 28-29, 1972.

24. Fox Butterfield, "Thieu Presses Formation of a New Political Party," *The New York Times*, Nov. 18, 1972.

25. Fox Butterfield, "Village Cadres Now Aid Thieu Party," ibid., June 12, 1973. The new Minister was Nguyen Van Ngai, who sought to denigrate Col. Be by charges of embezzlement. Col. Be's replacement was Col. Quach Huynh Ha.

26. Ibid.

27. Fox Butterfield, "Union Leader Dies in Vietnam Prison," ibid., July 4, 1973.

28. Personal interview of March 1972.
29. For an analysis of the Ngo regime's political organizations and a comparison
    of its approach to the organizing of political support with that of President
    Thieu through early 1970, see John C. Donnell, "Expanding Political Parti-
    cipation: the Long Haul from Villagism to Nationalism," *Asian Survey*,
    10:8 (August 1970); and for a depth treatment of this, including the role
    of Thieu's Democracy party, see my *Vietnam: The Politics of Manipula-
    tion* (forthcoming).
        In this period, two Saigon dailies (*Chinh Luan*, Feb. 11 and *Song
    Than*, Feb. 17, 1972) reported noncommittally on a *Newsweek* magazine
    item of February 14, 1972, p. 15, describing the new party in essentially
    the above terms. It predicted that Thieu would use "another secret organ-
    ization. . . to enforce party discipline" and remarked, "This structure,
    already in covert form, looks dangerously like the repressive and clandes-
    tine Can Lao 'party' " set up by the Ngos earlier.
30. Personal interviews with Hoang Duc Nha and Nguyen Phu Duc in Saigon,
    March, 1972. Incidentally, these informal remarks were made some six
    months before President Chung Hee Park declared martial law in *that*
    country on October 19, 1972.
31. South Korean elections feature the organization of essentially symbolic
    mass political participation to lend formalistic legitimization to authori-
    tarian rule. And there, as in South Vietnam, electoral participation is
    much higher in rural areas and lower in the urban, where many of the
    relatively well educated, younger citizens have been politically alienated.
    C.I. Eugene Kim, Youngwha Kihl, and Doock-kyou Chung, "Voter Turnout
    and the Meaning of Elections in South Korea," *Asian Survey*, 13:11 (Nov-
    ember 1973), pp. 1062–74, especially pp. 1073–74.
32. See the Tai-Silverman chapter in this volume. Briefly, a party had to
    organize chapters in at least half the forty-four provinces and/or the ten
    autonomous cities, and in these places it had to set up branches in at least
    one-quarter of the villages and city wards. It had to roster a membership
    of at least 5 percent of the voters in each province and city where it had
    branches. Finally, it had to nominate candidates in all National Assembly
    elections, and its candidates had to win at least 20 percent of the seats in
    any Lower House election and 20 percent of the votes cast in a Senate
    election. Optionally, it could also nominate candidates in presidential
    elections, but if it did so, its slate had to win at least 20 percent of votes
    cast.
33. National associations were obliged to have at least one hundred members
    and those operating at only the city or provincial level were required to
    have at least fifty or go out of existence. "Thieu Fixes Curbs on Clubs,"
    The New York Times, January 7, 1973.

34. "Saigon Catholic Group Forms Pro-Government Political Party," ibid., January 5, 1973. For further details, see the Tai-Silverman chapter in this volume and also "Peace Candidate Freed by Saigon," *The New York Times*, March 30, 1973.

35. The group threatening to go underground apparently was one of the VNQDD factions. (CBS morning newscast from Saigon heard in the U.S. on April 4, 1973). These excluded groups are discussed further below.

36. See the Tai-Silverman chapter for further details of this statement.

37. Ibid. This deposit was equivalent to about U.S. $4234 at the then current rate of exchange.

38. The first two slates were headed by cabinet ministers whom Thieu had asked to take leave of absence to perform this task, namely Dr. Tran Minh Tung, minister of public health and also secretary-general of the Democracy party, and Tran Van Lam, foreign minister. Joseph B. Treaster, "Candidates All Pro-Thieu in Senate Race," *The New York Times*, August 7, 1973.

39. James M. Markham, "Saigon Reports Big Vote Turnout," ibid., August 27, 1973.

40. David K. Shipler, "Thieu's Non-Communist Opponents Say They Feel Powerless," ibid., September 15, 1973.

41. Ibid.

42. Ibid. See also the account of the present writer's 1972 interviews on this subject in Saigon, supra.

43. This analysis is further developed in a manuscript by Jerry M. Silverman, a shortened version of which appeared as "South Vietnam and the Return to Political Struggle," *Asian Survey*, 14:1 (January, 1974).

44. Data from field research conducted by the writer in 1972.

45. James M. Markham, "After 11 Months of Battles Since Truce, Saigon Troop Morale Is Sagging Badly," *The New York Times*, December 14, 1973.

Appendix

The Role of Elections in Vietnamese Political Development: Seminar Report
Charles A. Joiner

The first seminar topic concerned influences of Vietnamese political culture upon the election process. Cultural effects on individual and group perceptions of elections as legitimate avenues for leadership selection were analyzed. Walter Slote's "Intra-Familial Dynamics and Their Implication for Vietnamese Politics" reported on his study of familial influence as a personal acculturation process affecting individual orientations toward relationships with "relevant" others, including those involved in political processes. The Slote thesis assumed various Vietnamese familial influences upon political socialization: siblings repress adverse sentiments towards parents, especially toward the father, the principal object of authority and deference; anger is deflected toward nonpurent objects, first in childhood but continuing through adulthood; delayed independence of children affects male self-perceptions so they may never lose their sense of the father's authority and never view themselves as men in their own right.

The political consequence, Slote observed, is seen in ambivalence of many political personalities in roles of authority, an ambivalence seen in swings between extremes and by arbitrary (and stern but benign Confucianist) use of authority. Further, for all Vietnamese, the nation is equated with an extension of the family. Avoidance of direct, open confrontation, e.g., in the form of political party rivalries, and a uniquely Vietnamese propensity for martyrdom, or self-sacrifice to manipulate others as a political tactic, are reflections of familial behaviors discouraging sibling rivalry. These familial influences are products of a cultural system more difficult to revolutionize than the nation's political structure. This has social and political repercussions in a nation attempting to integrate values associated with familial norms of respect and deference with values associated with modernizing effort.

Stephen Young's paper, "The Mandate and Political Competition in Vietnam," was presented next.

Milton Sacks's presentation was "Problems of Representative Government in Vietnam." While agreeing that cultural variables affect potential for success of representative government, Sacks said legitimacy in the Third World (including Vietnam) is confirmed only by electoral processes. This refutes the argument that military dictatorship or totalitarianism is necessary for development in these cases. Representative government is a significant mechanism for getting things done and for stability. It provides the only ground for resolution of crises situations, i.e., a bargaining arena. The important question is whether electoral processes are only plebiscites whereby power-holders use the mechanism, as did

173

Ngo Dinh Diem, and Nguyen Van Thieu in 1971, to provide a formalistic mandate from the society or whether real choices are offered concerning issues. The latter will occur in Vietnam only when there is real opposition with real rights to contest elections. Lack of legitimacy for political parties as institutions and continued high incidence of political violence have lessened chances for real choices.

Despite this and ancillary problems, such as the regional character of much of the nation's election of most candidates by pluralities rather than majorities, plethora of candidates, and the fact the 1971 presidential election (unlike previous legislative elections) would have been fixed even if it had been contested, there are nonetheless signs representative government may become a viable institution. The efficiency of much electoral administration is a fact. Electoral experiences have performed socialization functions to the extent that all Vietnamese political leaders must recognize electoral processes as established institutional phenomena.

True representative government, according to Sacks, will be possible only when there is more of a balance between the presidency and the legislature. Such a balance will not require strict separation of powers, partly because there is consensus that a presidential system with commensurate executive authority is appropriate for Vietnam (a point stressed by varied interest groups when the Constitution was written). This does not change the fact that a definite imbalance exists in the Vietnamese political system. Thieu's actions have damaged the legislative process, and as development of representative government is of the first order of importance, a reordering of the balance of power is essential. To an extent, the functional role of legislators is now recognized; it has resulted in some improved administration and in establishing links between representatives and their constituencies. If legislators were elected by majority rather than plurality vote and if opposition groups institutionalized their positions, chances for a more balanced polity would be improved. Representative government has made advances under the present constitutional system. Even pro-Thieu personalities criticized the 1971 one-man presidential election in their need to defend the system itself. Once there is greater legislative (and judicial) responsibility vis-à-vis the executive, there can be opportunity for effective representative government.

Analyses of the Slote, Young, and Sacks positions stressed several points. First, Ithiel de Sola Pool noted, presidential elections, while a "new tradition" in Vietnam, were inconsistent with Vietnamese cultural attributes that attempt to disguise conflict and avoid direct confrontation, something incompatible with a winner-take-all electoral process. Few nations have adopted an electoral form of gladiatorial combat; most have opted for indirect selection of the chief executive and top leadership. Presidential selection by a parliamentary method would be more harmonious with tradition.

Second, granting the significance of culture in political behavior, Douglas

Pike questioned the uniqueness of this influence in Vietnam. Emphasis on the virtue of the ruler is also Jeffersonian. The two worlds of tradition and modern politics, which Vietnamese political figures walk into and out of daily, are witnessed elsewhere also, perhaps everywhere.

Third, Senator Tran Quang Thuan observed that one presumably culturally affected phenomenon frequently considered significant, the phenomenon of "face," has been overemphasized. General Duong Van Minh, for example, did not withdraw from the 1971 presidential election because he feared losing "face." He was willing to lose. His decision was based upon objective facts of known unfair electoral practices in the provinces and of Thieu's refusal to make specific policy and personnel changes (province chiefs, foreign service officers) prior to the election.

He also questioned existence of a uniquely Vietnamese style of politics, although the mandate and communal autonomy with village elders making policy have historically been prominent factors. Recent history has shown an effective wedding of democracy and historical precedents is possible at the village level and freely elected bodies can function effectively there. The success of the village example can be emulated at the province level.

Fourth, Professor Nguyen Ngoc Huy emphasized the transitional nature of contemporary Vietnamese politics, which are moving from a Confucianist to a modern-democratic basis. While the population can choose leaders, psychologically and materially democracy is not yet possible. His political party, the Progressive Nationalist Movement (PNM), has adopted the strategy of attempting to improve things within the system (one tactic of which was supporting Thieu in 1971) in order to effect real power and attain progressive government based upon a balance between tradition and democracy.

The second broad subject was "Electoral Behavior in Vietnam Since the Mid-Sixties." With nine national elections from 1967 to 1971, and a series of local elections, important experiences have been accumulated by political figures and the electorate. There was general agreement that these experiences affected political development, particularly political party development, although party weakness was considered a deficiency in the political picture.

A summary of the nine national elections was presented by Theresa Tull in "Elections from 1967 to 1971—An Overview." Local elections were then analyzed by Richard Ehrlich's "Village and Hamlet Elections as a Means of Political Socialization." Two of his major hypotheses were: village as a basis for popular participation had come full cycle in Vietnamese history after Diem; and five groups (Viet Minh-NLF, Buddhists, Catholics, Hoa Hao, and Cao Dai) have been the only forces in recent Vietnamese history with genuine local constituencies. The historic assumption of village autonomy with its underlying base of collective responsibility had been undermined by the French and by the Diem regime, and peasants were prepared to opt for an alternative form of governance. For many the Viet Minh provided such an option, but to adherents of the other four groups their own institutions provided an alternative. Political parties had little opportunity to evolve. The big five continue to have distinct advantages in electoral competition: village organization, village-district-province-national-level hierarchies (the Hoa Hao has leadership for each level), ability to recruit leaders at the village level and provide certain upward mobility for them, a policy of welcoming adherents without regard to socio-economic status, and a devotion to specific ethical value systems.

Ehrlich asserted each of the five can perform all political functions (socialization and recruitment, communication, aggregation, and rule making-application-adjudication) especially at the village level where such functions are considered legitimate and relevant by most Vietnamese. In fact, there are no effective new village councils not tied to one of the five. Because of these roles, a built-in village system for accommodating ex-officials and defeated candidates, and increased powers granted village councils in financial and security matters, local elections are becoming increasingly meaningful for villagers. If provincial elections follow the village pattern, the present system based on military appointment will be undermined. If military personnel continue to assume dominant provincial and district administrative positions, the political socialization of masses of voters resulting from local elections could produce urban-village civilian coalitions competing with the military-controlled, appointed system of the existing administration.

Several points of disagreement were stressed in critiques of electoral behavior since the mid-sixties. Huy agreed with Ehrlich that the local level is primary in development of Vietnamese democracy. The critical problem is organizing politics at the village level. Political parties have been plagued in attempts to do this by traditional perceptions and by the GVN. Previously, when new men came to power they destroyed the previous governing apparatus. The ideas of competition and of elected officials representing their own constituencies and presumably the entire population are still not generally understood. The PNM has been criticized for compromising, for attempting to attain reforms without struggling for a complete system change. Difficulties stemming from such perceptions have been compounded by GVN (and renewed NLF) attempts to influence village government to attain a position of strength vis-à-vis political party organizations. Where villages have been organized by groups and parties the GVN found them resistant to its attempts to control local elections and councils.

Sacks's interpretation of recent electoral behavior differed from those of Tull and Ehrlich concerning the structure of the "big five." He considered several developments important: the An Quang Buddhists' return to political involvement, the Diemist revival, the relatively progovernment but somewhat aloof stance of the union movement, regional splits among Catholics, the relative decline in electoral fortunes of several parties such as the VNQDD, Revolutionary Dai Viets, and Hoa Hao (Phan Ba Cam faction), and success of a newer approach to electoral behavior represented by the PNM. Concerning the big five, Sacks recognized their continued importance though they are run from the top down. Hoa Hao deputies, for instance, act in conjunction with leadership in the Saigon area. Upward mobility occurs, but the local boy who makes good is likely to be a Rhodes scholar type who moves upward through the existing structure.

Ehrlich's position on the big five, however, was seconded by Stephen Young. He stressed that often a group's candidate is representative of established socioeconomic forces, e.g., a Hoa Hao council member also is the grandson of a distinguished local person. The Diemist revival ramifies in communal politics and ties among friends and families. Locally, these inherent forces were strengthened by pacification; the king who can pacify provides a certain prosperity and formal control obtains the mandate. In this context, elections have made a significant difference locally. Among political parties, it is the Dai Viet party (in all its aspects including the PNM) which, building upon bases provided by pacification and elections, has had the greatest impact.

This assessment of the Dai Viet role was not accepted by Thuan. He noted the An Quang Buddhists had made important electoral gains against the old Dai Viet and the VNQDD in 1971. This important shift in political party strength occurred, first, because his group, after disdaining to contest the Dai Viets in 1967, had actively contended in the 1971 election, and, second, because the GVN had become disillusioned with the old nationalist party. He believed that experience had sharpened his group's campaign techniques, as electoral competition at all levels, except for the presidency, had done for other groups. Yet, despite this and other advances in party development he associated with the increased electoral experience, he also stressed the negative impact of the GVN party and political development generally. By cheating to obtain election of certain candidates and by lining up certain deputies through bribery and other forms of corruption, the government undermines representative government and threatens the viability of the political system. Further, GVN attempts to influence politics in villages which have no party organizations have also fostered corruption. In thwarting the growth of representative government at all levels, the GVN plays into the hands of the NLF, who can infiltrate a corrupt system all the more easily.

The third general topic, "Elections and Legislative Development," centered upon presentations by Wesley R. Fishel and Goodman. The former provided tentative findings from his "Significant Changes in Legislative Composition from Diem to Thieu." Goodman provided a critique of the developing role of the National Assembly, particularly of its autonomy and its members' internal and external alignments and constituent services. His presentation was "What Went Wrong in Saigon: The Emperor's New Clothes or Allan Goodman's New Clothes." His underlying theme centered around the fact that little change actually occurred in South Vietnam, including changes in popular participation.

He underscored that 1971 manifested how little the war—and the United States—had affected political party *modus operandi.* Suspicion, hatred, and jealousy remain predominant. Frequently, still, threat of a coup is viewed as the only method for bringing about political change. Mobilization of support requisite for maintaining political system viability remains an elusive goal despite recurrent political crises. National-level internal divisions and lack of top leadership prestige have continued.

From earlier study, Goodman had anticipated the evolution by stages of a responsible legislative system—none of which occurred. He expected development of political organization at a pace commensurate with increased electoral behavior; a deputy's experience should have shown the importance of mobilizing and testing group organization for the 1971 elections. Politics and administration should have become increasingly civilianized at the province and district levels, with deputies working for reform legislation to restrict the number of candidates and thereby make local elections more meaningful. Goodman asked: "What went wrong? Why has the range of reforms been so small? Why have elections often been rituals ratifying personal rivalries?" He felt perhaps his own expectations were at fault. For instance, he assumed the fair conduct of elections and that candidates would focus on issues. While many candidates said they would not run if an election was rigged, in practice candidates only raised the issue of rigging if they felt they could not win. Too many advocated aggression as the road to power, for fear of their chances at the ballot box.

Further, Goodman had predicted opposition participation in elections would become significant. While the opposition regularly participates in elections, running candidates for public office continues to be viewed as less important than other aspects of political participation; locality, profession, and religion continue to be more important aspects of political participation than elections. These factors, combined with continued lack of rural-urban linkages and clear-cut governing majorities, raise the question whether South Vietnam is simply a praetorian polity (where raw power is used as long as competition remains weak) and is likely to remain one. Corruption, tyranny, and inflation have provided political parties with issues; they have not stimulated parties to devise and develop urban-rural linkages. Even in urban areas, no organizations strive for political mobilization, and, generally, urban centers do not appear likely foci for development of significant political movements.

In view of failure to develop along lines he predicted, Goodman asked what the implications were for the younger legislators. He suggested several: a willingness to bargain their legislative function of helping to make GVN policies appear legitimate in return for power to run local areas; refusal to develop legislative blocs into political parties that the GVN could suppress, and instead, an emphasis on functional fields less easily coerced and forming blocs around issues; a demand for local reform legislative packages; and a willingness to combat executive dominance, thus aiding legislators to promote coordination among diverse groups represented in the legislative branch. Above all, younger legislators should not simply imitate mores of older politicians and should avoid becoming enmeshed in a web of regime co-optation.

Commenting on Goodman's presentation, Thuan observed that the Lower House is aware it cannot challenge the executive effectively. The problem remains excessive executive dominance, the main flaw in the present political system. A true balance of power is essential. He stressed political party development and law making must be kept separate. His group is prepared to support some GVN bills while striving to attain needed reforms; cooperation with pro-GVN deputies on this basis is possible.

Thuan's view was generally accepted by Huy, who noted the legislature's role was not solely one of opposition. The PNM was opposed to the GVN's buying support in the legislature, not to its having a majority in that body. A cardinal weakness of the National Assembly elected in 1967 was that a number of deputies opposed the government as individuals rather than organizing to oppose specific programs. One positive aspect of the 1971 election was that certain extreme oppositionists as well as certain persons closely identified with the GVN lost. Thuan said some of the "extreme" opposition candidates would have been elected in fair elections and that a number of "extreme" pro-GVN deputies were defeated because the GVN made choices among progovernment candidates in specific contests. This, he believed, could result in enhanced legislative responsibility and greater concern for constituency interests. Thus, the new legislature may be an improvement, and there is potential for better organized blocs. In fact, the An Quang group and the PNM could well cooperate on specific issues.

Both Sacks and Tull took issue with Goodman's "what went wrong" thesis. They felt it was incorrect to conclude there had been no progress in developing the legislative role. Goodman responded he did not imply the legislature was a sham but only that significant possibilities for its development had not materialized. Sacks felt the increased numbers of opposition members in the Lower House after the 1971 election was important, especially since many so-called pro-GVN deputies were not completely pro-Thieu. Certainly the PNM, often called pro-GVN, is not a captive group. Moreover, for the first time Buddhists devised an electoral machine and an organization to build a legislative bloc. The primary problem is the possibility Thieu will buy out the opposition. The question is whether legislators and political parties can influence Thieu to make political reforms.

Tull believed Goodman's expectations had been too idealistic. It would be unrealistic to assume that a strong political party could be formed from a loose legislative bloc, although blocs now could help reinforce parties. The fact that both progovernment candidates in 1971 and the leadership of the new Lower House were distinct improvements was an indirect effect of the opposition role in the legislature.

In addition to these critiques of Goodman's statement, there was discussion of the term *praetorian* in the Samuel Huntington sense of application of raw power by the military in the political arena when other politicized social forces lack institutional political channels to compete with the military. Pike's view that there was no Junker class in Vietnam but rather political leaders in khaki who might not fully appreciate the meaning of electoral behavior seemed generally supported. However, Thuan noted Thieu's consultations with the Armed Forces Council still took priority over those he held with the cabinet. But Thuan agreed with Huy and Stephen Young that the generals are not a unified group. Young pointed out the military represented an interest group in Vietnamese politics and some leaders (mostly Catholics) are a special economic interest group, linked with particular Chinese leaders. Huy added the military is a divided faction including pro-Thieu and pro-Ky figures as well as supporters of the VNQDD, the Dai Viets, and the Worker-Farmer party. He believed Thieu himself does not have an essentially military orientation toward politics. Rather, Thieu is prepared to accept some electoral opposition as witnessed by his recognition of the Buddhists' political role in central Vietnam, even though they had withheld support from him after he lost Revolutionary Dai Viet support.

The fourth major topic, "The Elections and the Prospects for Political Development," dealt with potential for political mobilization through party development and possibilities for future roles of opposition parties, including the NLF. The perspectives of two significant forces were presented by Huy and Thuan, while Pike discussed political options of the NLF.

Huy described PNM methods of operations, programs, and goals in his "Elections and Political Mobilization: Prospects for Party Development and More Significant Competition."

Thuan next discussed "Actual and Potential Role of Opposition Forces in Elections and Political Development." He critiqued the status of oppositionists. Being in the opposition is in fashion even for persons elected with GVN backing. In fact, there are no genuine progovernment parties; some parties shift almost daily from a pro to an opposition stance. None of the parties has a real platform or direction by national leaders for broad purposes, and all concentrate only on single issues as these attract attention. The opposition has thus far failed because it has not articulated a position vis-à-vis either the GVN or the masses. Oppositionists, including An Quang, find a constructive stance difficult to attain. An Quang is prepared to support the GVN on some measures in order to manifest its good will and has tried to improve its knowledge by asking government officials to explain their positions to An Quang leaders prior to making policy decisions.

Thuan suggested additional legislation is required to permit the opposition to operate more effectively. Thus, province-level security councils should be abolished and power to imprison by government decree (for two years, renewable

indefinitely) eliminated. Government financial assistance to political parties
would also aid party development. Thuan placed emphasis upon the An Quang's
current efforts to strengthen its organization. Placing adherents of its movement in government positions and proselytization among government officials
is necessary for party development. Family and friendship ties are employed
extensively to influence officials to adopt and implement An Quang policies.
Because technical expertise is required for any regime, his group believes it
important to cultivate technicians and even persuade them to run for office.

Formation of various pressure groups for making viewpoints known to the
government is another significant function. Student organizations, farmers'
unions, and peasant groups are being formed as a base for village council elections. The group is also working on a platform and on appointment of a shadow
cabinet to follow activities of the ministries. Also, the group is attempting
through leadership classes to educate its leaders concerning their responsibilities.
These steps toward organization building must be supplemented by approaches
to other opposition parties with similar platforms to develop greater cohesiveness through alliances.

Thuan stressed that building strong parties through these methods is essential to organize An Quang adherents for the struggle with the communists and
for future national stability because only a freely elected government can achieve
stability. Although An Quang has been in the vanguard of the opposition for
many years, it had never considered Thieu, Ky, or other GVN leaders as enemies.
The group had used restraint and on several occasions cooperated with various
regimes to promote stability. Demonstrations and direct confrontation with
the GVN occurred only when there was no choice. He observed the present
is not the time to struggle aggressively against the GVN, because of serious problems posed by the communists. Cooperation between the opposition and the
GVN should occur in furtherance of the highest priority objective of national
survival. However, Thieu's strategy stands in the path of such cooperation; his
policy is not to have a GVN party and to weaken existing parties. Also, the
mass media is used by the GVN to attack vocal critics and to accuse those
relatively silent of lacking courage. The GVN's behavior shows it does not
understand the principles of representative government. He concluded: "If the
government remains narrowminded, where is the possibility for political development in South Vietnam?"

Douglas Pike's study was "The Possible Role of Elections in a Political
Settlement with the NLF." There appeared to be general agreement with Pike's
assumptions that the NLF was unlikely to agree to elections as part of a political
settlement and that at the present time it could not win an open national election. Joseph Zasloff, however, questioned whether NLF weaknesses would continue in light of South Vietnam's economic problems and increased withdrawal
of U.S. military and economic assistance. Zasloff felt Pike had presented an
overly optimistic view of the GVN's position, especially considering the continued

corruption, widespread antipathy to military rule, the effect of failures in Laos and Cambodia or politics in South Vietnam, the great remaining strength of the DRV, and the NLF's potential to expand organizationally in urban areas as well as in the countryside. Sacks did not believe it possible now for the NLF to pursue anything but low-level warfare or limited political activity. Pike responded that the NLF's weakness as an indigenous force, its current tactic of making its areas a "big classroom" for training while administering a holding operation until Saigon has major troubles, the weakened condition of the DRV and its unwillingness to permit NLF participation in electoral processes—all militate against disaster for either the GVN or the DRV-NLF for at least two years.

Huy pointed out the DRV is unlikely to accept elections in South Vietnam, as this would eliminate legal claims it has made against the South; only Moscow and Peking could persuade Hanoi to agree to such elections, and this is highly unlikely. He believed Thieu might accept an NLF role in future elections as part of a political settlement. This would be simple in a formal sense as Article 4 of the Constitution (forbidding communists to participate in elections) could be amended, and the NLF has never openly professed to be a communist organization anyway.

Sacks agreed Article 4 should be made inoperative. Elections could then serve to legitimate the communists' return to legal political processes without formal agreements or surrender. He believed the NLF might perceive this to be an easier means of subverting the existing political mechanisms. To the extent the NLF members can be guaranteed survival, the organization's leaders can tell followers there is a payoff operating within the political system.

Commenting it was amazing there still could be discussion of the significant possibility for representative government, even potentially involving the NLF, in South Vietnam after the years of strife, Kenneth Young stated that political parties constitute the one way out of the stalemate, which may continue for some years. Elections could be part of a settlement but not a precondition for a settlement. If the NLF is indeed reduced to the strength of but one of the sects and if there is a movement toward political equilibrium of the five or six major groupings in South Vietnam, it would appear Huy's concept of three or so broad coalitions—with the NLF part of a process of coalescence—is a definite possibility. This position was basically accepted by Thuan, who observed the NLF cannot win an election on a national basis and therefore wants a nonelectorally imposed coalition government.

Thuan expressed the view electoral experiences thus far have caused all political groups to believe it expedient to advocate popular self-determination; this increases the possibility for elections to become an integral element in any future political system. Not only have elections sharpened techniques of current party political maneuvering, but they might serve as a method for breaking the impasse at the Paris talks. An Quang wanted General Minh elected president because he could rally nationalist forces, bring about greater cohesiveness, and prove to the NLF there is nationalist unity. The NLF would then have been more obliged to consider nationalist conditions for a political settlement. Unfortunately, Thieu has not yet recognized the significance of electoral processes and representative government for political development. The one-man presidential election was such a mistake because it damaged popular faith in the legal political system and aided the NLF. If all political parties and major interests, including the GVN, cooperate, then political system viability is possible. In the absence of such cooperation, especially if Thieu does not develop trust in the political party system, Thuan commented, there is no hope.

A select list of the major assumptions discussed by the seminar on the role of elections in Vietnamese political development must be subject to arbitrary inclusions and exclusions. The following summary hypotheses are therefore attributable solely to interpretations of the reporter, Charles A. Joiner, who assumes full responsibility for their representativeness, accuracy, and scope. Only three assumptions can be considered as generally positive ones with qualifications pertaining primarily to regional variations.

1. There has been significant political development at the village level. Participation and access have increased. Party activities have been enhanced.

2. Electoral processes have been accepted as one form of legitimizing succession despite persistence of cultural norms blocking acceptance of some aspects of electoral behavior.

3. Organization-building by a select number of parties and interest groups has become more extensive and political parties enjoy greater viability than previously.

The other general presumptions were either negative ones or were highly qualified viewpoints concerning relative successes of political institutions.

1. Political parties are still not cohesive, have not established broad bases through alignments, have experienced serious organizational problems, and have not received official support required for development. The GVN and Thieu have undermined more than strengthened the growth of a party system.

2. Increased political maturity has developed among members of the legislature, at least in the forms of greater constituency orientation, increase in the number of actual and quasi-oppositionist members, and somewhat greater willingness to cooperate on issues. This has often been offset by executive intrusion stemming from Thieu's lack of appreciation of representative government, and the weaknesses of intralegislative organization and legislators' inability to cope with executive pressures.

3. Linkage between Saigon and the villages remains weak and tenuous for any organized group, including government-sponsored political leaders.

4. The GVN has failed to develop political structures for articulating interests of loyal supporters or to stimulate cohesiveness among loyal oppositionists.

5. The Saigon government continues to rule primarily by personality

politics and by dividing potential interest aggregating groups, i.e., it manipulates individual political personalities in a relatively structureless vacuum at the national level.

6. Where feasible the GVN has undermined political party development at the village level to retain a shifting but manipulatable governing elite locally.

7. All elections, while generally efficiently administered in a technical sense, have been subject to electoral manipulation. In most locations the GVN has influenced voters' choices.

8. It is unlikely the NLF will agree to participate in any open national electoral process, even if procedural fairness could be guaranteed and if bona fide choices for candidates or proposals are provided. The NLF is likely to engage only in elections to ratify previously agreed upon candidates and formats for the political system. Possibly the NLF might participate in future elections, especially at the local level, but it may not overtly admit this and may do so through localized political accommodations.

9. The one-man election for president in 1971 was a setback to political development in South Vietnam. An opportunity for political parties to co-operate in an open competition was lost. The existing degree of popular belief in representative government was lessened. Development of mature, nonclandestine, responsible, and articulate loyal opposition did not occur.

10. The role of elections in Vietnamese political development has been positive and potentially could become quite significant. Increased pride and electoral-representative experience have strengthened nationalist parties. Their combative, clandestine, and personalistic orientations have not necessarily been eliminated, but some have made strides toward construction of better organized and more competitive structures capable of extensive political mobilization. Continued military governance would both decrease their potential and be dysfunctional to future political system stability. Political parties and interest groups can become increasingly representative and effective locally, stimulating participation and commitment and political development generally at that level. This could be augmented by effective constituency activities by members of the National Assembly. Such development is also possible at the provincial level if the GVN and the military permit open electoral processes. Nationally, only alliances of parties with similar interests can provide for political development. Even such alliances can develop cohesion and effectiveness only if there is real execution of constitutional provisions for separation of powers and legal broadening of the electorate to permit electoral participation by persons currently classified as members of the illegal opposition.

Participants

Jerome R. Bass, The Asia Society-SEADAG
Arthur Dommen, University of Maryland

John C. Donnell, Temple University, Seminar Chairman
Richard Ehrlich, Department of State
Wesley Fishel, Michigan State University
Allan E. Goodman, Clark University
Nguyen Ngoc Huy, National Progressive Movement, Saigon
Charles A. Joiner, Temple University, Seminar Co-Chairman and Reporter
Sven Kraemer, Executive Office of the White House
Robert Nooter, Agency for International Development
Douglas Pike, U.S. Information Agency
Ithiel de Sola Pool, Massachusetts Institute of Technology
I. Milton Sacks, Brandeis University
Walter Slote, Columbia University
Tran Quang Thuan, National Assembly, Saigon
Theresa Tull, Department of State
Kenneth T. Young, Council on Foreign Relations
Stephen Young, Harvard University
Joseph J. Zasloff, University of Pittsburgh, Chairman, SEADAG Vietnam-
    Laos-Cambodia Panel

Asia House
December 10-11, 1971
New York, New York

Index

Index

Abrams, Creighton W., General, 79
Accountability in elections, 36
Acculturation, process of, 173
Adjudication of disputes, 115. *See also*
    Justice
Administration: Chinese, 26; district, 176;
    local, 1, 4, 31, 158; military, 4, 90;
    revolution in, 126. *See also* specific type
    of administration
Aerial combat, 58, 62, 65
Age groupings in elections, 45, 47
Agency for International Development
    (AID, 83, 86, 89–90
Agi-prop. *See* Cadres, Agi-prop.
Agricultural Bank, 86, 89–90
Agriculture, Ministry of, 87, 96
Alliance of National, Democratic and
    Peace Forces, 109n
Ambushes, strategy of, 116
An Giang province, 50, 139, 141–143
An Loc city, besieged, 58
An Quang Buddhists, political opposition
    group, 35, 39, 43–45, 48–51, 73, 91,
    104–105, 130–134, 144, 161–162, 176–
    182
An Quang pagoda, monks in, 56, 59, 63–
    70. *See also* Buddhists
An Xuyen province, 51, 139, 141–143
Ancestor worship, 13–14
Animism, 45
Anti-Communist Invaders' Front, 55
Armed Forces Council, 180
Army of the Republic of Vietnam (ARVN),
    112, 116; morale of, 24
Arrests of political opponents, 53–56
Asia Society, 2, 184
Asian Bishops, Council of, 26
Assistance, United States: economic, 3,
    56, 60, 65, 73, 80, 83, 86, 88, 96, 106,
    181; military, 1, 65
Astrology, influence of, 14, 17–18
Attentism, position of, 27
Au Truong Thanh, minister of economics,
    60–61
Authoritarianism, heritage of, 2, 9, 78,
    84, 106, 151–152
Authority, executive, 174; presidential,
    93, 125; village, 23, 82
Autocracy, system of, 78, 94, 96
Autonomy, 177; of cities, 100, 141–143;
    from Saigon, 92; village, 175

Ba Xuyen province, 139, 141–143

Bac Lieu province, 50–51, 104, 139,
    141–143
Bach Tuong (White Elephant), 135
Balance of power, 5, 179
Bao Dai, Emperor, 29, 93
Bass, Jerome R., cited, 184
Behavior: electoral, 3; guide to, 15–17, 28
Benedict, Ruth, cited, 13
Bien Hoa province, 50–51, 137–138,
    140, 142–143
Bien Tuy province, 139–140, 142–143
Binh Dinh province, 10, 31, 74, 138, 140,
    142–143
Binh Duong province, 38, 138, 140,
    142–143
Binh Long province, 50, 112, 138, 140,
    142–143
Binh Thuan province, 50, 138, 140,
    142–143
Bipartisan party system, 129
Bishops, Council of, 130
Bloc voting by military units, 5, 31, 41
Book of Songs, The, 14–17, 30
Bread-and-butter campaign issues, 49–50
Bribery, charges of, 5–6, 64, 95, 177
Buddhists: antigovernment faction, 56, 64,
    137, 152, 175; beliefs of, 13; against
    Diem, 21; in Danang, 58, 69; in Hue, 58,
    69; and Ky, 21; and leftist monks, 53; in
    Military Region I, 105; militant, 5–6, 8,
    69; political movement of 3, 9–10, 105–
    106, 130, 134, 161, 179; and self control,
    17; in 1967 elections, 38, 42, 47; in
    1970 elections, 45; in 1971 elections, 51
Budget development and allocations, 82–
    84, 89, 92–95
Budget and Foreign Aid, Director General
    of, 89
Bunker, Ellsworth, Ambassador, 20, 60,
    62, 65–66, 74
Bureaucracy and bureaucrats, 14, 34, 85,
    92, 95, 157

Cadres: agi-prop, 117–120; communist,
    68–69; lower level, 155; National Libera-
    tion Front, 7–8, 118; People's Revolu-
    tionary Party, 117; quality of, 118; quotas
    set for, 115; structure and development
    of, 82, 93, 95, 102, 125, 158; under-
    cover, 93. *See also* Administration
Cam Ranh province, 138, 140, 142–143
Cambodia, relations with, 18–19, 114

189

About the Editors

John C. Donnell is Professor of Political Science at Temple University; he has also taught at Dartmouth College and Columbia University and has been employed by the RAND Corporation. He has spent over eleven years in Asia (including six years in North and South Vietnam) with the U.S. Department of State, USIA, and later on contract and independent research. Professor Donnell has contributed chapters to *The Communist Revolution in Asia, Problems of Freedom: South Vietnam Since Independence,* and *Vietnam: Anatomy of a Conflict*; he has published articles in *Asian Survey, Journal of Asia Studies, Pacific Affairs,* and *Problems of Communism.*

Charles A. Joiner is Professor of Political Science and former Chairman and Director of the Public Administration Program, Temple University. He has been a consultant to the National Institute of Administration of South Vietnam, the University of Lebanon, and the Civil Service Commission of Lebanon. He is the author of *Politics of Massacre: Political Processes in South Vietnam, Fedayeen: Palestinian Resistance Movement and Arab World Politics, Saigon: Public Administration in the Saigon Metropolitan Area, Organizational Analysis, Dynamics of Administrative Situations, Civil Service Education and Training in Lebanon,* and numerous monographs on politics and administration in Indochina, Lebanon, and the United States. Professor Joiner has contributed many articles on South Vietnam to professional journals, including *Administrative Science Quarterly, Asian Survey, Economic Times, Current History, Journal of Southeast Asian History, Southeast Asia,* and *Vietnam Perspectives.*